Foreword

Luvern L. Cunningham
Novice G. Fawcett Professor Emeritus
The Ohio State University

Nothing in my first year as a local school superintendent, 1949-50, compares remotely with the experiences of the 18 beginners in the Carolyn Hughes Chapman study. At age 24, in the back of a saloon on a Saturday night, I was hired by a three-person, all-male school board to be superintendent. My first-year challenges were to find and hire enough teachers to fill the classrooms and make sure that the boilers would work when the blizzardy days of winter arrived. My proposal to reorganize local school districts for dollar savings and improved education was politely disregarded when advanced in December 1949. There were no protests, racial conflicts, instances of sexual harassment, taxpayer revolts, strikes, gangs, or campus shootings.

Albeit this superintendency was in a small, rural Nebraska community. The contrast between then and now is simply enormous and is testimony to the profound social, economic, cultural, and political changes that are underway in the United States and around the world. The Democrat Harry Truman gave way to the Republican Dwight Eisenhower in 1952. Most people slept well; they were tired of war and deprivation and just wanted to get along with having homes, raising families, and cheering the New York Yankees or the St. Louis Cardinals. Obviously, this is an oversimplification; there were deep, deep problems within American society. But for a few years, there was tranquility and satisfaction, for the most part, with a simpler life.

In the mid-1960s, Raymond E. Callahan gave the Alfred D. Simpson Lecture on Administration at Harvard University. Callahan, in fact, focused on 100 years of the American school superintendency, analyzing the evolution of the office from 1865 through 1964. He noted, as did Thomas Glass in this book, that the first superintendencies were established as much as 30 years earlier but were only coming to prominence in the 1860s. Callahan, in the mid-1960s, divided a century of superintendency development into four periods: The Superintendent as a Scholarly Educational Leader, 1865-1909; The Superintendent as a Business Manager, 1910-1929; The Superintendent as Educational Statesman in a Democratic School, 1930-1953; and The Superintendent as Educational Realist, 1954-1965.

Now, Carolyn Hughes Chapman's important book, *Becoming a Superintendent: Challenges of School Leadership*, captures the features of context that must be understood by those who enter the superintendency in the twilight of this century. The period 1965-1996 might be titled The Superintendent as Practitioner of Survival.

Callahan wrote a significant volume, cited in this book, entitled *Education and the Cult of Efficiency* (Chicago: University of Chicago Press, 1961), which documented the impact of business, especially the incorporation of the principles of scientific management, into the everyday administration of public schools in the United States. Scientific management had substantial taxpayer appeal during times of heavy growth in enrollments, fueled in part by liberal national immigration policies. A by-product of this movement was a wave of criticism aimed at public schools, stimulated by the belief that the running of schools was inefficient and filled with wasteful managerial practices. It is no surprise in the 1990s, therefore, to find that superintendents, beginning and seasoned, are mired in similar criticism. The National Alliance of Business and the Business Roundtable, joined by many governors and legislative leaders, are today's voices of efficiency at the national and state levels, with strident counterparts at local levels. Their calls for the elimination of waste and better management, joined by legions of antitax advocates, are generating intensive pressure on local school authorities. History is repeating itself, catching the new superintendents in its web, as the Chapman book documents. It must be noted, however, that there was then and is now reason for highlighting shoddy management and calling the profession to task.

As authors of *The Organization and Control of American Schools* (Columbus: Merrill Publishing Company), Roald F. Campbell, Raphael O. Nystrand, Michael D. Usdan, and I struggled to project in each edition what the future of the school superintendency was likely to be. In the final edition (1990), we projected some of the volatility and chaos that would surround the office, but we grossly underestimated the range and intensity of internal and external forces that would swirl about public education, coming to rest on the superintendency. The superintendent talent pool is shallow, and there are dwindling numbers of newcomers knocking at the door. Moreover, there is an apparent disjuncture between the preparation of administrators and the realities of everyday practice—witness the stories of the 18 beginners. Certainly, preparation, both pre-entry and continuing, is a matter of professional and public concern. A major contribution of this book is the light it sheds on the discrepancy between preparation and the exigencies of practice, as well as the position's significance as a public matter.

After four decades of responsibility for shaping and administering superintendency preparation programs, I find locating the center of gravity for preparation to be more elusive than ever. Having lived through periods of concentration on principles of administration, administrative tasks, democratic administration ideology, social sciences, and administration and the accompanying "theory movement," and more recently, ethics and values, the problem of correspondence or discrepancy between job demands and training looms larger and larger. The discrepancy phenomenon is not limited to the superintendency by any means, for it exists within most professions, but its social importance for children and youth cannot be minimized.

Thus, as the Chapman study indicates, those who are fashioning preparation programs have a major problem on their hands. As the early architects of public education were at work in the seventeenth, eighteenth, and nineteenth centuries, they relied heavily on philosophy, law, history, theology, and primitive pedagogy as sources of enlightenment. Later, other and newer fields of scholarship, such as sociology,

BECOMING A SUPERINTENDENT

Challenges of School District Leadership

CAROLYN HUGHES CHAPMAN
University of Nevada, Reno

Merrill,
an imprint of Prentice Hall
Upper Saddle River, New Jersey   *Columbus, Ohio*

Library of Congress Cataloging-in-Publication Data

Becoming a superintendent : challenges of school district leadership / [edited and compiled by] Carolyn Hughes Chapman.

    p. cm.

    Includes bibliographical references and indexes.

    ISBN 0-13-398173-8 (alk. paper)

    1. School superintendents—United States. 2. School management and organization—United States. 3. Educational leadership—United States.   I. Chapman, Carolyn Hughes.

    LB2831.72.B43   1997

    371.2´011´0973—dc20

96-23190
CIP

Cover photo: © D. Petku/H. Armstrong Roberts
Editor: Debra A. Stollenwerk
Production Editor: Alexandrina Benedicto Wolf
Design Coordinator: Julia Zonneveld Van Hook
Cover & Text Designer: Anne Flanagan
Production Manager: Deidra M. Schwartz
Electronic Text Management: Marilyn Wilson Phelps, Matthew Williams, Karen L. Bretz, Tracey Ward
Director of Marketing: Kevin Flanagan
Advertising/Marketing Coordinator: Julie Shough

This book was set in Zapf International by Prentice Hall and was printed and bound by R. R. Donnelley & Sons. The cover was printed by Phoenix Color Corp.

 © 1997 by Prentice-Hall, Inc.
Simon & Schuster/A Viacom Company
Upper Saddle River, New Jersey 07458

Printed in the United States of America

10 9 8 7 6 5 4 3 2 1

ISBN: 0-13-398173-8

Prentice-Hall International (UK) Limited, *London*
Prentice-Hall of Australia Pty. Limited, *Sydney*
Prentice-Hall of Canada, Inc., *Toronto*
Prentice-Hall Hispanoamericana, S. A., *Mexico*
Prentice-Hall of India Private Limited, *New Delhi*
Prentice-Hall of Japan, Inc., *Tokyo*
Simon & Schuster Asia Pte. Ltd., *Singapore*
Editora Prentice-Hall do Brasil, Ltda., *Rio de Janeiro*

psychology, social psychology, ethics, economics, political science, and anthropology, were factored into the thinking of the designers of preparation programs for school administrators. Of significance to all of the professions, too, was the arrival of professional schools, such as business, law, education, social work, medicine, nursing, architecture, pharmacy, public administration, and journalism. The admission to practice (licensing, certifying, orientation, the bar) within and among the professions was spawned through a curious mixture of public and private interests involving the "public," the organized professions (ABA, AMA, NEA, AFT), professional schools, and basic disciplines. The professionalization of the professions has become a field of scholarship unto itself.

Now, American society is entering a new era of large-scale institutional transformations, including public and, to some extent, private education and the professional training of those who practice there. The professional practice and admission to practice of professionals in most fields has been tied to informing disciplines and the translation of the content from those knowledge reservoirs into day-to-day work with clients, students, patients, or parishioners. Today, the question that this book helps raise is, Do those disciplines still have meaning for the training of superintendents? Or other professionals? If they do, which or what parts? If they do not, where are the foundations for professional practice in the superintendency for 1997 and 2007?

Anticipating varying sentiments surrounding these questions, it is fair to ask which of the traditional disciplines still have merit? And which of the emerging centers of intellectual ferment have promise and can be expected to inform reform of preparation programs? Where can we turn for intellectual help? Where are the genuinely new and different intellectual systems that can frame the transformation of preparation of future generations of school superintendents?

Preface

Though the superintendent in most school districts enjoys recognition, prestige, and a relatively high salary, news coverage of school affairs leads one to conclude that the superintendent is the lightning rod that can draw electrical charges from the board of education, parents, teachers, administrators, and students. Even in this era of emphasis on site-based management, the superintendent remains the person held responsible. Teachers and administrators are protected in their positions by contracts and tenure laws, but the superintendent, like the coach of a losing football team, is the one whose job is on the line. Those who function as Monday morning quarterbacks in a school district may not understand the complex factors that lead to decisions. Furthermore, even school board members and central office administrators generally know little about what the superintendent's life is like.

Becoming a Superintendent: Challenges of School District Leadership introduces readers to the superintendency by inviting them to share the lives and perceptions of individuals who are in their first year as superintendents of school districts. The text will be of primary interest to those who aspire to be superintendents or who are new superintendents. Learning about the challenges faced by superintendents can help them assess their own skills, dispositions, attitudes, and interests in relation to those required in a superintendency. School board members who select, work with, and evaluate superintendents will also find this book helpful and revealing, as will those responsible for the preparation of superintendents in universities.

Recognizing that lack of experience is a handicap all first-time superintendents share, this book was written to provide vicarious experiences and perspectives that can help overcome this handicap. Superintendents are often expected to initiate action or develop strategic plans. They need to know what other superintendents have done in similar circumstances. Reflecting on the experiences of others can enable readers to see alternatives for addressing critical incidents and assess consequences.

The Research Base

This book emerged from a research project known as the Beginning Superintendent Study (BSS). Because of their belief that the short tenure of many superintendents was an impediment to sustained efforts to improve schools and school districts, a research team conducted a comprehensive, qualitative research study of beginning, first-time superintendents. The 18 superintendents who were the subjects of the BSS were selected to provide diversity by representing rural, town, suburban, and urban districts in 12 states in widely scattered areas of the United States. Half of the BSS superintendents were women and one third were minorities.

The research team included 12 professors of educational leadership or educational administration in universities throughout the United States. In addition to conducting monthly interviews with each superintendent, the researchers visited the school districts, attended board meetings, and analyzed board meeting minutes and local news coverage of the schools.

The heart of this book is the case studies of actual beginning superintendents written with the sensitivity and insight of professors of educational leadership who are also veteran administrators. The case studies provide opportunities for readers to build bridges connecting their own prior knowledge of schools and of leadership with the real world experiences of new superintendents.

Though leadership theory is not the primary focus of this book, the authors describe the experiences of superintendents in terms of relevant theories. In addition, Chapter 16, "Through the Lens of Leadership Theory," provides a comprehensive analysis of the conceptual frameworks for leadership evident in the work of the beginning superintendents. Professors who want to place a greater emphasis on theoretical aspects of the superintendency may wish to adopt a book on leadership theory as a companion text.

This book is not a cookbook with a set of recipes for becoming a successful superintendent. Superintendents need to be reflective practitioners if they are to respond effectively to emerging situations and to assess potential consequences of initiatives. To provide a "how-to-do-it manual" with a set of "right answers" would deprecate the complex challenges of educational leadership.

To the Professor

You may wish to vary the order of reading assignments in *Becoming a Superintendent* to fit your teaching style and preferences. By assigning Chapter 1 first, you will provide an advance organizer for the qualitative research underpinning the case studies. However, Chapter 2 includes not only a history of the superintendency but also a broad spectrum of quantitative data about the superintendency. You may prefer to have your students read this chapter late in the term rather than near the beginning.

You will find that the **case study chapters (Chapters 3 through 13)** begin with small, rural districts and then move to larger and more complex urban and suburban districts. These chapters conclude with another small, rural district. Because the case studies are largely independent of one another, you can easily vary their sequence to fit the interests of your classes as well as the demographics of your area. The **abstract provided at the beginning of each chapter** will assist you in making sequencing decisions.

The case chapters in this book lead to **four cross-case analysis chapters** at the end. Although building from specific instances to general principles may fit the teaching style of many professors, others may prefer that students read these chapters before the case studies to provide frameworks for considering the individual situations.

To aid readers in their growth as reflective practitioners, each chapter ends with **Questions for Reflection and Discussion.** These questions have been carefully designed to actively engage readers in analyzing the experiences and information presented.

Acknowledgments

The heroes of this book are the 18 first-year superintendents who wrenched precious hours from demanding schedules for multiple interviews with research team members. Their willingness to share frankly their challenging, and sometimes painful, experiences has given this book its reality.

The members of the BSS research team made this study possible. They were invited to participate based on their expertise and interest, and in some cases on their geographic proximity to the school districts served by first-time superintendents. Without any source of external funding, these people believed so strongly in the need for the research that they were willing not only to contribute their time and expertise but also to assume their own expenses. While continuing their work as full-time university faculty members, they used their own resources for telephone, audiotaping, clerical, and significant travel costs as they gathered and analyzed data about first-time superintendents. Four of them moved across the country to accept new university teaching assignments during the study, but continued their commitment to the project. More information about the BSS research team is provided at the end of this preface.

The design of the Beginning Superintendent Study is modeled after the Beginning Principal Study, described in *Becoming a Principal: The Challenges of Beginning Leadership* by Forrest W. Parkay and Gene E. Hall. Both of these individuals were helpful and encouraging as this study was being conceived and developed.

Identification of a pool of 400 first-time superintendents from which to select the 18 participants in the BSS was made possible through the cooperation of the American Association of School Administrators (AASA) and its state affiliates, state departments of education, state school board associations, and superintendent search consultants.

Far too many people were important to me in the writing of this book to acknowledge all of them adequately. Interactions with superintendents and former superintendents helped to develop the research questions and to refine perceptions during the analysis of data. Special appreciation for such contributions is expressed to Dick Foster, Karl Plath, Dick Boyd, Luvern Cunningham, Gordon Cawelti, Bill Anderson, Gloria Griffin, Betty Mason, Sharon Lease, Hawthorne Faison, Jeff Maddox, Arthur Steller, and Guy Sconzo. In addition to these contributions, Luvern Cunningham reviewed the entire manuscript and added his unique perspectives by writing the Foreword. His valuable insights emerge from his long experience as superintendent, scholar, and Dean of Education at The Ohio State University.

Colleagues in the Department of Educational Leadership at the University of Nevada, Reno, have been consistently supportive and encouraging. Graduate assistant Chima Igwe spent many hours in the library, helping to verify the accuracy of citations throughout the text and troubleshooting a host of collateral issues. Emerging news articles on the superintendency were located and organized by my daughter, Lisa Campbell. Many of these were so significant that they found their way into the book.

Debbie Stollenwerk, Alex Wolf, Marie Maes, and Penny Burleson of Prentice Hall have been most helpful in their systematic contributions throughout the process of bringing this book to life. The following reviewers provided invaluable insights and guidance in refining the book to strengthen its usefulness as a textbook: Gary M. Crow, University of Utah; John C. Daresh, Illinois State University; Glen I. Earthman, Virginia Polytech Institute and State University; Beverly B. Geltner, Eastern Michigan University; Spencer Maxcy, Louisiana State University; Cynthia J. Norris, University of Houston; John B. Peper, University of Texas at El Paso; and James S. Rinehart, University of Kentucky.

Most of all, appreciation is expressed to my husband and colleague, Samuel G. Chapman, for his enthusiastic support and encouragement throughout the research and writing process. His insights as a political scientist and former administrator, in addition to his skills as an author and editor, have made significant contributions to the quality of this work.

Carolyn Hughes Chapman

The BSS Research Team

Charles M. Achilles is Professor of Educational Leadership at Eastern Michigan University. He previously served for 21 years on the faculty of educational administration and as Coordinator of Field Services in the Bureau of Educational Research and Services at the University of Tennessee, Knoxville. He is best known for his research on class size and student achievement, public confidence in schools, and preparation programs for school administrators.

Freddie A. Banks, Jr. is Associate Professor of Educational Administration at Eastern Illinois University. He was previously a teacher, guidance counselor, principal, and superintendent of schools. Dr. Banks is the founder and advisor of the Minority Teacher Education Association and is the project director for the Minority Teacher Identification and Enrichment Program at Eastern Illinois University.

Ira E. Bogotch is Associate Professor of Educational Leadership at the University of New Orleans. He has over 20 years of administrative experience in government, education, and non-profit organizations. Though his earlier research focused on school-based management, his more recent research has been on central office administration.

Edward W. Chance is Professor of Educational Administration at the University of Nevada at Las Vegas. He previously served for 7 years on the faculty of the University of Oklahoma. He has been a classroom teacher and school administrator in both rural and urban settings. His research interests are in the areas of leadership development, rural education, and organizational change.

Carolyn Hughes Chapman, designer and coordinator of the Beginning Superintendent Study, is Associate Professor of Educational Leadership at the University of Nevada, Reno. She served as a supervisor in Parma, Ohio, as a principal in Shaker Heights, Ohio, and as assistant superintendent for curriculum and program development in Oklahoma City. She is best known for her leadership in the movement to incorporate the teaching of thinking into school curriculum and instruction. In 1985-86 she was president of the Association for Supervision and Curriculum Development (ASCD).

Samuel G. Chapman is Professor Emeritus of Political Science at the University of Oklahoma. Besides teaching in public administration and law enforcement administration for 28 years, he was a city councilman in Norman, Oklahoma; a police officer in Berkeley, California; police chief of Multnomah County (Portland), Oregon; and assistant director of the President's Commission on Law Enforcement and Administration of Justice appointed by Lyndon B. Johnson.

Joan L. Curcio is Associate Professor of Educational Administration and program director for the College of Education at the Northern Virginia Graduate Center of Virginia Tech University. She is a former high school principal and assistant superintendent. Dr. Curcio served as a member of the research team for the Beginning Principal Study while teaching at the University of Florida. Her experiences on the principal study provided insights that were helpful to the BSS.

Larry L. Dlugosh is Chair of the Department of Educational Administration at the University of Nebraska, Lincoln. Before joining the department, he served for 23 years as a Nebraska school administrator. Of those years, 13 were invested in district-level leadership, including 4 years as an associate superintendent for curriculum and instruction and 9 years as a superintendent of schools. Dr. Dlugosh coauthored *The School Superintendency: New Responsibilities, New Leadership* (1996).

Thomas E. Glass is Professor of Educational Administration at Northern Illinois University. He conducted *The 1992 Study of the American School Superintendency* for AASA. Dr. Glass has conducted extensive research on effective superintendents, and he is one of the authors of *Selecting, Preparing, and Developing the School District Superintendent* (1993).

William M. Gordon is Professor of Educational Leadership in the College of Education at Wright State University in Dayton, Ohio. He is also a practicing attorney. In addition, as the Director of the Center for Program Design in Saluda, North Carolina, he works with school districts on governance, policy, supervision, and desegregation matters. Dr. Gordon has been a principal and has taught not only in the United States but also in universities in Botswana and Sierra Leone.

Doris A. Henry is Assistant Professor of Leadership at the University of Memphis, where she is internship coordinator for the K-12 School Administration and Supervision Program. Dr. Henry served as a principal in Phoenix and in Oklahoma City. She started the first Superintendents' Leadership Development Program for West Tennessee. Her research efforts focus on change in school leadership.

John L. Keedy is Associate Professor of Educational Administration and Higher Education at the University of Louisville. He gained administrative experience both as a principal and as assistant superintendent for instruction. His research interests include school improvement, organizational change, and teacher and administrator theory building.

Mary Woods Scherr is Associate Professor of Education at the University of San Diego. Her 10 years of service as a school board member as well as her experiences as a teacher and administrator contribute to her understanding of educational leadership. She is a specialist in qualitative research with a focus on women as educational leaders.

Brief Contents

Contents

3

Jackie: Big Time Challenges in a Rural District   41

4

Hank: Chief, Coach, Superintendent   55

5
Chad: System Entry Sets the Stage   67

6
Kathleen: Whirlwind Courtship, Passionate Honeymoon, Quick Divorce?   81

7

Jeena: Out of the Peace Corps, Into the Fire for an Elected Superintendent   99

8

Eugene and Keith: A Tale of Two Suburbs   111

17
The Road to the Superintendency   233

BECOMING A SUPERINTENDENT

Challenges of School District Leadership

BEGINNING SUPERINTENDENTS AND THE CHALLENGES OF LEADERSHIP

Carolyn Hughes Chapman, The University of Nevada, Reno

ABSTRACT.   The educational reform movement that began in the 1980s drew public attention to the need to improve American schools. Though the overall impact of the reform movement is open to debate, one clear outcome was recognition of an urgent need to strengthen school leadership. Individuals who become superintendents of schools enter a world where their actions impact entire school districts and are constantly subject to public scrutiny. Recognizing the unique demands facing new superintendents, a research study of first-time superintendents was conducted to enhance the understandings of aspiring superintendents, school board members who will choose superintendents, and those responsible for their preparation. This book is based on comprehensive,

---

NOTE: The information in this chapter that first appeared in the article "A Study of Beginning Superintendents: Preliminary Implications for Leading and Learning" in the *Record in Educational Leadership*, Vol. 15, No. 1, is used here with the permission of Frederick Gies and Leadership Services International, Inc.

in-depth case studies and analyses of the vicarious experiences those case studies provide.

America's children have entrusted us with their dreams. They come to us able, brave, and willing. We are the stewards of their future, as they are of ours."
(Bullard & Taylor, 1993, p. 410)

Since the time of Thomas Jefferson, Americans have turned to the schools to help them achieve their dreams for their children and for the nation. Building on Jefferson's legacy, Horace Mann and other common school crusaders in the nineteenth century spoke with missionary zeal as they promoted schools that would be publicly financed and governed to serve all students. As the twentieth century approached, schools became larger and more complex, and the educational administration profession evolved. A person called *superintendent* became the pivot point between the schools and the public that was represented by that uniquely American institution—the board of education.

A prominent early superintendent and pioneer professor of educational administration, Ellwood Cubberley, described the dynamic calling of public education:

The administration of education each year becomes a more important and a more dignified piece of work. . . . To engage in it is to enlist in the nation's service. Its call is for those who would dedicate themselves in a noble way. Those who would serve must be of the world, with red blood in their veins; they must know the world, its needs and its problems; they must have largeness of vision, and the courage to do and dare (Cubberley, 1909, pp. 60, 68).

The American Association of School Administrators (AASA) conducts national studies of the superintendency every 10 years, as described in Chapter 2. The 1952 AASA 10-year study expressed perceptions similar to Cubberley's when it stated the following:

It is the superintendent of great heart and courageous spirit, possessed of sound judgment and deep understanding, who will carry the profession and the schools forward. . . . His spirit and his devotion to education will be magnified many times through the teachers, principals, pupils, and citizens of his community. His world will be immeasurably enriched by his service and leadership (AASA, 1952, p. 437).

HEROES WANTED!

Though these descriptions of superintendents may sound corny to modern ears, they are echoed in Deal and Kennedy's (1982) description of heroes in their widely read book, *Corporate Cultures*. They define heroes in corporations as those people who "personify the culture's values and as such provide tangible role models" (1982, p. 14). Deal and Kennedy explain the functions of heroes in organizations:

> Heroes are pivotal figures in a strong culture. . . . The hero is the great motivator, the magician, the person everyone will count on when things get tough. They have unshakable character and style. . . . Heroes are symbolic figures whose deeds are out of the ordinary, but not too far out. They show—often dramatically—that the ideal of success lies within human capacity (p. 37).

What ceremonies can you put into your place your image here?

Though school superintendents have seldom been heralded as heroes in recent years, few would argue that heroes are needed to rescue embattled public education. The vision that superintendents still can be heroes is expressed in the titles of books such as Tyack and Hansot's *Managers of Virtue* (1982) and Kowalski's *Keepers of the Flame* (1995). What makes the role of superintendent appealing to some educators, even in times of conflict, has been described as

> the opportunity to be involved in the whole flow of events that make a school district tick. It's seeing people, particularly adults, learn and grow and knowing that you've influenced their development. It's testing your skills against situations that sometimes seem unchangeable. It's seeing things happen in your district and knowing that, though your role may have been behind the scenes, without you they wouldn't have happened (Blumberg, 1985, p. 216).

Some superintendents have been remarkably successful in helping schools become more effective. Bullard and Taylor vividly describe these modern heroes in their book *Making School Reform Happen* (1993). However, in recent years, the rapid turnover of superintendents has increasingly been identified as a significant deterrent to sustained efforts by a school district to improve its schools (Bennett, 1991; Kerr, 1988; Murphy, 1991). For instance, in one 18-month period in the early 1990s, 27 of the 47 city school districts that belong to the Council of Great City Schools needed to replace a superintendent (Daley, 1990). Six different people served as chancellor (superintendent) of the New York City Schools in 11 years (Scherer, 1995).

> Only two superintendents out of those running the country's 47 largest city school districts have been in the post more than three years. . . . City schools have been squeezed between a rock and a hard place for years. Politicians demand speedy improvements, while budgets are slashed and social problems escalate. Residents flee to the suburbs the minute they can afford to, leaving the cities with dropping standards, growing racial tensions and runaway levels of violence and drug abuse (In the U.S. . . . , 1994, p. 12).

Some city school boards, in the mid-1990s, sought chief executive officers (CEOs) from the business world to run their schools. Because of the low salaries, compared with those in the corporate world, they had trouble finding CEOs who were interested. A Chicago school board member summed up the problems of attracting CEOs to the superintendency: "Number one, we don't pay them enough; number two, they get treated like garbage; . . . and number three, they get run out of town" (Jones, 1994, p. 24).

The problem of rapid turnover in the superintendency is by no means endemic to large cities. For example, a study of rural Oklahoma school districts identified 41 districts that had 3 or more superintendents in a 5-year period (Chance & Capps, 1990). A study of the American superintendency, released by the AASA in 1992, indicated that the average length of a superintendency is 6.47 years. This period is even shorter in very small and in very large districts (Glass, 1992).

A study by Giles and Giles (1990) revealed that 62% of persons appointed to superintendencies in California in 1988–89 were first-time superintendents. After examining directories of California superintendents over a 15-year period, Giles and Giles reported that 25% of California superintendents held their positions for 2 years or less. The Giles' findings were consistent with similar percentages reported for North Carolina and Indiana (Sorohan, 1990).

Given the need for capable superintendents to lead our nation's schools and given the rapid turnover of superintendents, surprisingly little is known about the experiences of those who become superintendents of schools. Sergiovanni, Burlingame, Coombs, and Thurston (1992) noted that few qualitative studies of superintendents' lives have been done, though many such studies have been published on the lives of teachers and principals. The Beginning Superintendent Study was designed to help fill this void.

(Lack of experience) is often the greatest handicap first-time superintendents suffer. This handicap is exacerbated by the relative isolation of the superintendency and the fact that many are not only new to the role but also new to the school district. This book provides a tool for overcoming lack of experience by allowing readers to live vicariously the experiences of novice superintendents.

DESIGN OF THE BEGINNING SUPERINTENDENT STUDY

The Beginning Superintendent Study (BSS) was developed in response to the need for research to strengthen the preparation of superintendents, as well as to enhance their understandings and increase their ability to provide long-term leadership for school districts. A primary focus of the BSS was the developing professional identity of the first-year superintendent of schools.

In recommending methodology for research on superintendents' professional experiences, Miklos (1988) pointed out the need for

> in depth case studies . . . that would penetrate the depths of how these processes are actually experienced by people who aspire to or actually hold administrative positions. The naturalistic, qualitative, interpretive approaches to research hold potential for yielding insights that would contribute to advancing basic understandings and to developing new conceptualizations of the processes through which people become administrators (p. 69).

In 1992, Carolyn Hughes Chapman, Associate Professor of Educational Leadership at the University of Nevada, Reno, brought together a team of professors who recognized the need for such research and were interested in exploring beginning first-time superintendents' experiences. The study of beginning principals conducted by Forrest W. Parkay and Gene E. Hall (1992) provided a model research design.

The Beginning Superintendent Study (BSS) is based on extensive, in-depth case studies of 18 first-time school superintendents. A pool of first-time superintendents, from which to select participants, was compiled from a variety of sources. One of these was a survey of all participants in the AASA Superintendents Academy over a 3-year period. In addition, state affiliates of AASA, state affiliates of the National School Board Association, state departments of education, and superintendent search consultants were asked to submit names of newly appointed first-time superintendents.

These varied sources provided a pool of nearly 400 superintendents of whom 18 were invited to participate in the BSS. Their selection was guided by a desire for balance in gender and ethnicity, as well as for geographic diversity and inclusion of different kinds of districts.

The research team included 12 professors of educational leadership or educational administration in universities from across the United States. Each professor worked with one or two superintendents through their first 12 months of tenure. Superintendents were assured that confidentiality would be respected. Confidentiality has been maintained throughout this book through the use of pseudonyms for superintendents and for their districts.

The case studies were developed through a series of interviews with the first-time superintendents, visits to their school districts, and evaluation of relevant documents. Research team members visited the new superintendents in their districts, attended board meetings, and subscribed to local newspapers to follow news coverage of the school districts. Interviews were conducted, either in person or by telephone, approximately once a month throughout the superintendent's first year of service. Researchers used uniform interview guides to ensure that data collected were consistent, though they followed up on unique information as it emerged during the structured interviews. (Interview guides are shown in the Appendix.)

Analysis of data by the research team was conducted according to the procedures of grounded theory research, seeking to identify patterns, themes, or trends that characterize how superintendents shape their professional identities as they face the challenges of leading school districts. Transcriptions or other written accounts of the interviews were shared among research team members. This process ensured that data were analyzed by more than one team member. Portfolios for the school districts were developed, including documents such as school memos, newspaper articles, board agendas, and board minutes. Though other questions emerged during the course of the investigation, the following questions guided the initial analyses:

1. What are the keys to successful entry into the role of superintendent?
2. What strategies do beginning superintendents use to establish their professional identities, and what sources of support help them to accomplish that aim?
3. What time management issues confront beginning superintendents, and how do they set priorities and develop strategies for coping with such issues?
4. What kinds of job-related stress do first-time superintendents report, and what strategies enable them to manage that stress effectively?
5. What critical events do first-time superintendents encounter, and what consequences do these events have for their ability to provide long-term leadership for the school district?

CONTEXT OF THE BEGINNING SUPERINTENDENT STUDY (BSS)

The 18 beginning superintendents were employed by rural, town, suburban, and urban school districts ranging in enrollment from 512 to 127,000 students. Their school districts are located in 12 states from the Atlantic to the Pacific and from the Canadian border to the Gulf of Mexico. Balance in gender and race came about by including 9 female and 6 minority superintendents in the group of 18. Table 1-1 provides further information about the superintendents and the districts that employed them.

A broader context for the case study data was provided by analysis of surveys from 107 first-year superintendents, who were among the 1,748 respondents to a nationwide survey conducted for the 1992 AASA 10-year study of the superintendency (Glass, 1992). Data stemming from the 10-year study and comparisons of the national samples with the 18 participants in the Beginning Superintendent Study are presented in Chapter 2.

PREVIEW OF THE FINDINGS

1.   What Are the Keys to Successful Entry Into the Role of Superintendent?

To learn about the district and community, superintendents who were new to their districts focused much of their initial time on structured inquiry. Many of them arranged a series of meetings not only with administrative staff and board members but also with school and community groups for what one superintendent termed "in-depth briefings." These meetings typically included sessions with civic and religious leaders, public officials, corporate business partners, teachers, and parent groups. The superintendents asked lots of questions and listened thoughtfully. Their ability to listen helped them get to know the district and community quickly and to develop a "big picture" of the situation.

In two instances, the process of learning about the district and community was included in formal entry plans, which the superintendents developed and presented to their boards for approval. One superintendent negotiated with the board a 150-day entry plan based on ideas in the book *Entry* (Jentz et al., 1982). Jentz describes what he calls "structured collaborative inquiry" as a means of getting to know the system and gathering the information and opinions that help to set an agenda for action. Another superintendent said:

The board approved my entry plan document, which identifies a whole series of things that I was committing myself to do to get grounded here. I am very much committed to that plan; it's pretty ambitious, but it does have in it the kinds of things that I hope will give me a good base to understand where we've been and how things work now.

Though other first-time superintendents did not present a formal plan for board approval, it was evident that learning about the district and community was their first priority early in their superintendencies.

TABLE 1-1
The Beginning Superintendents and Their Districts.

Name	Age	Race/Gender	Previous Position	District Setting*	Enrollment	Minority Students, %	Low SES Students, %
Philbert	43	White male	High school principal	Rural, east	1,425	< 1	19.0
Keith	40	White male	Assistant superintendent	Suburb, central	1,500	7	0.003
Hank	56	Indian male	Assistant superintendent	Town, west	1,650	29	41.0
Bob	43	White male	Assistant superintendent	Town, east	3,400	49	40.0
Chad	39	White male	Assistant superintendent	Suburb, east	4,100	5	25.0
Eugene	47	Black male	Assistant superintendent	Suburb, central	4,400	84	23.5
Don	47	White male	Area superintendent	Town, east	6,100	45	55.0
Tomas	46	Hispanic male	Assistant superintendent	Suburb, west	8,700	35	25.0
Myron	53	Black male	Assistant superintendent	City, central	22,000	20	20.0
Jackie	54	White female	Curriculum director	Rural, west	512	10	27.0
Laura	49	White female	Assistant superintendent	City, west	2,500	59	74.0
Martha	51	White female	Assistant superintendent	Town, west	8,000	46	53.0
Lucy	49	White female	Assistant superintendent	Suburb, east	8,100	48	15.0
Jeena	42	White female	Classroom teacher	Town, east	13,000	35	60.0
Theresa	47	White female	Assistant superintendent	City, central	25,000	17	13.0
Kathleen	51	White female	Assistant superintendent	Suburb, central	55,000	48	55.7
Susan	50	Black female	Assistant state superintendent	City, east	72,000	70	70.0
Marilyn	59	Black female	Assistant superintendent	City, west	127,000	67	50.0

*The district settings were classified according to the code developed by Frank H. Johnson (1989) of the Office of Educational Research and Improvement of the National Center for Educational Statistics: city (urban) districts are in the central city of a Metropolitan Statistical Area (MSA); suburban (urban fringe) districts are within an MSA but not the central city; town districts are not in an MSA and are in communities whose population equals or exceeds 2,500 people; and rural districts are in communities with less than 2,500 people or having a ZIP code designated rural by the Census Bureau.

Another beginning superintendent described how his predecessor and written documents assisted him during this process:

The superintendent who was here was wonderful. He put together planning packets of information for me. I've been reading the local papers and local newsletters from all the schools. I've been going back through budget, planning, staffing, and enrollment patterns. . . . I'm just trying to familiarize myself with every single aspect of the district. . . . I've tried to look at the processes that they used to make decisions and the people that they work with. All those kinds of things, I think, are the most important for me to know. Whether I like it or not, I'm coming into a very well-established culture.

Developing good working relationships with the immediate central office staff was also a priority. One superintendent approached this process directly:

The first thing I did was to go right to my secretary and say, "Let's sit down together. I want to do whatever I can do to earn your respect, loyalty, and friendship. I am going to have a close working relationship with you. I want us to be of the same mind and feel like we work positively."

The collaborative aspect of the entry period was especially important in several districts whose boards, during the hiring process, had expressed their desire to have the districts work more collaboratively than they had in the past. Demonstrating a collaborative style and respect for the ideas of all constituencies was part of setting the tone for future action. One minority superintendent put it this way:

There has been an entrenched bureaucracy. I do not believe it serves the schools well, nor has it, in general, served the community well. It certainly hasn't served the students well. . . . It's been a top-down arrangement where you had to get clearance from the superintendent, the blessing of the superintendent, and somehow work through the old boys' network. That course didn't work very well. . . . We've got to find ways to engage people here in the decision-making process and take it out of the hands of the superintendent alone.

Another said:

They had been used to a very centralized approach, and the board and staff want to move toward a more decentralized approach. . . . We want to see a collaborative consensus-making organizational approach developed and implemented by the end of the year.

Though it occurred before individuals were employed as superintendents, many of them declared that a key to successful entry into the superintendency is extensive prior experience in school administration. This is consistent with the findings in Tom Glass' study of career paths of exemplary superintendents (Carter, Glass, & Hord, 1993). Glass reported: "The exemplary superintendents were far more likely to spend a few years in central office positions before acquiring appointments as superintendents" (p. 61). The 1992 AASA 10-year study found that about 50% of superintendents had prior experience in central office positions. Central office experience, including those positions responsible for curriculum and instruction and staff development, seemed to provide valuable communication and planning skills.

More than 70% of the superintendents included in the Beginning Superintendent Study had prior experience in central office positions; most of them had served as deputy or assistant superintendents in larger districts. Four had been assistant superintendents in the district where they became superintendents. One, who had not been an assistant superintendent, had served as an administrator for 18 years, including 13 years as a high school principal in other districts.

Other descriptions of the keys to successful entry into the role of superintendent included: "knowing what you want to accomplish"; "ability to listen to all constituencies without being defensive"; "willingness to keep my mouth shut and listen—being a very willing student, especially about school finance"; "developing strategies for change, but without a pre-set agenda"; and "careful contract development to cover every possible situation anticipated." Each of the superintendents who were appointed with prior experience in the district pointed out the importance of knowing the community and staff and of having contacts within the community to provide needed information. These observations underscored the wisdom of superintendents appointed from outside the district taking time to learn and build collaborative relationships.

2. What Strategies Do Beginning Superintendents Use to Establish Their Professional Identities, and What Sources of Support Help Them to Accomplish That Aim?

One entry strategy served a dual purpose. Meetings with community leaders and school groups not only helped the superintendent learn about the district but also helped to establish the professional identity of the superintendent and a base of support. One superintendent described her strategy as building outward from the children to the parents to the school system to the community. She used what she called "up-front-and-out there strategies." She said, "I asked the parents to work with me. . . . I stand up in front of them and make an impassioned plea to work with me." Of her contacts with community leaders, she said:

I have been to see every elected official in the district; I have gone to see and speak before every body, every board. . . . I have spoken before all of these groups of people introducing myself, telling them what my hopes and aspirations are for this school system, pledging the cooperation of the school board, and asking them to work with us so that we don't necessarily have to spend more money but that when we pool our resources, this energy takes place, and we can get a whole lot more for our dollars by working together than we can by working as separate entities.

Another superintendent who also spoke formally with the primary civic, service, and religious groups in the community said she was striving to set the tone for working together and for involving community members in strategic planning. Having been hired by a reform board with the challenge to "turn the district around," she began by striving for *a couple of short-term successes that would be visible and symbolic of good things to come . . . a pilot program to target two or three things that relate to instruction where we think we have a chance of getting positive movement . . . or getting two or three faculties to buy into doing something unique in terms of dropout prevention.*

Planned visiting to schools in a large district helped one superintendent establish her identity. She visited one school on her first official day on the job. Then she visited every school at a rate of ten per month until all schools and every work site were visited within a few months. These visits also helped to develop her understanding of the district staff and students and their needs.

Some beginning superintendents used professional colleagues from outside the district as a base of support, as a sounding board, and as mentors. In other districts, school board members provided primary support for their superintendent's developing professional identity. Sometimes board members helped the superintendents establish support or advisory groups. One such group was called a Town Forum and was comprised of teachers, parents, community members, and business leaders.

One superintendent turned to professional literature for strategies for establishing his professional identity. Phil Schlechty (1990), Stephen Covey (1989), Ann Lieberman and Lynn Miller (1984), and Peter Senge (1990) all had substantial influence on this first-year superintendent's efforts to make sense of his work. He often got up at 5 A.M. to read and write. He described some of his conclusions:

We can't make progress unless we replace the traditional bureaucratic culture in schooling—programs that are merely cyclical (replaced by new ones). The new culture has three pieces: structural (new roles and relationships for school people); curriculum (exit outcomes, task analysis); and student quality work (identified by teacher work teams with the help of consultants).

Other superintendents shaped their identity by developing wide-based school improvement or strategic planning teams, stressing open communication and involvement. They invited school personnel, parents, and community members to participate. They provided training for the planning teams and followed up throughout the year.

Whether superintendents served small or very large districts, they shaped their professional identities through high visibility, providing a vision of improved education for students, and developing the means to achieve the vision through collaborative planning.

3. What Time Management Issues Confront Beginning Superintendents, and How Do They Set Priorities and Develop Strategies for Coping With Such Issues?

Beginning superintendents were often, at first, overwhelmed by the magnitude of the job. This was especially true in very small districts with little or no support staff and in large districts when key assistant superintendent positions were vacant. One superintendent declared that he had no idea of the time commitment when assuming the position.

Daytimers

Superintendents were willing to devote whatever time was needed to get the tasks done. However, such devotion came at the price of time for themselves and their families. One beginning superintendent described the impact by saying, "I feel as if I've become a monk." Several of the female superintendents participating in the study were living in states or cities distant from their husbands. Time with spouses was limited to occasional visits and telephone contact, but they stated that this enabled them to concentrate fully on the job. Those superintendents who were single also found that their freedom from family responsibilities allowed them to spend more time on the job. When asked what they did for recreation or for themselves, most of the superintendents found it difficult to identify such activities.

Even when living with their families, beginning superintendents reported that many evenings and weekends were spent on the job. Some superintendents in smaller districts tried to be at all school functions at each of the buildings but found this simply did not work. Bond issues or school referendum elections consumed huge chunks of time for some of the superintendents. In one district, a bond issue, which had failed three times before the superintendent came, would fail twice more during the superintendent's first year. He participated in more than 50 meetings on this bond issue during his first year, faithfully making himself available to the public at each meeting until the last question was asked and answered.

One superintendent stated that her typical work day extended from 7:30 A.M. to 9 or 9:30 P.M. She said:

When I ran out of time during the regular day on my calendar, I started meeting people for lunch and meeting people for dinner. So I've been getting home at 9 or 9:30 every evening, and my planning time is being usurped. I know this can be deadly; it can be a deadly mistake.

The pressure of time management issues was highlighted when she found that even this time commitment was not sufficient to keep some staff members satisfied. She reported:

I've heard through the grapevine, from a board member, that some of the members of the central staff are feeling isolated, but that's just because everybody's vying for my time. I have to balance that. I know the importance of making sure everybody feels included, but my purpose is not to make sure everybody in the organization has a piece of my time and is assured they have a job. I have to balance that with the community needing to see me, and my main mission is not for them to feel secure. I know full well that ultimately I'm going to have the people in the organization feeling good about the mission, but my purpose is not to serve the central office per se. . . .

In my former position, I learned a lot about large organizations and what happens when people in the bowels of the organization don't feel the same sense of urgency the top staff member does, and they want to cut through all the layers and have access to the top staff member. I didn't have a lot of patience for that, but then finally I realized that I wasn't going to get anything done unless I could make those people feel as I do. So I began doing some very deliberate things to do that, putting in place a high performance organizational model and spending time working on the organization *itself. I didn't really want to do that but realized I had to. Once I took the time to do it, things started turning around. There's no way I could have done that here in a month, but it was a little disheartening to hear it's happening already.*

Even in her frustration, this superintendent identified a key for coping with time management issues: prioritizing with an eye to primary mission. Other superintendents spoke of prioritizing systemic goals—those crucial to the entire system. Spending time on such goals helps to institute procedures that ultimately free up time for a longer range focus. Some superintendents set priorities according to strategic plans, emphasizing students and schools. One research team member noted that for her superintendents the movement from normalcy to crisis to normalcy was only for relatively short periods. "They brought the district back to calm waters as quickly as possible, focusing on the long-range plan to set priorities."

The team was surprised to learn that some superintendents were, for the first time, using a systematic scheduling system such as Daytimer or Franklin Day Planner and were just discovering how valuable such an approach can be. One superintendent had the advantage of an administrative assistant in charge of the calendar and monitoring the superintendent's time. The availability of support personnel and the ability to delegate and hold subordinates responsible for completing tasks appeared to enable some superintendents to cope with time management issues smoothly.

4. What Kinds of Job-Related Stress Do First-Time Superintendents Report, and What Strategies Enable Them to Manage Stress Effectively?

In addition to the time management issue addressed above, a wide variety of other demands also created stress for first-time superintendents. A partial listing of these stressors includes the following:

"Being a highly visible, public figure" who is "always on stage and always quoted"

Frequent requests to make speeches

The need to respond to multiple, diverse constituencies with different priorities

School board elections

People unwilling to change when the board expects that changes will be made

The need to terminate incompetent employees

Dealing with employees charged with sexual assault

New people in key positions

Pressure from fundamentalist, right-wing religious groups

Getting to know the people in the schools and communities

Gang violence in schools or involving students

Fiscal emergencies

Deciding who to trust

Lack of people in whom to confide

The issue of trust was particularly critical in districts where key administrators from inside the district had competed unsuccessfully for the superintendency. The new superintendents knew these individuals might be hoping they would fail. In one such district, each of the two assistant superintendents secured employment with other school districts within a month of the superintendent's arrival. Although the new superintendent needed to learn key information from them before their departure, he could not depend on the accuracy of what they reported.

One superintendent identified three sources of stress:

First, the superintendency is an entirely new job that requires a new definition; it could blow up in your face at any time. . . . Second, because of growing violence, drug use, and social changes, teachers and administrators have less control over what and how students behave and learn in schools. . . . Third, education is a tough career and some teachers and administrators are not going to make it.

Strategies for handling stress were both professional and personal in nature. A proactive coping strategy was improving communication with all stakeholders, to prevent or defuse problems before they become serious. Building up commitment and trust in professional judgments with administrators, teachers, parents, and staffers was a priority. Developing commitment and involvement by social service agencies in addressing problems with students or staff was also important for some districts. Another proactive strategy was working with attorneys and senior staff to design fair, equitable evaluation systems.

Keeping a diary of work was used by some to reflect on events, on the progress toward goals, and on the impact being made. Most of the superintendents commented about the value of regular communication with the BSS researcher. Communicating with a knowledgeable, objective fellow professional with whom they felt free to share confidential events and problems proved to be an important strategy for coping with stress.

Personal coping strategies used by the superintendents included assuring that time was set aside for family and self and physical exercise, with exercise patterns varying from daily to four days a week to one day a week. Some found the commuting time between the district office and home helpful for reflection. Others found that just driving out of the community helped them to regain perspective. Although one superintendent went fishing, he found that time for such interests was extremely limited. Another addressed the matter of stress directly by visiting a therapist.

5. What Critical Events Do First-Time Superintendents Encounter, and What Consequences Do These Events Have for Their Ability to Provide Long-Term Leadership for the District?

The critical events encountered by the superintendents participating in the study were as diverse as the districts they served. Two kinds of critical events occurred in many of the districts. One related to fiscal problems and was not unexpected. The other, impacting a surprising number of districts, centered on charges of sexual abuse or molestation of students by educators.

Sometimes the superintendent and board were well aware of major fiscal problems during the interview process. The residents of one district had defeated a desperately needed bond issue three times before the superintendent was employed. Even with heroic efforts on the part of the superintendent, the bond issue failed twice more before passing.

In another district, the superintendent, when assuming office, recognized the need for added funding in both operating and capital improvement budgets. However, even with this knowledge, it was a shock to discover buildings in total disrepair and to hear at board meetings vociferous complaints from parents and school personnel. Rather than doing "quick fixes" on the buildings where protests were the loudest, she made a careful analysis of needs and resources and reported her findings to the board. She said:

What made the presentation, I think, so impressive is that I gave them a report that indicated that we really had $600 million worth of capital needs, and we had only $8 million on hand. The $600 million estimate was made by the state two years ago, but evidently no one here ever did anything with it.

This was far from the only district where board members had not been fully or accurately informed of fiscal needs by previous superintendents. In a smaller district, though the dollar amount involved was less, the new superintendent was dismayed to discover that $500,000 of state funds had been misappropriated and needed to be replaced from an already strapped local budget.

One new superintendent believed he was coming to a district with ample resources because it spent nearly $2,000 more per pupil than his previous district. He was amazed to discover that his new district was financially strapped. Spending close to $3,000 less per pupil than its surrounding districts limited the educational opportunities it could provide.

State funding crises, delays in state education appropriations, changes in state aid formulas, significant population shifts due to military cutbacks, and even a tornado produced unanticipated critical events for other superintendents. In these cases, even careful planning and responsible management by their predecessors were not sufficient to avert the pressures caused by the lack of needed funds.

Board members seemed to recognize that the fiscal crises were neither created by the new superintendents nor within their power to correct immediately. In retrospect, it appears that facing a fiscal crisis with a school district provides an opportunity for a new superintendent to build alliances and demonstrate leadership. New superintendents applied systematic collaborative problem solving processes to the fiscal emergencies, seeking to keep the board of education and the public informed of the facts in each situation. This openness and collaboration set a tone for addressing future issues within the districts.

The number of districts where charges of sexual abuse or molestation emerged was surprising to the research team. Although each event had unique circumstances, in several instances it seemed apparent that prior administrators had knowledge of the situation but had neither documented it nor acted to resolve it. In one instance, a suspect teacher attempted suicide when his behavior became known; in another instance, a teacher was formally charged, convicted, and subsequently imprisoned; and in still another case a male teacher with more than 20 years of tenure was said to have been inappropriately involved with a male student. One superintendent needed to deal with a teacher who was also a coach and who had an affair with a high school student. When confronted with the accusation and some evidence, he acknowledged the situation and resigned before the board acted to terminate him.

Each of these circumstances created a need for the superintendent to scrupulously protect the due process and privacy rights of the individuals involved while keeping the board informed and taking appropriate action. It appears that a long-term effect of needing to face such delicate personnel issues early in a superintendency would be to build a board's confidence in the superintendent as a leader whom they can trust to do the right thing for students while respecting human dignity.

OVERVIEW OF BECOMING A SUPERINTENDENT

This book invites the reader to explore the complex world of the beginning superintendent through both wide-angle and telephoto lenses. A national survey provides wide-angle perspectives on first-year superintendents and how they compare with their more experienced peers. In Chapter 2, Tom Glass provides a historical perspective on the superintendency and examines findings of the *Study of the American School Superintendency*, which he conducted for the AASA in 1992. He compares the 107 first-year superintendents included in that survey with the subjects of the Beginning Superintendent Study as well as with a national sample of more than 1,700 superintendents.

Close-up, telephoto lens images of beginning superintendents are provided in the case studies presented in Chapters 3 through 13. These superintendents are diverse in their gender, ethnicity, geography, and size of school district. Readers are invited to share their lives as they encountered the demanding and often unexpected challenges of their first superintendencies.

Cross-case analyses in Chapters 14 through 17 provide wide-angle perspectives on the political, ethical, legal, and theoretical dimensions of the superintendency, as well as pitfalls that complicate the lives of first-time superintendents. In Chapter 14, Bill Gordon analyzes mistakes beginning superintendents made, providing a guide to "rocks in the roadway" other first-timers will want to avoid. Harsh realities superintendents encountered when faced with political games and with evidence of immoral and unethical behavior are examined by Sam and Carolyn Chapman in Chapter 15.

Mary Scherr focuses the lens of leadership theory on the experiences of first-time superintendents in Chapter 16, showing how they illustrate or contradict prior understandings of leadership. Finally, in Chapter 17, Doris Henry and Chuck Achilles explore the preparation of superintendents, drawing from the experiences of the beginning superintendents. New and innovative programs that have emerged in recent years are examined as models for preparing superintendents for the challenges of the twenty-first century.

QUESTIONS FOR REFLECTION AND DISCUSSION

1. In seeking to learn about the superintendency, what are the benefits and the liabilities of studying superintendents with diversity in ethnicity and gender, considering that
   only a small fraction of superintendents are
   minorities or females?

2. What patterns do you see between the characteristics of districts employing first-time
   superintendents in relation to their gender
   and ethnicity? What hypotheses do you have
   about why such patterns may have emerged?

3. How does rapid turnover of superintendents
   affect the attitudes and behavior of parents,
   teachers, and administrators in a school
   district?

4. Considering your own experiences with
   and observations of superintendents, what
   characteristics would you look for if you
   were on a search committee to select a
   superintendent?

REFERENCES

American Association of School Administrators.
(1952). *The American school superintendency*. Washington, DC: Author.

Bennett, D. (1991, April). Big city blues. *American
School Board Journal, 178*, 22–24.

Blumberg, A. with Blumberg, P. (1985). *The school
superintendent: Living with conflict*. New
York: Teachers College Press.

Bullard, P., & Taylor, B. O. (1993). *Making school
reform happen*. Boston: Allyn & Bacon.

Carter, D. S. G., Glass, T. E., & Hord, S. M. (1993).
*Selecting, preparing and developing the school
district superintendent*. Washington, DC:
Falmer Press.

Chance, E. W., & Capps, J. L. (1990, October).
*Administrator stability in rural schools:
The school board factor*. Paper presented at
the Annual Meeting of the National Rural
Education Association, Colorado Springs.

Covey, S. R. (1989). *The seven habits of highly
effective people*. New York: Simon & Schuster.

Cubberley, E. L. (1909). *Changing conceptions of
education*. Boston: Houghton Mifflin.

Daley, S. (1990, December 26). School chiefs dropping out, plagued by urban problems. *New
York Times*, p.1.

Deal, T. E., & Kennedy, A. A. (1982). *Corporate
cultures: The rites and rituals of corporate
life*. Reading, MA: Addison-Wesley.

Giles, S., & Giles, D. E. (1990). *Superintendent
turnover: Crisis facing California schools.*

(Report No. EA 022 484). California. (ERIC
Document Reproduction Service No. ED 325
981)

Glass, T. E. (1992). *The 1992 study of the American
school superintendency: American's education leaders in a time of reform*. Arlington,
VA: American Association of School Administrators.

In the U.S. its tough to keep those superintendent
positions filled. (1994, Winter). *The International Educator, 9*, 12.

Jentz, B., Cheever, D. S., Jr., Fisher, S. B., Jones,
M. H., Kelleher, P., & Wofford, J. W. (1982).
*Entry: The hiring, start-up, and super-vision
of administrators*. New York: McGraw-Hill.

Johnson, F. (1989). *Assigning type of locale codes to
the 1987-88 CCD public school universe*.
(Report No. CS 89-194). Washington, DC:
National Center for Education Statistics.

Jones, R. (1994, April). Instant superintendent:
Can a candidate with business savvy but no
education experience really handle the job?
The American School Board Journal, 188,
23–26.

Kerr, R. P. (1988, December). Superintendents best
serve their schools by staying put. *Executive
Educator, 10*, 20—21.

Kowalski, T. J. (1995). *Keepers of the flame: Contemporary urban superintendents*. Thousand
Oaks, CA: Sage.

Lieberman, A., & Miller, L. (1984). *Teachers,
their world, and their work*. Alexandria, VA:

Association for Supervision and Curriculum Development.

Miklos, E. (1988). Administrator selection, career patterns, succession, and socialization. In N. J. Boyan (Ed.), *Handbook of Research on Educational Administration*. New York: Longman.

Murphy, J. T. (March, 1991). Superintendents as saviors: From the terminator to Pogo. *Phi Delta Kappan*, 72, 507—513.

Parkay, F. W., & Hall, G. E. (1992). *Becoming a principal: The challenge of beginning leadership*. Boston: Allyn & Bacon.

Scherer, R. (1995, June 19). Big city school superintendents are posting high dropout rate. *The Christian Science Monitor*, pp. 1, 18.

Schlechty, P. C. (1990). *Schools for the twenty-first century: Leadership imperatives for educational reform*. San Francisco: Jossey-Bass.

Senge, P. M. (1990). *The fifth discipline: The art and practice of the learning organization*. New York: Doubleday.

Sergiovanni, T. J., Burlingame, M., Coombs, F. S., & Thurston, P. W. (1992). *Educational governance and administration* (3rd ed.). Boston: Allyn & Bacon.

Sorohan, E. G. (1990, January). Plan now for the coming shortage of administrators. *School Board News*, 10, 8.

Tyack, D., & Hansot, E. (1982). *Managers of virtue: Public school leadership in America, 1820-1980*. New York: Basic Books.

2

THE SUPERINTENDENCY
Yesterday, Today, and Tomorrow

Thomas E. Glass, Northern Illinois University

ABSTRACT. Comparisons between beginning superintendents and more experienced colleagues add new images to the portrait of the superintendency that has been evolving over the past 150 years in American school districts. These comparisons and the historical context provide a broad picture of the superintendents in the United States in terms of their backgrounds, districts, school boards, and sources of support, stress, and satisfaction.

T he 15,000 men and women scattered across the nation who hold positions as public school district superintendents have attracted increasing interest in the past several years. School reformists, legislators, and the private sector have become increasingly aware of superintendents' importance not only in day-to-day operations but also in the transition of school systems into the next century.

Understanding the superintendency requires a look at *yesterday* to gain a historical perspective on the changing role of superintendents and their place in American public education. A portrait of *today*'s superintendency is supplied by the 1992 National Study of the American School Superintendency (Glass, 1992), which is based on responses from 1,748 superintendents. Anticipation of the superintendency of *tomorrow* is provided by analysis of responses from the 107 first-year superintendents within the national study as well as responses from the 18 participants in the Beginning Superintendents Study (BSS). The generalizability of data from the BSS superintendents was enhanced by including superintendents who were diverse in gender and ethnicity and who served rural, town, suburban, and urban school districts scattered from coast to coast.

HISTORICAL PERSPECTIVE

The profession of the superintendency slowly evolved within American public education during the mid-1800s as cities grew during the industrial revolution. Larger towns with larger populations had many "schoolhouses," and school boards found it necessary to hire an educator to coordinate day-to-day operations. Administration of these early school districts was shared between the board, the superintendent, and, sometimes, a business manager independently reporting to the board.

By the Civil War, 27 large eastern and midwestern cities had established a superintendent as the chief administrative officer. As cities grew after the Civil War, the number of superintendencies grew parallel to increases in school population. However, the day-to-day governance in thousands of small rural districts was left in the hands of farmer-populated school boards (Callahan, 1966).

The early pioneering superintendents, especially those in the large cities, faced almost insurmountable challenges to provide adequate school funding and to keep city politics away from the schoolhouse door. At times, the very existence of the common school movement was threatened.

With few exceptions, early superintendents were men, as single women typically stayed in the classroom. In the nineteenth century, married women were rarely allowed even to teach in American public schools.

Several states did not develop a free public education system until the first and second decades of the twentieth century. Thus, many early superintendents, resembling circuit riding preachers, traveled far away from their cities and school districts to preach the gospel of a free public education. These pioneers were moral role models, champions of the democratic ethic, and, perhaps most importantly, builders of the American dream.

The American superintendency has greatly changed since the early days of the common school movement. Today, in most school districts, superintendents are administrators responsible for managerial matters such as finance, capital expenditures, coordination with the state board of education, and public relations. Most no longer worry about coal for stoves and whether teachers have a place to board during the school year, important concerns their professional forefathers shared with their rural school boards. However, the transition in responsibilities is still evident as superintendents today struggle to prevent boards from trying to micromanage day-to-day operations. In summary, the superintendency and superintendents have substantially changed as America has evolved from a rural agrarian society to a nation of urban dwellers.

Establishing Professionalism

Superintendents did not immediately wrest day-to-day control of school districts from school boards. This contest was described by Ellwood Cubberley (1922), one of the pioneer educational administrators, as the struggle of superintendents to be *professional.*

The relationship between school boards and superintendents has been a continuing subject of discussion and research over the years. This partnership and the ways boards of education function are thought by most writers to be key elements in the effectiveness of a school district. Certainly, board-superintendent relations have been of highest concern to superintendents.

School boards in the early days were often the nemesis of superintendents. The superintendent pioneers, such as Cubberly, George Strayer, and Frank Spaulding, not only championed the cause of the common school movement but also wrestled with boards who saw school dollars and jobs as political spoils to be spread among their lackeys. Deciding who would be employed and what textbooks, supplies, and food would be purchased were political issues to the party machines of Chicago, New York, and Boston (Callahan, 1966).

While pioneer superintendents worked to establish the concept of the common school district and differentiate the roles of the superintendent and school board, they were also greatly concerned with the professional preparation of future superintendents. Some of the early and best known superintendents soon found their way into university teaching and founded departments of educational administration. One of the most notable of these was Ellwood Cubberly at Stanford University. Though he had never taken an administration course, he wrote over 20 books about school administration!

Era of Scientific Management

In the early 1900s, the superintendency was established and legitimized with school boards and the public. At the same time, a great wave of "scientific management," based on the work of Frederick Taylor, swept private sector corporate management.

This approach was by no means limited to the business world. The predecessor of the American Association of School Administrators (AASA), the Department of Superintendence of the National Education Association, at its 1913 conference, featured an address on the "Underlying Principles of Scientific Management." Building on this address, Frank Spaulding, superintendent of schools at Newton, Massachusetts, reported on the "marvelous results" of applying scientific management in the "educational industry" (Callahan, 1961, p. 68).

Daniel Griffiths, in his 1966 book *The School Superintendent*, discusses the induction of the principles of scientific management to school management. Griffiths asserts that schools were forged into "industrial models." One reason that superintendents saw scientific management positively was that it advocated shifting decision making from laypersons on untrained boards of education to trained "industrial" managers, namely to professionals, like themselves. The influence of scientific management is still evident, though many current writers declare that its highly centralized, hierarchial bureaucracy and organizational chain of command are primary obstacles to reform and restructuring.

Superintendents in cities, whose burgeoning populations were fueled by the industrial revolution, saw scientific management as a way to tie together their ever expanding organizations and to measure production. Many thought this was the way they could be accountable to taxpayers.

A sidelight to scientific management was that, by the 1930s, most states had spelled out in statute the role of the local school superintendent and the board of education. Codification more clearly drew lines of authority, making the superintendent responsible to the board of education, thereby specifying the current organizational form for today's school districts.

Superintendents as "Experts"

From the 1920s, superintendents and principals were recognized as the educational "experts" of local school districts and were seldom challenged unless a political question was at hand. Beginning in the 1960s, during the civil rights movement, the "expertness" of many school administrators was severely questioned. The school reformers of the 1960s and 1970s especially questioned the scientific management model of the urban school organization, which, some said, failed to provide adequate education to minority children.

School reformists in the 1980s and 1990s are still questioning the highly centralized nature of many districts and are targeting the organizational structure and culture of individual schools as keys to reform. Secondary schools, most of which epitomize scientific management, have not changed organizationally since the early 1900s.

School boards still look to superintendents for expert opinion. However, as Arthur Blumberg points out, modern day superintendents must be politically astute, leaving less time to impact teaching and learning (Blumberg, 1985). Unfortunately, this reality often puts superintendents in a role conflict as boards expect superintendents to be politicians, managers, curriculum specialists, counselors, and personnel supervisors—"A man or woman for all seasons." Unrealistic expectations held for superintendents by school boards are serious problems in many districts today.

Practice into Theory: A Revolution in Training

A third phase in the development of the superintendency began in the late 1950s and is just now fading away. Daniel Griffiths and Jacob Getzels describe this phase as one aspect of the move toward "professionalism" (described earlier). So what should superintendents be trained to do? Many of the early day professors, such as Strayer and Spaulding, were large-city superintendents before turning to the university classroom to train future superintendents. These early professors were mostly interested in training students in the skills and practices that they "knew from experience" worked successfully.

In the 1960s, the professors of educational administration took the training of school administrators from the world of "real life" into the theory bases of sociology and psychology. Many of these professors had had no previous experience as superintendents and principals. Yet, by the 1970s, they were the dominant group in the educational administration professorate (Sass, 1989).

In many instances, "superintendent social scientists" were taught theoretical models of management and instructed on how to test them in a field setting. This was a far cry from the days where practitioners taught practitioners the skills of educational administration as an applied craft (Sclafani, 1987).

Challenges in the 1960s and 1970s

The social conflicts of the 1960s and 1970s significantly impacted the nation's school districts and their superintendents. One of the most interesting developments of this era was the changing composition of school boards. Many board members came into their roles bearing special interest platforms. In previous decades, school boards were generally comprised of businessmen and professional people interested in public education for the general welfare. However, beginning in the 1960s and 1970s, more blue-collar workers, homemakers, and others were elected as single issue candidates intent on changing the system (Getzels, Liphan, & Campbell, 1968, pp. 352–358).

Unfortunately, few superintendents have written about their experiences during this tumultuous period. However, one did. Larry Cuban (1988) provided the most significant picture of this period of the superintendency in *The Managerial Imperative and the Practice of Leadership in Schools.* He pointedly identifies how the social tensions in the community spilled into the schools.

Social unrest and conflict during this period did change the superintendency. It's probable that boards began to infringe more on the previous domain of policy making held by superintendents (Campbell, Cunningham, Nystrand, & Usdan, 1990).

Superintendents Under Fire

When parents or community members become disenchanted with their school district, the first person to hear about it is usually the superintendent. Board members may get phone calls, but it is usually the superintendent who bears the daily criticism. This criticism is compounded by complaints of unhappy employees and unions often at odds with the school board and other community interest groups. Hence, superintendents are frequently caught between hotly and bitterly competing groups (Tucker & Zeigler, 1980).

Once caught in a web of competing interests, superintendents may see their contracts terminated. One reason these superintendents do not survive is because boards of education feel that by changing superintendents they can deflect or delay further public criticism. It is like changing baseball managers. Theodore Kowalski (1995), in his book *Keepers of the Flame*, describes webs of conflict in urban school districts where dissatisfaction and controversy are constant.

Superintendents in an Era of Reform

The 1980s and 1990s have been an era of continual attempts to reform America's schools. Unfortunately, not a great deal has happened to alter the basic unit of public education, namely the schoolroom. If reform is to penetrate the doors of teachers' classrooms, school culture must be changed. Usually, the process of culture change is led jointly by the formal and informal leaders both in schools and in districts (Conley, 1993, p. 322).

Most reform efforts have been top-down mandates by legislatures and state boards of education to oblige local school districts to comply with new directives. Even at the local level some reforms have been top-down mandates by boards of education.

Much of the 1980s school reform literature pointed a finger at superintendents as the culprits who stand in the way of true reform. Superintendents were not only caught between competing interests in their school districts but also criticized by reformists as being blockers of reform. What confused many superintendents was that they perceived themselves as change agents in their school districts and as true school reformers.

In recent years, a second wave of school reform has recognized the importance of the role of the superintendent and principals in a school district. This more constructive wave of reform emerged in the late 1980s as the media, influential national organizations, and the world of professional education called for better preparation of superintendents and principals.

The 1990s have seen the emergence of charter schools across the country and advocacy for other forms of control at the local level by principals, parents, teachers, and students themselves. In a few notable instances, state or city officials, rather than local school boards, have appointed chief executive officers (CEOs) to operate large city districts, and some school boards have contracted with private, for-profit firms to run schools, bringing new challenges to superintendents' authority and policy making leadership.

STUDYING THE FIRST-YEAR SUPERINTENDENT

In recent years, the American school superintendency, much like similar leadership positions in the private sector, has become a more specialized and complex role. Close scrutiny of public schools by politicians, parents, and voters, along with a myriad of new governmental regulations, laws, administrative mandates, and employee union concerns, have created a leadership scenario far different from 20 years ago.

The traditional organizational structure of school districts and the manner in which states delegate operational responsibility identify the superintendent as the chief developer and implementer of policy. Even though site-based management might decidedly change the operation of a local school budget process, legislative statutes and state agency regulations still hold the superintendent responsible for budget management. Despite what reformists may desire, the "buck stops here" still characterizes the office of the superintendent.

The superintendent's role will be critical to twenty-first century school district leadership, and hence it is imperative to know something about the women and men who will furnish that leadership. Their personalities, training, concerns, goals, and actions will have a dramatic impact on furthering reform necessary to enable this country to be globally competitive in the twenty-first century.

THE AASA'S 10-YEAR STUDIES OF THE SUPERINTENDENCY

Every 10 years, the American Association of School Administrators (AASA) conducts a National Study of the American School Superintendency. In 1990, the seventh such in-depth study was conducted by the author of this chapter, with the assistance of staff at AASA. A nationwide survey was distributed to over 2,700 superintendents with 1,748 responding. Throughout this chapter, these 1,748 superintendents are referred to in the tables and text as the national sample. Of this *national sample*, 107 were first-year beginning superintendents; they are designated in this chapter as the *first-year sample* within the total group of AASA respondents. The demographics and opinions of this group are considered here as representative of first-year superintendents nationwide during the early 1990s (Glass, 1992).

This chapter compares the 18 first-year superintendents who were participants in the Beginning Superintendent Study (BSS), with the first-year sample and their more experienced colleagues in the AASA study. The 18 BSS project participants, designated in this chapter as the *BSS group*, each completed the AASA survey, in addition to providing ethnographic data for the research team. Data from these three groups of superintendents, the national sample, the first-year sample, and the BSS group, provide a context for the case studies, which appear in succeeding chapters of this book.

GENDER, RACE, AND ACADEMIC PREPARATION OF SUPERINTENDENTS

The gender of school administrators has been the subject of considerable writing in the past few years. The AASA National Study found that 15% of first-year superintendents were women, as shown in Table 2-1. This was much higher than the national sample in which only 6.6% were women. In future years, a higher percentage of women are likely to be entering the superintendency as well as the principalship. A good example of this trend occurred in the early 1990s in Illinois, where the number of women superintendents has increased from 27 to 67 in four years (Glass, 1995). Recognizing the trend and the need to learn more about female superintendents, the Beginning Superintendent Study was designed with gender balance by including equal numbers of males and females.

In the United States today, most minority students attend schools in large urban districts. These districts are frequently led by minority superintendents (Rist, 1991). As indicated in Table 2-2, only 3.9% of the national sample were minorities. However, minorities comprised 8.6% of the first-year superintendent group. The minority representation among first-year superintendents probably represents future trends, as

TABLE 2-1
Gender of Superintendents.

	National Sample		First Year Sample		BSS Group	
Gender	N	%	N	%	N	%
Males	1,600	93.4	91	85.0	9	50.0
Females	113	6.6	16	15.0	9	50.0
TOTAL	1,713	100.0	107	100.0	18	100.0

TABLE 2-2
Race of Superintendents.

	National Sample		First Year Sample		BSS Group	
Race	N	%	N	%	N	%
White	1,648	96.1	96	91.4	12	66.7
Minority	66	3.9	9	8.6	6	33.3
TOTAL	1,714	100.0	105	100.0	18	100.0

more minorities gain access to principalships and superintendencies. The BSS design included one-third minorities.

The types of districts minority superintendents will serve is an important issue. Today, minority superintendents are most frequently seen in large urban districts and minority populated districts. This might be viewed as a kind of reverse discrimination because minority superintendents seem to be "locked" into minority districts.

The possession of a doctoral degree appears to have been an important factor in the entry of women and minorities to the superintendency. The AASA study found that, while 44% of the national sample held doctoral degrees, 51.8% of women superintendents and 62.1% of minority superintendents had earned doctorates (Glass, 1992, p. 66).

More first-year and BSS project superintendents had doctoral degrees than the national sample, as shown in Table 2-3. This is not surprising as possession of the doctoral degree makes an inexperienced candidate more marketable as a candidate for a vacancy. The possession of a doctorate is consistent with an emerging trend for boards of education to seek superintendents who are expert instructional leaders. In the past 10 years, the number of superintendents possessing doctorates has risen dramatically in almost all states (Glass, 1995).

TABLE 2-3
Highest Degree Held by Superintendents.

	National Sample		First Year Sample		BSS Group	
Highest Degree	N	%	N	%	N	%
Bachelor's	13	0.8	1	0.9	0	0.0
Master's	644	37.9	36	33.6	4	2.2
Specialist	266	15.8	15	14.0	1	5.6
Doctorate	754	44.4	54	50.6	13	72.2
Some Other Degree	21	1.2	1	0.9	0	0.0
TOTAL	1,698	100.0	107	100.0	18	100.0

EXPERIENCES BEFORE THE SUPERINTENDENCY

The AASA study found that nearly 70% of both first-year superintendents and their more experienced colleagues were raised in rural areas or small towns. This is probably because most school districts are located in rural areas or small towns, and school boards tend to prefer superintendents who share their social values. However, this factor may inhibit mobility of small-town superintendents who wish to move to larger districts in suburbs or cities.

While half of the BSS group also had their roots in rural or small-town areas, nearly 40% of them were raised in large cities. This may be related to the fact that two thirds of the BSS superintendents were employed by city or suburban districts.

A majority of superintendents were former secondary teachers and administrators. Only about 30% were former elementary teachers, as indicated in Table 2-4, though a majority of female superintendents were former elementary teachers. Secondary social studies, science, math, and English were the most often encountered teaching areas of superintendents. Less than 7% of superintendents had been physical education teachers, thus debunking the prevailing myth that coaches dominate appointments to superintendencies.

Approximately half of all superintendents in the study entered school administration by the time they were age 30, and 80% were administrators by age 35. Typically, a teacher with several years experience enrolled on a part-time basis in a university-based program leading to principal certification and a master's degree program in educational administration.

The first administrative position for superintendents was usually a principalship or assistant principalship. However, as shown in Table 2-5, one third of the BSS project superintendents entered administration as central office coordinators or directors, positions more commonly held by women, due to their expertise in curriculum and instruction.

The most common career path for superintendents, as indicated in Table 2-6, was a progression from teacher to principal to central office to superintendent.

TABLE 2-4
Subjects Taught in First Full-Time Teaching Positions.

	National Sample		First Year Sample		BSS Group	
Subjects	**N**	**%**	**N**	**%**	**N**	**%**
Elementary	407	28.5	24	26.7	6	33.3
Social Studies	273	19.1	12	13.3	4	22.2
Science	157	11.0	11	12.2	2	11.1
Math	132	9.3	11	12.2	1	5.6
English	131	9.2	7	7.8	2	11.1
Foreign Language	13	0.9	4	4.4	2	11.1
P.E./Health	67	4.7	6	6.7	0	0.0
Business Education	57	4.0	2	2.2	0	0.0
Special Education	39	2.7	7	7.8	1	5.6
Other Subjects	142	10.0	6	6.7	0	0.0
No Teaching	8	0.6	0	0.0	0	0.0
TOTAL	1,426	100.0	90	100.0	18	100.0

TABLE 2-5
First Administrative or Supervisory Position.

First Position	National Sample		First Year Sample		BSS Group	
	N	%	N	%	N	%
Assistant Principal or Dean of Students	547	32.2	39	36.8	7	38.9
Principal	708	41.7	39	36.8	3	16.7
Director-Coordinator	220	13.0	15	14.1	6	33.3
State Agency, Business Office, or Other	223	13.1	13	12.3	2	11.1
TOTAL	1,698	100.0	106	100.0	18	100.0

This path was followed by almost 40% of superintendents in the AASA Study and 61% in the BSS study. In the national sample, about 35% became superintendents after experience as teachers and principals. This pattern is more likely to be true for superintendents in small districts. On the other hand, a more typical career track for administrators in larger districts was to spend a number of years in central office working in personnel, finance, or curriculum before becoming a superintendent. Still another pattern is illustrated by some central office administrators in large districts who successfully compete for small district superintendencies in order to break into the ranks.

Regardless of the specific positions individuals filled in their path to the superintendency, about 90% of them worked in more than one school district before becoming superintendents. Only 7.1% of the first-year sample and 11.8% of the BSS group reported spending their entire educational career in one school district.

TABLE 2-6
Career Pattern Prior to the Superintendency.

Career Pattern	National Sample		First Year Sample		BSS Group	
	N	%	N	%	N	%
Teacher Only	94	5.9	4	4.0	1	5.6
Principal	65	4.0	2	2.0	0	0.0
Central Office Only	32	2.0	1	1.0	1	5.6
Teacher and Principal	585	36.4	34	34.3	2	11.1
Teacher and Central Office	166	10.3	16	16.2	2	11.1
Principal and Central Office	59	3.7	3	3.0	0	0.0
Teacher, Principal, and Central Office	605	37.7	39	39.5	11	61.0
Other	0	0.0	0	0.0	1	5.6
TOTAL	1,606	100.0	99	100.0	18	100.0

BECOMING A SUPERINTENDENT

A superintendent vacancy in large, well paying districts generally attracts 40 to 60 applicants. For positions in smaller districts, there are often few applicants. Many superintendents find richer contracts and suburban living more attractive than living in an isolated small town that is losing population and tax base.

Of the first-year superintendents in the AASA study, 42.1% were hired from within. A disadvantage of being hired from within is that there is generally no honeymoon or grace period. However, family finances and a spouse with a desirable job often deter candidates from applying for jobs outside their districts. About two thirds of the national sample of superintendents and of the BSS superintendents were outside candidates, as shown in Table 2-7. Some of these may have been hired as change agents, though data reported in Table 2-8 indicate that this was most often true of the BSS group. Research indicates that outsiders typically are more change agent minded and perform better on the average than insiders, a view first put forth by Richard Carlson (1972) and tested often since.

Why did superintendents think they were selected by their school boards? About 40% of the superintendents in the AASA study reported that they had been hired because of their personal characteristics. Just over 25% of the AASA samples and 55.5% of the BSS superintendents reported that they had been hired as change agents. The representation of women in the BSS group may have impacted this. Women superintendents have been reported in other studies to see themselves as experienced

TABLE 2-7
Superintendents Hired From Within School Districts.

Successor Type	National Sample		First Year Sample		BSS Group	
	N	%	N	%	N	%
Insider	616	36.0	45	42.1	6	33.3
Outsider	1,094	64.0	62	57.9	12	67.7
TOTAL	1,710	100.0	107	100.0	18	100.0

TABLE 2-8
Reasons Given by Superintendents for Their Selection.

Reason for Selection	National Sample		First Year Sample		BSS Group	
	N	%	N	%	N	%
Personal Characteristics	636	38.5	44	42.3	5	27.8
Change Agent	452	27.4	27	26.0	10	55.5
Instructional Leader	368	22.3	22	21.2	3	16.7
Maintain Status Quo	35	2.1	1	0.9	0	0.0
Specific Task or No Particular Reason	161	9.7	10	9.6	0	0.0
TOTAL	1,652	100.0	104	100.0	18	100.0

TABLE 2-9
Age of Superintendents.

Age Group	National Sample		First Year Sample		BSS Group	
	N	%	N	%	N	%
Below 40	123	7.1	20	18.7	2	11.1
41–45	325	18.9	41	38.3	3	16.7
46–50	463	26.9	23	21.5	7	38.8
51–55	417	24.2	18	16.8	4	22.3
56–60	294	17.1	4	3.8	2	11.1
Over 60	100	5.8	1	0.9	0	0.0
TOTAL	1,722	100.0	107	100.0	18	100.0

classroom teachers and instructional leaders who wish to be superintendent in order to improve the instructional program. Male superintendents have traditionally seen themselves as administrators of resources rather than instructional leaders.

The national average age of a superintendent was near 50 (Glass, 1992). The superintendents in the first-year sample were most frequently between the ages of 42 and 45, as shown in Table 2-9. However, the national sample was only slightly older, half being between the ages of 46 and 55. It appears that first-year superintendents are a bit older than in past decades. Of the BSS project group, 77.8% were between the ages of 41 and 55.

Most superintendent careers are 15 to 17 years, with retirement at about age 57 (Glass, 1992), but early retirement programs in many states are inducing current superintendents to retire. This may lead to a younger cadre of superintendents. In Illinois, the number of superintendents in their first contract year has increased three-fold in recent years (Glass, 1995).

In most communities, school superintendents are paid well in both salary and benefits, compared with other local management positions. An interesting aspect of the salaries, reported in Table 2-10, is that first-year superintendents were making more than their more experienced colleagues. More than a third of the first-year sample and 77.8% of the BSS group were making in excess of $69,000. Their benefit

TABLE 2-10
Salaries of Superintendents.

Salary	National Sample		First Year Sample		BSS Group	
	N	%	N	%	N	%
Less than $29,000	198	11.7	4	3.8	0	0.0
$29,000–$38,999	229	13.5	9	8.5	0	0.0
$39,000–$48,999	342	20.2	22	20.7	0	0.0
$49,000–$58,999	330	19.4	16	15.1	2	11.1
$59,000–$68,999	232	13.7	18	17.0	2	11.1
$69,000 and Higher	364	21.5	37	34.9	14	77.8
TOTAL	1,695	100.0	106	100.0	18	100.0

packages were generally worth at least a third more in actual dollars. It appears that districts employing more experienced superintendents in the national sample have not kept pace with salaries in districts that have employed new superintendents. These senior superintendents may have been reluctant to ask for salary increases in recognition of fiscal constraints in their districts. The relatively high salaries of the BSS group reflect the fact that several of their districts had advertised a high salary to attract quality candidates to seek work in a "tough" district.

SUPERINTENDENTS AND THEIR SCHOOL DISTRICTS

The average American public school district serves fewer than 2,500 students. Not surprisingly, nearly two thirds of the first-year sample found their first superintendency in a district with fewer than 3,000 students. Importantly, almost one fourth of them began in districts with fewer than 300 students, as indicated in Table 2-11. This means the beginning superintendent was probably also serving as principal and business manager.

Probably, the superintendents in the first-year sample, who entered the superintendency in districts having more than 25,000 students, had previously served as deputy or assistant superintendents in large urban districts. This was certainly true of the BSS group. Interestingly, the four BSS superintendents who began in districts of more than 25,000 students were all female. Minority and low socioeconomic students made up substantial percentages of their enrollments.

Understanding that superintendents typically begin their careers in small districts, it is important to learn whether these districts are gaining or losing enrollment. Leading a district that is losing enrollment is not an enviable task, as such districts almost always must reduce budgets. This can create many virtual life or death dilemmas for the superintendent.

As indicated in Table 2-12, over 50% of first-year superintendents found themselves in districts with declining enrollments. This is not uncommon in small towns and rural areas, which, according to the 1990 Census, are in population decline. The 1990s baby "boomlet" does not seem to be occurring in the districts most often served by first-year superintendents. However, half of the BSS superintendents were in growing districts.

TABLE 2-11
Size of District.

Pupil Enrollment	All School Districts		National Sample		First Year Sample		BSS Group	
	N	%	N	%	N	%	N	%
25,000 or More	172	1.1	145	8.4	8	7.5	4	22.2
3,000–24,999	2,706	17.6	610	35.4	32	29.9	9	50.0
300–2,999	8,255	53.4	716	41.5	41	38.3	5	27.8
Fewer than 300	4,316	27.9	253	14.7	26	24.3	0	0.0
TOTAL	15,499	100.0	1,724	100.0	107	100.0	18	100.0

TABLE 2-12
Change in Enrollment.

Enrollment Change	National Sample		First Year Sample		BSS Group	
	N	%	N	%	N	%
Increased 25% or More	178	11.2	7	5.1	2	11.8
Increased 15–24%	130	8.2	9	6.6	3	17.6
Increased 5–14%	265	16.7	15	11.0	4	23.5
Changed Less than 5%	256	16.1	16	11.8	1	5.9
Decreased 5–14%	375	23.6	31	47.1	6	35.3
Decreased 15–24%	239	15.1	17	12.5	1	5.9
Decreased 25% or More	145	9.1	8	5.9	0	0.0
TOTAL	1,588	100.0	103	100.0	17	100.0

WORKING WITH THE BOARD AND THE COMMUNITY

The experienced superintendents saw the general management of their districts as the boards' primary expectation, as shown in Table 2-13. However, first-year superintendents, saw instructional leadership as being primary. This was a most significant difference between the two groups.

It is interesting to compare these expectations with the importance of factors used in board evaluations of superintendents and with the reasons superintendents believed they were selected for their positions. All three groups of superintendents reported that the most important criterion in their yearly evaluations was "general effectiveness," as reflected in Table 2-14. Relationships with the school board were seen as second highest in importance.

First-year superintendents ranked leadership as their board's most important expectation, but experienced superintendents saw it as less crucial than general management and human relations skills. However, all three groups ranked leadership higher as a board expectation than as an evaluation criterion. Interestingly, although superintendents frequently cited personal characteristics as reasons they were selected, as was shown in Table 2-8, they saw these characteristics as of only minor importance in their evaluations.

The need to more clearly link board expectations and superintendent evaluation was illuminated when superintendents were asked if they were evaluated according to the criteria on their formal job descriptions. Although the majority of superintendents reported that were evaluated on the basis of their formal job descriptions, between one third and one half of the superintendents reported that they were not, as illustrated in Table 2-15. Some superintendents perceived that whether they were retained was based on personal preferences or biases of individual board members.

First-year superintendents say they take the lead in developing district policy almost as often as their more experienced colleagues. As shown in Table 2-16, more than 60% of superintendents see themselves dominating policy initiatives. This

TABLE 2-13
Boards' Primary Expectations
of Superintendents.

Primary Expectation	National Sample Rank	First Year Sample Rank	BSS Group Rank
General Management	1	2	2
Human Relations Skills	2	4	3
Instructional Leadership	3	1	1
Knowledge of Finance and Budget	4	3	6
Community Relations	5	5	4
Planning Strategy	6	6	5

TABLE 2-14
Importance of Factors Used in Board Evaluations.

Evaluation Factors	National Sample Rank	First Year Sample Rank	BSS Group Rank
General Effectiveness	1	1	1.0
Board/Superintendent Relationships	2	2	2.0
Management Functions	3	4	5.0
Budget Development/Implementation	4	6	8.0
Educational Leadership/Knowledge	5	3	6.5
Community/Superintendent Relationships	6	5	3.5
Staff/Superintendent Relationships	7	7	3.5
Personal Characteristics	8	8	6.5
Personnel Recruitment and Supervision	9	9	9.0
Student/Superintendent Relationships	10	10	10.0

TABLE 2-15
Are Superintendent Evaluations
Based on Job Descriptions?

Are Evaluations Based on Job Descriptions?	National Sample N	National Sample %	First Year Sample N	First Year Sample %	BSS Group N	BSS Group %
Yes	864	56.9	58	66.7	9	52.9
No	654	43.1	29	33.3	8	47.1
TOTAL	1,518	100.0	87	100.0	17	100.0

practice may contain both positive and negative aspects. Just over a third of first-year superintendents say policy is a shared function—probably a politically safer road.

A very important task of the superintendency is the preparation of the board meeting agenda. In fact, the sequencing of the board agenda has much to do with whether or not board meetings run smoothly. Also, the selection of items is important. About three quarters of experienced and first-year superintendents prepare board agendas by themselves, as indicated in Table 2-17. More BSS superintendents—nearly 40%—shared this task, presumably with the board chair.

The development of the board agenda is also a key time for communication with individual board members, as a savvy superintendent needs to know in advance whether there is disagreement among board members on proposed agenda items. Split votes occurring in formal board meetings usually do not promote the image of an effective board or good leadership on the part of the superintendent.

A historical premise in public education is that the public should be consulted. More than 80% of superintendents in each of the three groups reported that they sought community participation "frequently" or "all the time," as shown in Table 2-18. Both experienced and first-year superintendents felt that community participation in district decision making was more important in the 1990s than in the previous decade. This demonstrates increasing recognition of the fact that community members should be consulted on a frequent and sincere basis by superintendents.

TABLE 2-16
Who Takes the Lead in Developing Policy?

	National Sample		First Year Sample		BSS Group	
Policy Development Leader	N	%	N	%	N	%
School Board or Board Chair	67	3.9	4	3.8	0	0.0
Superintendent	1,158	67.1	66	62.2	11	61.1
Shared Leadership	489	28.3	36	34.0	7	38.9
Other	11	0.7	0	0.0	0	0.0
TOTAL	1,725	100.0	106	100.0	18	100.0

TABLE 2-17
Who Prepares the Agenda for Board Meetings?

	National Sample		First Year Sample		BSS Group	
Board Meeting Agenda Preparer	N	%	N	%	N	%
Superintendent	1,314	76.6	80	74.8	11	61.1
Board Chairperson	4	0.2	0	0.0	0	0.0
Shared Responsibility	385	22.4	27	25.2	7	38.9
Other	14	0.8	0	0.0	0	0.0
TOTAL	1,717	100.0	107	100.0	18	100.0

Superintendents were asked to check program areas where they seek community involvement in planning or advisory capacities. Data reported in Table 2-19 reveal that responses for first-year and experienced superintendents were highly congruent. The importance of the question is reflected in the areas in which most superintendents involved the community, for instance, setting objectives and priorities, curriculum, and fund raising where voter support is obviously needed in bond or tax rate elections.

Inadequate school finances were identified not only as the most serious problem facing boards of education but also as the factor that most inhibits superintendent effectiveness, as shown in Table 2-20. Other factors superintendents reported as deterrents to their effectiveness included too many insignificant demands, state reform mandates, and collective bargaining agreements. The inhibiting effect of collective bargaining agreements was particularly evident among the BSS superintendents, many of whom served in very large school districts.

TABLE 2-18
Do Superintendents Actively Seek Community Participation?

Community Participation is Sought	National Sample		First Year Sample		BSS Group	
	N	%	N	%	N	%
All the Time	433	25.2	35	32.7	6	33.3
Frequently	946	55.2	58	54.2	11	61.1
When Required	281	16.4	9	8.4	1	5.6
Seldom or Never	55	3.2	5	4.6	0	0.0
TOTAL	1,715	100.0	107	100.0	18	100.0

TABLE 2-19
Areas in Which Superintendents Involved Community.

Areas of Community Involvement	National Sample		First Year Sample		BSS Group	
	N	%*	N	%*	N	%*
Objectives/Priorities	1,256	73.7	73	69.5	15	83.3
Program/Curriculum	1,119	65.6	62	59.0	15	83.3
Student Activities	865	50.7	55	52.4	10	55.6
Student Behavior/Rights	714	41.9	41	39.0	8	44.4
Finance and Budget	539	31.6	33	31.4	9	50.0
Evaluation of Programs	599	35.1	30	28.6	9	50.0
Fund Raising	1,077	63.2	70	66.7	8	44.4
Strategic Planning	852	50.0	41	39.0	13	72.0

* Superintendents were asked to check all relevant areas. The percentages given indicate the portion of the responding superintendents who reported that they involved community in those areas.

TABLE 2-20
Factors That Inhibit Superintendents' Effectiveness.

Factors Inhibiting Effectiveness	National Sample		First Year Sample		BSS Group	
	N	%*	N	%*	N	%*
Inadequate Financing	1,018	59.0	91	85.0	10	55.6
Too Many Insignificant Demands	895	51.9	47	38.3	13	72.2
State Reform Mandates	655	38.0	35	32.7	4	22.2
Collective Bargaining Agreements	438	25.4	20	18.7	8	44.4
Racial/Ethnic Problems	38	2.2	3	2.8	1	5.6
Too Much Added Responsibility	306	17.7	13	12.1	5	27.8
Insufficient Administrative Support	292	16.9	23	21.5	4	22.2
Poor Relations with Board Members	243	14.1	13	12.1	4	22.2
Ineffective Staff Members	142	8.2	23	21.5	5	27.8
District Too Small	141	8.2	8	7.5	2	11.1
Lack of Community Support	114	6.6	4	3.7	1	5.6
Drug Problems	31	1.8	3	2.8	2	11.1

* Percentage of responding superintendents reporting these factors.

SUPPORT, STRESS, AND SATISFACTION OF SUPERINTENDENTS

Superintendents are in some respects "alone and lonely" in their positions, as they are technically the supervisors for all educators and non-educators in the district. Their participation in professional organizations is one means of networking and socializing with other superintendents. These organizational memberships provide professional development activities and useful professional networking. Such networking can be helpful in seeking a next position because many who work for superintendent search firms actively participate in these professional associations.

Most first-year superintendents belong to the American Association of School Administrators (AASA) or one of its state affiliates, as indicated in Table 2-21. The other professional organization to which large numbers of superintendents belong is the Association for Supervision and Curriculum Development (ASCD). A significant difference exists between the national group and the first-year sample in terms of membership in ASCD. It appears that first-year superintendents, of whom almost two thirds belong to ASCD, are more interested in curriculum matters than older and more experienced colleagues, less than half of whom belong to ASCD.

TABLE 2-21
Memberships in Professional Organizations.

Organization	National Sample		First Year Sample		BSS Group	
	N	%	N	%	N	%
AASA	1,321	76.6	70	68.6	17	94.4
ASCD	781	45.3	66	64.4	8	44.4
STATE AASA	1,140	66.1	58	56.9	9	50.0

TABLE 2-22
Superintendents Having
Mentors for the Superin-
tendency.

Mentors	National Sample		First Year Sample		BSS Group	
	N	%	N	%	N	%
Yes	842	49.1	58	54.2	14	77.8
No	836	48.7	48	44.9	4	22.2
Don't Know	38	2.2	1	0.9	0	0.0
TOTAL	1,716	100.0	107	100.0	18	100.0

Superintendents also belong to a number of other professional organizations, ranging from those for elementary and secondary principals to those for school business officials and public relations people. These varied affiliations probably indicate prior responsibilities of the superintendents.

As shown in Table 2-22, a few more than half of the sample of first-year superintendents indicated they had the assistance of mentors as they prepared for and sought to gain their first superintendency. More than three fourths of the BSS group reported having mentors, including *all* of the minority superintendents.

The AASA study reported that females and minorities in the national sample were more likely to have mentors than nonminority males. In contrast to male superintendents, of whom 48% reported having mentors, 59.5% of female superintendents had mentors. Ethnic minority superintendents had mentors 55.2% of the time in comparison with 48.5% for ethnic nonminorities (Glass, 1992, p. 61).

In some states, mentoring programs have been implemented to assist individuals interested in the superintendency. Perhaps, the most positive step that could be taken to increase the competency levels of future superintendents is through effective mentoring programs. This seems especially important to recruiting highly qualified women and minority superintendents.

Most first-year superintendents and experienced colleagues see the superintendency as a moderately to considerably stressful occupation, as revealed in Table 2-23. However, few see it as being a job in which stress becomes disabling. Superintendents in the BSS group felt higher levels of stress as compared with the other two study groups, which may be related to the fact that more of them were in very large districts.

TABLE 2-23
The Superintendency as a Stressful Occupation.

Stress	National Sample		First Year Sample		BSS Group	
	N	%	N	%	N	%
Little or None	139	8.1	3	2.8	0	0.0
Moderate	713	41.7	54	50.5	7	38.9
Considerable	724	42.3	42	39.3	7	38.9
Very Great	134	7.8	8	7.5	4	22.2
TOTAL	1,710	99.9	107	100.0	18	100.0

TABLE 2-24
Degree of Self-Fulfillment in the Superintendency.

Self-Fulfillment	National Sample		First Year Sample		BSS Group	
	N	%	N	%	N	%
Little or None	55	0.4	3	2.8	0	0.0
Moderate	587	34.3	26	24.5	5	27.8
Considerable	1,069	62.5	77	72.6	13	72.2
TOTAL	1,711	100.1	106	100.0	18	100.0

In spite of the stress inherent in the superintendency, a large majority of superintendents found considerable fulfillment in the job. As reported in Table 2-24, first-year superintendents found somewhat more fulfillment than their more experienced colleagues.

Superintendents are like other professions where a little griping and complaining can be heard at professional meetings. But in the privacy of putting on paper the levels of fulfillment they obtain in their jobs, a much more positive response is given.

Even though many superintendents serve districts with inadequate finances, community pressure, aggressive unions, and numbing state bureaucracy, they remain emotionally attached to the superintendency. All three groups strongly indicated they would again choose the superintendency as a career. This is a bit more true for first-year superintendents, even though some of them did not survive in their job for a second and third year.

SUMMARY

The profiles and opinions of first-year superintendents and their more experienced colleagues are not radically different. However, there are some subtle differences that should be noted. The first-year sample and BSS project superintendents possess more formal education, earn higher salaries, and are more interested in instructional leadership. More women and minorities are in evidence among the first-year superintendents. Though these groups are still grossly underrepresented in the superintendency, having a doctoral degree and mentoring appear to be significant factors in opening the doors of the superintendency for women and minorities.

QUESTIONS FOR REFLECTION AND DISCUSSION

1. As you reflect on the history of the superintendency, what changes have you noticed in the role of the superintendent in districts where you have lived or worked?

2. What factors have contributed to changing expectations for superintendents over the past century?

3. How do you think changing expectations impact the kind of preparation needed to be a successful superintendent in the coming decade?

4. How can entering the superintendency in a small town or rural district be both an asset and a liability to upward mobility?

5. What problems may arise from the contrast between the primary reasons superintendents are selected and the criteria on which they are later evaluated?

REFERENCES

Blumberg, A. (1985). *The school superintendent: Living with conflict.* New York: Teachers College Press.

Callahan, R. E. (1961). *Education and the cult of efficiency.* Chicago: University of Chicago Press.

Callahan, R. E. (1966). *The superintendent of schools: A historical analysis.* St. Louis: Washington University. (ERIC Document Reproduction Service No. ED-010-410).

Campbell, R. E., Cunningham, L. L., Nystrand, R. O., & Usdan, M. D. (1990). *Organization and control of American schools* (6th ed.). Columbus, Ohio: Charles E. Merrill.

Carlson, R. O. (1972). *School superintendents: Careers and performance.* Columbus, OH: Merrill.

Conley, D.T. (1993) *Roadmap to restructuring: Policies, practices, and the emerging visions of schooling.* Washington, DC: Office of Educational Research and Improvement. (ERIC Document Reproduction Service No. ED 359 593)

Cuban, L. (1988). *The managerial imperative and the practice of leadership in schools.* Albany, NY: SUNY Press.

Cubberley, E. P. (1922). *Public school administration.* Boston: Houghton Mifflin.

Getzels, J., Liphan, J. M., & Campbell, R. F. (1968). *Educational administration as a social process: Theory, research and practice.* New York: Harper and Row.

Glass, T. E. (1992). *The study of the American school superintendency 1992: America's education leaders in a time of reform.* Arlington, VA: American Association of School Administrators.

Glass, T. E. (1995). *The 1994 survey of Illinois public school superintendent opinion on issues of importance.* Springfield, IL: Illinois Association of School Administrators.

Griffiths, D. E. (1966). *The school superintendent.* New York: Center for Applied Research.

Kowalski, T. J. (1995). *Keepers of the flame: Contemporary urban superintendents.* Thousand Oaks, CA: Corwin Press.

Rist, M.C. (1991, December). Race and Politics Rip Into the Urban Superintendency. *Executive Educator, 12,* 12–14.

Sass, M. (1989). *The AASA performance goal and skill areas: Importance to effective superintendency performance as viewed by practicing superintendents and professors of educational administration.* Unpublished doctoral dissertation, Northern Illinois University, De Kalb.

Sclafani, S. (1987). *AASA guidelines for preparation of school administrators: Do they represent the important job behaviors of superintendents?* Unpublished doctoral dissertation, University of Texas, Austin.

Tucker, H. J., & Zeigler, H. L. (1980). *Professionals versus the public: Attitudes, Communications, and response in school districts.* New York: Longman.

3

JACKIE
Big Time Challenges in a Rural District

Doris A. Henry, The University of Memphis

ABSTRACT.   Jackie's first superintendency was in a 10,000 square-mile mountainous rural district with 512 students in kindergarten through 12th grade. Because she saw the Vista School District as fiscally sound and one where people were concerned about children and willing to support schools, she willingly left her previous position in an urban area. Jackie's dream was to develop an outstanding, innovative educational system where "real education" could take place. But little did she know that as superintendent, she was to find a nightmare of fiscal crisis, incompetence, and sexual impropriety.

I magine considering a move from an urban area to become a first-time superintendent in a town of 1,200 people, set in the midst of an immense, beautiful, mountainous rural county. Moreover, with almost 80 personnel, the district was the county's largest employer. Jackie wondered if she would need different skills in a rural setting from those she had polished as an urban central office administrator. However, she anticipated that working in the Vista School District would be pleasant and less stressful than continuing to face the complex challenges of an urban core district.

One reason Dr. Jackie West agreed to participate in this study was a hope that her story would provide a connection for beginning superintendents between the theory learned through their academic studies and the reality of the job. She also expressed concern about the minuscule amount of professional literature on being a superintendent in a very small district. Though Glass reported that 27.9% of all school districts have less than 300 pupils (Table 2.11), Henry and Murphy's (1993) review of doctoral dissertation topics found few on rural superintendencies.

Of the 512 students in the Vista School District, 90% were Anglo and 10% Hispanic. They were served by 43 teachers, 3 principals, and 32 support staff, in an elementary, a middle, and a high school. Classes were small, averaging 12 to 13 students. A graduation rate of 82% in the year prior to Jackie's arrival reflected the fact that six students did not graduate.

The seven board members, four women and three men, were elected at November general elections. All but one of the board members were employed outside the district; the exception was the secretary at the middle school. The teachers' organization was very informal with few, if any, negotiations, procedures or demands. The teachers' organization and the school board worked cooperatively.

THE INTERVIEW PROCESS

Of the 50 applicants for the Vista superintendency, 2 were women. Reference checks were made on all 10 semifinalists, and then 5 finalists were selected. They included three male superintendents, a male high school principal, and Dr. West, a 54-year old female, who was a curriculum director in a large urban district in the state.

Jackie was the first finalist interviewed, a process that lasted for 12 hours. During the day, Dr. West met the retiring superintendent, visited the schools, met with the town committee, and had dinner with the school board. The board also questioned Dr. West's husband, an attorney, during the interview. When asked why she was selected, Dr. West said:

I never knew if it was better to interview first or last, but I guess it's one or the other. Since I was the first, they said that I was the standard to which they held the other people. It was my enthusiasm, my creativity, and my ideas that they liked. . . . my interest in technology, some of those sort of things, they're looking to achieve.

The board expressed some concern that Dr. West was not from the area. She, however, considered herself from the area because she had worked there on summer jobs while in college. She said:

It wasn't like I was coming in and not knowing what I was getting into. I lived up here and knew the people, so I did know the area and then we came . . . for the interview. We checked out the area, . . . the local paper. . . . We knew some of the issues they were dealing with, cutting back, and stuff like that. I didn't know anybody personally, but I knew of people in the area.

Dr. West had applied to two other, higher paying, districts, but she knew the others had major problems. She didn't "really think that going into my first superintendency I wanted to take on more than I could handle. . . . I felt more comfortable in a situation like this where I knew I could be successful."

Dr. West intuitively sensed board support. She saw the board members as being good, caring, honest people, without any agendas for power, and sincerely interested in education. Reflecting on questions she might have asked during the interview to help her better assess problems she would eventually face, she said she wished she had probed more into past personnel issues. "They could have explained to me . . . one issue last year where a person was let go because of sexual indiscretion toward a student. . . . They released him but they paid him off."

FINANCIAL ISSUES CONVERGE

The economic base of the area was agriculture and cattle. Although the majority of the population were not wealthy, the taxpayers were able to generate enough revenue to make the district eligible for minimal state support. According to Dr. West, the district was expected to provide the same academic opportunities as other districts in the state, even with little state support.

Though mining had once been important to the district's economic base, a decrease in mining operations over the past few years had led to a reduction in the amount of taxes paid based on smaller assessed valuation and a subsequent tax abatement of $310,000. The abatement issue, first brought to the board for discussion in August after Jackie became superintendent, put a significant portion of the total school budget at risk.

While 26 districts in the state were faced with abatements, Vista was the only one to raise the mill levy to counter the loss of monies. Facing a December 15 deadline, the board raised the millage even knowing that they might face litigation. The board took its bold action believing that if they did not do so, they would put the education of the community's young people in jeopardy. After the December decision, Jackie reported that the board was 100% supportive of the levy, even though, "It could be very bad politically, as well as personally, to be liable if they made a bad or wrong decision."

Another financial issue Dr. West faced during her first few months was the rapidly shrinking reserve fund. Every year a new bus needed to be purchased, and the reserve fund was the only available source of funds. Although other options for transporting students were being considered, another bus was needed to start the school year.

Jackie had recommended hiring an additional teacher, based on projected enrollment, but, instead, enrollment was down. The district had already frozen teachers' salaries, terminated the media specialist, and reduced some staff to half time in order to maintain the educational programs while meeting the budget constraints caused by the lost mining tax abatement dollars.

Proposed state budget cuts further complicated the financial picture. These cuts were in reaction to a failed state referendum on the November ballot for a 1% sales tax increase to support schools. The state's proposed budget cuts would mean a 30% to 35% revenue loss for the Vista School District. This revenue loss, in combination with the tax abatement, portended financial crisis.

As if these fiscal pressures were not enough, for the first time in the community's recorded history, a tornado touched down, blowing the roof off the elementary school and severely damaging the high school roof. With this calamity of nature, Dr. West had little choice but to recommend a bond election.

The requests for increased operating millage and the bond election came at a time of national, state, and local opposition to spending more money for education. The negative national sentiment was reflected in the Gallup poll of public attitudes toward schools (Elam, Rose, & Gallup, 1991). The failed sales tax referendum illustrated statewide views. Locally, the support for a bond election had been jeopardized when officials—NOT those of the Vista School District—mishandled a previous hospital bond issue. When it was discovered that the hospital had used monies for purposes other than those for which they had been intended, it was no surprise that the public was reluctant to pass other bond levies.

Dr. West realized that her lack of experience in conducting bond elections was also a handicap in the campaign. However, she knew that communication with stakeholders was going to be important to gaining the community's support of the bond election. Accordingly, she solicited support from the mayor and key community people. Unlike Hank, whose story is told in the following chapter, Jackie persuaded the principals to involve the teachers by calling parents after school hours to encourage their support. In addition, weekly public meetings were conducted where everything was described honestly. "One lady said she wasn't going to vote for it [the bond election] until after the meeting. She said, 'I decided you guys were honest; told it like it was and now I'm going to vote for it.'" Dr. West also asked the editor of the newspaper for support, and every time the editor supported schools in the newspaper, she wrote him a thank you note. Consistent to the end, Jackie wrote the editor a gracious letter thanking him for his support after the bond election passed.

BUILDING THE FOUNDATIONS FOR CHANGE

"While all changes have not resulted in school improvement, improvement is not likely to occur unless changes are attempted" (Goode, 1992, p. 46). One reason Dr. West was hired was because of her fresh, exciting, new ideas for improving the education for all the young people. She expressed her ideas clearly and enthusiastically during the interview. The board welcomed and supported this change from the comfortable routine with the former superintendent.

Recognizing that support is necessary to institute change, we will first consider the support Jackie gave and received as a new superintendent. Establishing a vision, developing a framework for implementing the vision, instituting communication channels, and developing strategies for meeting the challenges provide the basis for understanding the dynamics involved in Jackie West's first superintendency. West's compelling vision helped to provide the bedrock that enabled educational improvement to move forward even when besieged by the storms of controversy and crisis.

WHO GIVES SUPPORT TO THE SUPERINTENDENT?

In the beginning, Dr. West felt her strongest support from her husband and from two women in the district—the board president and the middle school principal whom Dr. West considered to be isolated like she. They supported her by embracing her ideas and encouraging her. Jackie was reluctant to talk extensively about her job to her husband because of the demands of a commuting marriage and her desire to enjoy their limited time together. Her sense of humor, even in the face of her isolation, was expressed when she said, "My dog listens real well!" When she needed to talk to someone else, she saw a therapist in the city where her husband lived.

An early priority for Jackie was to become familiar with her new district. She began immediately to participate in community activities. She spoke to community groups, drove through a portion of the 10,000-square-mile district each weekend, and visited each of the churches. She rode every school bus to see where her students lived and to experience the long journeys they endured to attend school. She listened to people and developed a sense about her support.

Dr. West categorized her community supporters in two areas: those who wanted change and supported her fresh ideas and those who helped her acclimate quickly. She did not have predetermined criteria for seeking people to support her, but found support intuitively. As she connected with the people in the community and found she related easily with them, she still did not feel she could speak without reservation. Even in her first month on the job, she pointed out, "You really have to face the fact that it's going to take a good two years of being pretty isolated until you begin to establish either friends or a support base within the community."

Dr. West also sought support from people who could assist her with specific tasks. For example, when preparing for the bond election, she called a colleague more seasoned in school finance for advice and received detailed instructions on how to proceed. She also contacted the area superintendent for advice. Jackie's professional network enabled her to access people who had specific expertise and whom she trusted.

Even with support, Dr. West soon felt the isolation that the superintendency entailed:

I really have to make sure that I get out of there and do things professionally. I'm probably going to try to attend AASA and ASCD. If I don't, I think I'll die here. Literally . . . you're really isolated in terms of professional development and I'm going to have to get out . . . and not lose the cutting edge. . . . I can see how you can become really stagnant here.

ESTABLISHING A VISION AND FRAMEWORK

Dr. West had a vision of developing this small, rural district into an island of excellence:

My vision is that every child coming out of third grade will be successful in reading and writing. . . . I'd like to see the graduation rate go to 95%, and . . . look at each child individually to see what she or he needs to be successful.

Jackie's actions demonstrated her understanding of the importance of combining a leader's vision with building a shared covenant to provide a sense of direction for the schools (Sergiovanni, 1990). She first shared her vision during the interview process, and then articulated it to the staff upon her arrival. Immediately she started gathering information, opening up channels of communication, infusing new ideas, and establishing a framework for making her vision a reality.

Dr. West continued the development of a shared vision by having the board president speak about the direction of the district to the teachers at the orientation meeting. No board member had ever addressed the teachers in the past.

The town manager and mayor met with Dr. West to discuss the important issues the district faced. Their suggestions, and those of other community leaders, were incorporated into the strategic plan she guided the board to develop. As early as July she realized that a collaborative team was needed if her dream was to become reality:

I'm going to have to build a team. . . . I don't know who will be on it. . . . I would have to involve the principals, but then to pick some other champions, so to speak, to help to create. . . . I'm just going to have to know people a little better before I proceed.

Jackie also recognized the importance of listening as a tool for developing a shared vision:

I have found the best thing to facilitate change is to go into a new place and be willing to spend a lot of time listening . . . helping support people personally . . . reinforcing people when they do something positive and recognizing them for their contributions. So, [I] listen carefully.

Meetings with a variety of people, both school personnel and community people during those first months, played an important part of communicating her vision. She visited all three schools to meet with staff members and listen to them. She met with the transportation director, maintenance people, the principals, the board, and the retiring superintendent. When Dr. West's secretary resigned because her family moved out of the community, Jackie took advantage of this opportunity to hire someone who was supportive of her philosophy and style of leadership.

Dr. West felt she did not make any major decisions the first couple of months as superintendent. However, by the end of the year, she realized that many of her early decisions were major because of their impact on how the district functioned.

OPENING COMMUNICATION CHANNELS

One of Grohe's (1983) suggestions for a successful new superintendency was to "streamline and generate communications. The worst thing a new superintendent can do is fail to talk to people—school personnel and community members alike" (p. 28). Dr. West was accustomed to a district where everyone was expected to communicate and keep appropriate people informed. When she arrived, she was surprised that the board president was the only person to contact her. She said, "None of them has called or anything. It's really weird." Jackie also discovered that the principals had "never before felt comfortable coming in and talking to the super-intendent. . . . [Now] they were so excited that somebody was listening."

Dr. West quickly learned the power of the media, especially in a small commu-nity. Anything she said was quoted in the local newspaper, a dramatic change from the urban newspapers where earlier she had competed for print space. She learned this in Vista after talking openly about the problem with the high school library. The next day she was astonished to read the newspaper's verbatim account of all com-ments she had made!

Dr. West was able to develop the channels of communication and build a rela-tionship with every board member by interviewing each member individually about his or her perceptions of the district. She communicated regularly with the board through informational packets or memoranda sent to them prior to board meetings. When crisis situations arose, Jackie telephoned each board member immediately. Appropriate district personnel who could assist with the situation were then called. She found that, in a small district, teams for addressing emerging situations are defined by whoever is available or who has expertise to address the issues. This was sharply variant from the urban district where Jackie had worked, because the large system had teams built into the structure, defined by positions of authority.

One example of the strategies Dr. West employed during a crisis situation was seen in how she handled the threatened 30% to 36% cut to the district's budget. The proposed cuts created a wave of anxiety among school people and throughout the community. Meetings were set up to air the situation and to garner suggestions from teachers, staff, board members, parents, and the accountability committee commu-nity people, as well as from others. Dr. West spearheaded the organization of a com-munity meeting with the area's state senator and representative. She also wrote the governor and commissioner of education to explain the impact the proposed budget cuts would have on her district. Dr. West believed that her meetings, letters, and tele-phone calls helped set the stage for an 11th-hour legislative decision in April, which cut only 4% from the district's budget instead of the threatened 30% to 36%.

In addition to addressing the fiscal crisis, Jackie developed other strategies to open lines of communication. She organized focus groups for community members and was encouraged when the first meeting drew 125 people. Two people from the state school board association were brought in to work with the groups, and Jackie described the public response as "very positive."

Jackie also opened communication channels with students. She visited all three schools frequently, often daily. She talked with students on their school buses, in their classes, and whenever she saw them in the community. She made herself known to them, and they felt free to open up to her.

Dr. West believed that continued communications were a key reason for her successes. Contacting the legislators during their debate on the proposed budget cuts was a part of the total portrait. "When a bill would come up that we wanted to support or oppose, I'd write or call them. I kept in contact with them all year long."

RISING TO CHALLENGES CREATED BY CRISES

After the first couple of weeks, Dr. West was responding to incidents and setting precedents. The first incident was $410 stolen from the high school locker room. The stolen money was a symptom of much larger problems that unraveled there throughout the year, described in the following paragraphs.

The high school library was missing over 1,500 books, but the more serious problem was that the majority of the books on the shelves predated 1970. Only 1 set of encyclopedias out of 13 was complete—and that was 1962 in vintage. Moreover, she found a closet full of unshelved books, and she estimated that $35,000 would be needed to update the library's holdings. Dr. West was shocked to learn that the librarian, who had been fired the year before, still had keys to the library and was seeking unemployment compensation of $6,500.

The high school principal failed not only to properly supervise the librarian but also to accurately calculate graduation rates for a state report, listing 64% instead of 82%. When the state department of education called Dr. West in November about the graduation rate, she confronted the high school principal. He claimed that it was "too much trouble to track the dropouts." Dr. West responded, "Give me a break, two kids!" The state report was corrected.

When a public meeting was held at the high school to promote the bond election, the high school principal did not attend, even though 70% of the bond issue would go to the high school. This principal sought to undermine Jackie as superintendent by constantly referring to conversations with the former superintendent. Jackie explained, "He and the former superintendent did not want me to come, so he sort of subverted me all year long, very subtly."

At the end of the school year, Dr. West requested that the board dismiss the high school principal. Concurrently, members of the principal's church organized an attempt to persuade the board to support a vote of no confidence in Dr. West. The board supported Dr. West after a compromise was struck. It called for Dr. West to assume the high school principalship while continuing in her role as superintendent. It also called for the high school principal to become the guidance counselor at the high school and middle school. The essence of the accord was to increase Dr. West's workload without relieving her of an employee whose behavior bordered on insubordination.

Another crisis erupted in January. Just as Jackie was basking in the accomplishment of the successful bond election, she was faced with an allegation that a male middle school teacher had sexually assaulted a female student.

The parents had brought this to the attention of the board in the past, but the administration didn't do anything about it. The parents figured it wasn't worth bringing it to the attention of the administration again until I came, and they brought it up again because they were going to test me and see what I did.

Jackie's investigation revealed that the charges did, indeed, have substance and that other girls in the middle school were aware of the sexual relationship between the teacher and the eighth-grade girl whose parents brought the issue to Jackie's attention. Dr. West believed she had to do what was right, so she confronted the teacher, suspended him with pay, and brought the case before the board, asking for the teacher's termination.

Simultaneously, the parents filed a police report. Special prosecutors were sent in to investigate the case, and criminal charges were filed. The teacher, when faced with the seriousness of his crime, negotiated a plea with the prosecutor, accepting a lesser sentence in return for not contesting the allegations.

Jackie was relieved that students did not have to testify in court. She was also relieved because she recognized that if the event were later brought before the court as a civil matter, the proceedings could cost the district between $50,000 and $100,000 to defend. As she reflected on the situation, West compared her role in the community to that of a therapist. All the feelings and emotions were spewing forth, and she was the one to whom everyone turned.

The middle school boys sought retribution against the girls, because the girls "got rid" of their favorite teacher, who allegedly sexually assaulted the girls. Jackie had a representative of the district attorney meet with the students to help them understand the dynamics of this complicated event. She also wrote a grant to bring in a consultant from the victim and sexual advocacy center to conduct a workshop for the community, middle and high school teachers, and students. The grant was funded, and the consultant met with the groups. The community became very emotional during the workshop. One minister yelled at the consultant; another minister started rumors. A bus driver resigned for fear of sexual assault. Jackie commented that the situation had the potential of a "witch hunt."

Even the usually supportive middle school principal began to wilt in the face of controversy, and Jackie needed to work with the principal to help her recognize the facts of the case. As a means of avoiding similar problems in the future, Dr. West developed a handbook that addressed sexual abuse and sexual harassment, based on the information she received at a session during the annual conference of the American Association of School Administrators.

Not surprisingly, pending budget cuts and decisive personnel actions caused morale to plummet. Keeping her verve and focusing on instructional issues were important to counter the low morale and move the district forward.

BECOMING A STRONG INSTRUCTIONAL LEADER

Paramount to realizing Dr. West's vision was improvement of the instructional program. Because principals were the key people, she began with them. She set new expectations for the principals. One was that they would write goals and plan for outcomes. When the goals were written, they would call her to set up times to discuss them. None of them called, so Jackie called them, only to be told that in the past the principals had neither written goals nor been evaluated.

Another new expectation was that the principals would attend to the operational details of their schools. For example, a teacher in one school had failed to renew his teaching certificate, and Dr. West had to intercede because neither the principal nor the teacher was concerned about the possible consequences. Jackie came to realize, "There's a total lack of awareness about what is legal, what is illegal."

In another example, a coach went to a clinic without prior board approval and then expected the board to reimburse him for attending. The high school principal, who was later demoted, had made a verbal commitment to allow the coach to attend the clinic, and Jackie had to sort out the predicament. This incident illustrated a pattern that Dr. West began discovering in her first months on the job: "There were a lot of loose ends, like in policies that had been read but not finished, not put in the books—just a lot of loose ends, organizational types of things that need to be done."

There was no policy or criteria for evaluating principals. Dr. West gave principals examples from other districts and asked them to develop criteria for their evaluations in the areas of leadership, supervision, communications, and personal qualities. They were to determine how the criteria could be demonstrated. Jackie asked them probing questions to stimulate their thinking, but she also realized that she might have to develop the instrument herself. She expressed her feelings about the issue when she said, "They're going to do it whether they like it or not, or I'll do it for them." Eventually she did develop the instrument, and they provided feedback.

The nonstop crises did not discourage Dr. West from pursuing her vision. She formed committees to develop a technology plan, design and implement a special program using nearby recreation areas for students at risk, develop social studies curriculum, and define student outcomes.

Another way Dr. West sought to improve instruction was through observing teachers. In October, she started classroom visitations, alternating among the three schools. Her purpose was to observe the articulation of the curriculum. She called the teachers in advance to set up the observation time. At the conclusion of each observation, she left a positive note.

A teacher evaluation council was established to examine the evaluation policies and restructure them. In addition to Dr. West, the council consisted of a teacher representative from each school, one principal, and one citizen from the community.

Seeking new resources was another of Jackie's strategies for improving instruction. She wrote several grants that were successful in acquiring new funds. Dr. West discovered that the district qualified for a federal energy impact grant that would give them the money to compensate for the tax abatement, thus postponing the need to take monies from educational programs. She also wrote a $500,000 technology preparation grant proposal for the districts in the region, driving through hazardous blizzard conditions to attend the meeting about the grant. She described her trip home at 11:30 at night:

I had to drive over the pass, with the snow, with the blizzard, and not one other car track on the path. It was really freaky. It was really above and beyond the call of duty. When you are a rural superintendent, sometimes you drive miles and miles in order to do anything. . . . It was 300 miles in one day just to go to a meeting. You don't think about that in the city.

The proposal called for linking the districts with interactive video, telecommunications, and other aspects of distance learning. She presented the proposal to the other districts for their approval. It was approved, submitted, and funded.

Another collaborative technology proposal provided additional subject matter opportunities for the students. Through interactive video, a teacher in another district began to teach Spanish to students in the Vista district, which created a stronger academic offering for students, at minimal cost.

As a means of increasing the capacity of the district to provide opportunities for students, West asked the board to approve seven staff development days in the teachers' calendar. This represented a change in a calendar that had never included any staff development days. It was a first step in enhancing instructional leadership. The next step was finding people who would deliver quality staff development training with limited funds. Jackie's solution was to call on friends to provide the training; happily, they were forthcoming. On one occasion she personally supervised all three schools so principals could attend an in-service session about 50 miles away.

Although focusing on academics was important, Jackie realized that athletics were a significant source of civic pride. Community members considered winning football and basketball teams as critical as bringing the schools into compliance with state accountability laws. When the high school basketball team went to the state tournament, it provided a needed morale boost for the entire community.

Dr. West faced urgent issues that could have distracted her from her vision for the Vista schools. One was the sense of having to do it alone: "I think it is just feeling like you have to do everything. I end up doing so much stuff. I feel like I'm spinning my wheels. On the other hand, no one else is here to do it."

On another front, she could have procrastinated because she did not feel she had adequate preparation to comfortably address the budgetary, managerial, and moral crises besetting her. Instead of being derailed, she choose to set priorities and continue with her plans to develop an outstanding innovative educational system.

JOYS OF THE SUPERINTENDENCY

Challenges and frustrations notwithstanding, Dr. West found joy in her work. The essence of her enthusiasm and continued energy was her love of young people and her ability to spend a great deal of time in the schools.

Gratifyingly, the board recognized Dr. West's accomplishments throughout the year. The first public recognition was at the September board meeting when one of the female board members said, "She is doing a really good job, and we're really proud of ourselves for hiring her." During a later September board meeting, a different female member said, "We are so glad you're here. When we were looking for a superintendent, we just never thought we could get anyone as good as you." At a November board meeting, Dr. West received a good evaluation from the board; and, at the local economic development council meeting, the town manager spoke of her saying, "They've [the district] got a winner."

People expressed appreciation for the organization and structure Dr. West gave the district. The bond issue was one of only seven that passed out of more than a hundred bond elections held in the state that year. The newspaper supported her recommendations, especially the bond election. She started the "Build a Generation" project, one of twelve from the state. She was appointed to the state school finance committee as 1 of 2 females on the 15-member committee. After the board presented her with a birthday cake in December, she commented:

I'm getting to know people, and they really seem to appreciate what I'm trying to do, especially with technology. They said if it weren't for you being here, we don't know what would happen. At least you're willing to look at change and look forward to different kinds of things to do so. That felt real good.

Jackie helped the community and the girls who were sexually abused to process their emotions. Some people told her that they were glad they had a woman for a superintendent to deal with such delicate issues.

Dr. West attended football and basketball games, the county fair, the Rotary Club, banquets, and numerous other local functions. She was invited to sit on community boards and to participate in community associations. Of these activities, she said, "I'm not aggressively pursuing it, but I am trying, whenever anyone asks, to be involved."

CONCLUSIONS

Dr. West described herself as a puzzle solver because she liked to investigate and find the solutions to problems. Her skills were constantly tested during her first year as superintendent. She felt the tenuous life of a superintendent as early as the fourth month:

You never know. Something could happen next week that'll change, but right now things are going pretty good. . . . I never expected I would be doing this stuff. I mean it's not practically any educational curriculum. It's all building, bidding, constructing. That's good, because that's the area I needed to learn. So, I guess I'm learning it.

Dr. West had a vision of creating an "island of excellence." She saw a rural community as an island because it has definite boundaries. The involvement of the community was not an option, but a necessity. Dr. West immersed herself in the whole community, through her communications and involvement with the town manager, mayor, parents, and citizens, to help resolve the problems it faced.

Financial concerns consumed most of her time, and it was the area where she felt she had the most modest skills and preparation. However, it was the people issues that were the toughest. When she recommended the termination of a teacher in January because of his sexual indiscretion, she said, "It was the biggest decision I've had to make in my whole life as an educator."

The school board members supported Dr. West throughout the year. "They have been a great board, excellent board. Even when the chips are down, even in spite of all the community upheaval, they [the school board] voted to support the decisions." These positive perceptions of the board may seem somewhat at variance with the compromise negotiated by the high school principal, but they reflect Jackie's ability to maintain an optimistic outlook.

The joys and successes Dr. West experienced were connected with improving the education of all young people. She faced financial crises, personnel problems, and personal isolation in the community, but she always created ways for students to benefit. The recreational program for students at risk, the technological advances, and the improvements to the physical plant made possible by the passage of the bond issue after the tornado were a few examples of the benefits for the students.

Developing people—the school board, the administrators, the teachers—was important. "Upgrading people's skills and bringing them into the 21st century . . . is the best thing you can do for a school district." Jackie brought a vision of what needed to be done and never wavered from that vision.

Trust is important, but who do you trust? How do you know you can trust someone? People, especially in rural communities, are suspicious of outsiders. Jackie found that relying on her intuitive sense about people was often all she had.

Throughout the year, Dr. West's vision did not falter in spite of the fiscal and noninstructional issues that demanded her attention. She saw her role as developing a collaborative team. Strategic planning, prioritizing, and remaining focused were the tools she used.

Understanding the anatomy of change was another crucial factor in Jackie's first year as superintendent. Though implementation of change takes time, by setting her goals and by guiding, and sometimes pushing others to set theirs, she was able to forge ahead.

Communication was another key to her successes. A great deal of her time was spent involving and informing the board, listening to people, and keeping everyone informed. Superintendents must develop a better understanding of the differences that men and women communicate. She described men as more linear, concrete, and directive communicators, and she saw women as more open and warm.

When asked in June if she would again choose to be a superintendent if she were making the choice again, Jackie West responded:

I don't know, to tell you honestly. I suppose yes, but I mean, it has been very hard both personally and professionally. And if really and truly I'd known what I was getting into—see my perception was that it was this nice little town that had a good financial base, etc., etc., and then it all just went to hell. It's taken . . . months, and so I don't know if I really would. I would probably think more seriously if I did.

The school district was similar to a dysfunctional family. When someone allows people to speak the truth, and that's my style, I tell the truth. All of a sudden everything else that's been hidden under the carpet comes out. It's sort of like, in psychological terms, an intervention where you just—people just start telling the truth and then every- thing explodes. But once it's out, it's out, and then you can go from there.

Dr. West faced stresses in her personal life as well as those on the job during her first year as superintendent. Both her marriage and her professional career nearly ended before the year was out. She survived, but not without extraordinary stress. Living in an isolated, small rural community was more difficult than she thought it would be. In addition to the isolation of the community, she felt very isolated as a superintendent. "You can't really make friends with the staff because they think you're brownnosing someone or vice versa." In a large district, there are specialized personnel to handle all the aspects of school operations, but in a small district you have to do it all yourself. Handling stress, especially when there is limited support, is very important. She found that every single month presented new crises or crucial decisions. She declared that having a therapist helped.

At the end of her first year on the job, Jackie West was asked to summarize her thoughts about the superintendency:

You know, if things turn around and I can really do what I want to do here, I could stay here, provided I have the kind of personal life I'd want, which right now, I don't. But it could be kind of exciting and fun to create out of this a really dynamic, neat, little school district.

QUESTIONS FOR REFLECTION AND DISCUSSION

1. As you consider the dilemmas Jackie faced, which do you think had their genesis in her moving from a very large school district to a very small one?

2. Many individuals who have been assistant superintendents in large districts gain their first superintendency in much smaller districts. Based on your knowledge of Jackie's first year, what recommendations would you give someone considering such a transition?

3. What effects did the development of a shared vision have on the district and on Jackie?

4. What were some indicators that Jackie was concerned with "doing the right thing" as well as "doing things right" in seeking to be both a leader and a manager?

5. What do you think may have been the long-term effects of the way Jackie handled financial crises and sexual misconduct?

REFERENCES

Elam, S. M., Rose, L. C., & Gallup, A. M. (1991, September). The 23rd Gallup poll of the public's attitudes toward the public schools. *Phi Delta Kappan, 43,* 41–56.

Goode, D. J. (1992, Spring/Summer). The superintendent: Planning for organizational change. *Record in Educational Administration and Supervision, 12,* 46–50.

Grohe, B. (1983, July). How I used candor to make my new superintendency a success. *The American School Board Journal,* 28–29.

Henry, D. E., & Murphy, J. F. (1993, Summer). Ways of knowing: An alternative framework for reviewing doctoral-level research on the school superintendency. *Record in Educational Administration and Supervision, 13,* 74–84.

Sergiovanni, T. J. (1990). *Value-added leadership: How to get extraordinary performance in schools.* San Diego: Harcourt Brace Jovanovich.

4

HANK
Chief, Coach, Superintendent

Edward W. Chance, The University of Nevada, Las Vegas

ABSTRACT.   *Hank Waters became the superintendent in a nationally recognized retirement community in the southwest. He had been involved in schools for many years, but this position represented his first and last superintendency, since he planned to retire within four years. Dr. Waters is a tall, imposing Native American, in his mid-50s, who had previously coached and taught in the school district. His initial year as superintendent of the Lake School District focused on gaining administrative control of a district that had been led in a laissez-faire manner by the previous superintendent. Hank also spent substantial time attempting to pass a bond issue, which eventually failed by a wide margin. The remainder of Hank's time focused on opening communication lines and dealing with state-mandated initiatives, a negative board member, personnel concerns, and legal problems created by his predecessor's administrative mistakes. Throughout his first year, Hank continued working to improve communication with the school and community and to create an image of a superintendent with a clear vision of who was in charge.*

THE DISTRICT AND COMMUNITY

The Lake School District is located on a large man-made lake in a southwestern state. The district is only 17 miles from one state border and approximately an hour drive from two other state borders. Though the Lake School District has a total population of 18,000 people, it centers on a town of 6,000 people, of whom some 75% are retired and have moved to the lake-front community from areas across the country.

The locale, identified as one of the most desirable retirement areas in the United States by the *Wall Street Journal*, was attracting growing numbers of retirees. This was forcing up property values, especially on land adjacent to the lake. For instance, a 700-square-foot cabin on the lake recently sold for $115,000. The lake has approximately 1,200 miles of shoreline and is a popular summer resort and vacation area. In fact, the population triples during the summer months because of recreational attractions such as boating and fishing.

The largest employer in the Lake community is the local hospital, which has 45 doctors on staff. The high number of physicians reflects the status of the community and the needs of its many retired residents. The second largest employer is the Lake School District, which has 123 certified personnel. The remainder of the local employers are small trade and service businesses and those directly related to the recreational enterprises. Financially, the community represents two extremes, from the very wealthy to the very poor, while supporting only a small middle class. The most influential groups in the community related to school issues are band parents and athletic boosters. The retirees are, of course, a force to be concerned about, as they traditionally respond negatively to any increase in local taxes.

The Lake School District includes four buildings serving 1,680 students in a preschool, an elementary school, a middle school, and a high school. The district's population was growing, having experienced a 7% increase during the school year prior to Hank's becoming superintendent. Student population growth was expected to continue into the twenty-first century.

Many of the students were children of local medical personnel or service workers, and many others were children of less affluent families. Of the students, 41% qualified for free or reduced price lunches. The elementary school was the largest of the four in the district, with 840 students in kindergarten through fifth grade. The high school senior class was the smallest class, with 90 students. The ethnic composition of the school included 1% Asian-American and Hispanic, 28% Native American, and 71% Caucasian.

The bonding capacity valuation in the community was $56 million. Because of recent state-mandated reforms, which focused primarily on salaries, the Lake district was having financial difficulty, as reflected in minimal carryover—less than 2% of the budget. As the school population continued to expand, the district's financial problems were expected to accelerate. By state law, no new taxes could be passed without a vote of the people. It was unlikely that a tax increase would be supported until schools were in dire straits.

The Lake School District covers 140 square miles, with 1,000 students riding buses daily. The school buses averaged 10 years of age, with some 100,000 miles on each. The school facilities were adequate, but continued student growth and the aging of facilities cast an ominous shadow for the future.

THE SUPERINTENDENT

Hank Waters holds a Ph.D. from a major southwestern research institution. He had coached and taught for several years prior to moving into school administration. Although this was his first superintendency, he had been preparing for such a position for several years.

Prior to accepting the job of superintendency, Hank had been an assistant superintendent for 15 years in a nearby urban school district. His responsibilities there focused on personnel and finance. His previous district was much larger than the Lake district, and much wealthier.

Early in his educational career, Hank had been a teacher and coach in the Lake district. The researcher noted that some individuals in the community and the schools called him "chief," others called him "coach," and still others called him "Dr. Waters." The variations in nomenclature reflected when the individuals had first known Hank.

Because the urban district where he worked was nearby, he believed he had been able to keep abreast of important events in Lake schools. Paradoxically, Hank was both an insider and an outsider. He was an insider because he knew the district fairly well and because many of his previous students were now community leaders; one was even a board member. He was an outsider because he was not part of the political or social milieu of the Lake community. As later became evident, Dr. Waters did not know the district as well as he thought.

Initially, Hank was very reticent with the researcher, providing minimal, superficial information. Only after the bond issue that he had championed so stridently failed did he begin to open up and discuss the problems of the district. It was as if Hank needed someone to talk with regarding the school district, and the researcher served in that capacity.

Hank Waters originally applied for the superintendent's position by submitting a resume at the request of the board. He never completed a formal application as other candidates were required to do, and he was the first person they interviewed. It appeared that Hank was a favored candidate from the beginning. He was interviewed on three later occasions, after the board had interviewed the other candidates. It was as if they were reaffirming their decision and beliefs regarding Hank.

Waters felt that his candidacy generated a great deal of community support. He indicated he believed the school "needed a firm hand" and that the board "wanted somebody that they knew would be in control and was not afraid to say no." He also believed that some members of the board felt the district teachers had too much freedom and thus "a boss was needed who would control them."

A couple of board members were concerned about why Dr. Waters would leave a larger system to come to the smaller Lake School District. Hank felt he alleviated their concern by focusing on the potential of Lake School District. He believed that much of this concern was based on his being in his mid-50s and speculation about whether he planned "to coast" to retirement. There were already three retired superintendents in the community, and the board did not want a person to come to the district only with plans to retire. Waters agreed to serve as superintendent for "at least three to five years" and not seek an early retirement.

There were some liabilities in accepting the Lake superintendent's position. Hank was forced to take a small reduction in salary and benefits, and he also had to sell his home in the adjacent community. While a new home was being built, Hank commuted to the Lake School District, leaving home at 5:45 A.M. to be in the district by 7:00 A.M. Early in the year he felt this drive beginning to wear on him physically and mentally, a feeling that intensified as the year progressed and as problems mounted.

Dr. Waters' initial contract provided him 20 days of vacation per year, but this was the only perk he received. He was hired on a 1-year contract as stipulated by state law. He received "no continuing employment or property rights" and could be reassigned by a majority vote of the board at any time for any reason. His salary as a new superintendent was $66,200.

VISION, INITIAL GOALS, AND DISTRICT CONCERNS

Hank Waters' vision for the school district was that it would become a leader in the use of technology. He also wanted to create a district that utilized a participatory approach to leadership and decision making. However, as his first year unfolded, Hank found he would not be able to focus on this vision. In fact, as will be seen, his vision often was lost in a multitude of critical incidents and managerial crises. He failed to fully share his vision with others and, indeed, often seemed to lose sight of it. Additionally, Hank's site administrators often had values that were at odds with his. This circumstance contrasts dramatically with the recommendations of Manasse (1985) and Sergiovanni (1992), who emphasize the need for a vision based on shared values.

Dr. Waters also identified two broad goals for himself and the school district. The first was to pass a $3.5 million bond issue that would primarily be used to construct additional classrooms, to purchase new buses, and to buy more computers for the district. His second goal was to work closely with the principals in order to "move them toward being educational leaders rather than managers."

After further discussion, Waters identified a third goal: to gain control over what he felt was teacher abuse of the district's leave policy. He stated that the teachers "took 1,000 and some odd days of leave—that's sick leave, personal leave, and professional leave" during the previous year. In his view, this abuse of leave negatively impacted time-on-task, and Hank was committed to controlling this. This issue also was important to the board and was discussed with Hank during his interviews.

Dr. Waters found the bond issue took a large percentage of his time, until early March when the initiative was defeated by an almost two-to-one margin. The bond issue campaign, discussed later in this chapter, faced stern opposition mounted by a religious group that was opposed to outcome-based education. In addition, some local farmers, retirees, and a board member vocally opposed the effort.

COMMUNICATION, A STRENGTH OR A LIABILITY?

Hank Waters repeatedly identified communication as one of his strengths, and it was this area that required much of his attention and focus. He began holding manager meetings with a group that included the cafeteria manager, transportation manager, and maintenance director, as well as the principals. He organized these meetings to deal with the excessive confusion and waste created by a lack of communication between the school organization's various components. For example, Hank stated:

The band is leaving town, the football team is leaving, and several groups are going some place. We are going to have 200 students missing lunch. It helps the cafeteria to know not to cook 200 chickens, and it helps the transportation man to know that they are going to be gone.

These management meetings, along with weekly administrator meetings, significantly improved the level of internal communication within Lake School District. Previously, there simply was no effective district-wide internal communication. The meetings also assisted in supplying information to the community because all activities were better coordinated. This need for better information was one of the concerns of the community, and Hank confirmed that the meetings had "helped us with public relations in the community."

These meetings provided an opportunity for two-way communication, but most of the information and direction was provided by Waters. Although this would weaken Hank's vision of participatory leadership, it may have been necessary because of the managers' lack of maturity and readiness. Situationally, according to Hersey and Blanchard's (1988) model, Hank Waters found it necessary to be more in the telling or directing stage. Although this style did not fit with Waters' espoused style of participatory leadership, it certainly addressed the board's mandate to establish more administrative control and Hank's desire to be in charge.

Additional areas of communication focused on working closely with the board and opening communication lines with the faculty. Waters sent a weekly letter and memos to all board members advising them of school related information. He also met regularly with individual board members to discuss the district. This served a dual purpose of informing the board of issues while educating board members about the role of the superintendent.

The importance of educating board members in this fashion became more evident when Hank discovered one board member was spending almost every day at the high school offering advice and complaining about certain teachers. The superintendent's office was at one end of the high school, so he saw much more of this board member than he wanted to. Dr. Waters was eventually forced to confront this member, and the problem eased after several meetings. He was concerned that the confrontation would change the level of support from the board member, but this did not happen. Hank Waters' leadership approach with this individual was highly directive and reflected what Reddin (1970) calls a benevolent autocrat approach. He achieved the result he sought without causing undue resentment.

Communication with board members was especially important because of one member, who simply refused to support the decisions of Hank or those of the board. This board member opposed the bond issue and contributed to its eventual failure. The member was also against hiring Hank as superintendent. When pushed to discuss the reason, Waters stated that "the board member was a problem when he was a student and carried a long-term grudge into his role on the board." The reason for the grudge, which will be discussed later in the chapter, became apparent to the researcher much later in the year. Hank eventually committed himself to improving working conditions with the individual and scheduled several one-on-one meetings that began to garner his support. However, the support was never more than superficial, because the board member simply was unable to put aside his personal animosity toward Hank.

WORKING WITH TEACHERS AND PRINCIPALS

Dr. Waters met periodically with teacher representatives. Many of these conversations focused on issues such as duty, leave, student discipline, and homework. Unlike some districts in the state, the Lake School District formally negotiated. Many areas of potential concern were covered by the master contract and, hence, were not discussed in these meetings. However, a stir was created when Waters told the teachers they could no longer leave school during their planning periods to shop or run errands. The board considered teacher control a major issue, and Hank indicated he "tackled it head on." He was highly directive in this regard, with a strong focus on the task of keeping the teachers at school. He indicated that the teachers would have to accept his changes, whether or not they supported them.

Although the teachers disliked the new policy, the community generally supported Dr. Waters' stand because they felt the "teachers were finally doing their job." Hank stated, "How do you expect people to feel when they see teachers downtown at all hours of the day?" This control over the use of planning time was eventually expanded to include the use of professional leave.

Miscommunication was evident when teachers misinterpreted, accidentally or on purpose, some of Hank's decisions. For instance, on one occasion he refused to allow the band to march in town prior to a big football game because of inadequate planning on the part of the band director. The band director implied to the students that the band could never march in town. As a result, many patrons complained to the board about the superintendent's arbitrary decision.

Throughout the year Dr. Waters worked to improve the supervisory skills and instructional leadership of the principals. This was not only one of his goals but also a community and board concern. He sent several principals to various types of training and discussed instructional strategies with them. A more formalized approach to improve their skills was not developed. By the end of the year, because of increased conflict between Hank and the high school principal, the principal resigned to accept a nearby superintendency. The school counselor was appointed as the new principal, with the understanding that he would focus on instruction. An assistant principal was hired with primary responsibility for management. During the spring, a 2-day retreat and several intensive "interaction sessions" were held to discuss administrative goals for the coming school year. These meetings were well received by those involved because they provided administrators an opportunity to plan for the future.

Not all of Hank Waters' initial goals were met; but some were, though often not in the manner he envisioned. The bond issue failed, but from this experience, he learned more about the community, the board, and the teachers. The goal of having the principals as instructional leaders was furthered because of administrative turnover. The teachers certainly were spending more time-on-task because of new policies regarding planning time and leave.

However, a series of time-consuming critical incidents dominated much of Hank's time and established the tone of his first year. Most of these incidents fell into one of three broad categories: (1) global board or district issues; (2) personnel matters; and (3) legal and fiscal concerns.

GLOBAL BOARD OR DISTRICT ISSUES

The most serious incident relating to the district was the failure of the bond issue. Hank Waters, spent six months preparing the community for this initiative. He spoke to more than 1,600 people. In October, he established a strategic planning committee consisting of board members, community and business leaders, and retirees. Interestingly, no administrators or teachers were on the committee, an oversight that eventually contributed to the bond issue's defeat. The planning committee met on a regular basis to discuss the bond election. According to state law, a bond issue needed a positive vote of 60% in order to pass. The Lake election fell far short of the required abnormal majority, being approved by only 35% of the voters. Hank Waters took the smashing bond defeat as a personal failure and continually referred to it in his conversations. But, he didn't give up. In fact, he planned an attempt to pass a revised bond proposal but indicated that "others will have to take the lead" in the campaign.

Waters remained amazed at the degree of opposition to the bond issue. He viewed the defeat as a result of "opposition to outcome-based education" and general opposition to tax increases. Perhaps the biggest problem related to the bond issue was that he spent too much time trying to convince the opposition rather than focusing on potential supporters. He especially sought to gain the support of retired citizens, a strategy that did not work. In addition, Hank assumed that teachers and administrators would support the bond proposal, which was not the case. In all likelihood, his approach backfired on him.

Another global issue concerned the board member with the grudge (mentioned earlier). After several months as superintendent, Dr. Waters discovered that the problem was a result of an incident that took place when he taught and coached in the district two decades earlier. It concerned a sophomore, one of Hank's students, who quit school to marry. Hank had tried to convince her otherwise. The person she married—the school board member—never forgave Waters, having carried this grudge against him for 20 years.

A third global district issue was that of outcome-based education (OBE). At the beginning of Hank's first year as superintendent, the state department of education viewed OBE as a vehicle for some of its reform efforts. Many schools invested heavily in training for OBE. By mid-year, there was a ground swell of opposition to OBE across the state, particularly by religious groups, who saw it as "humanistic." Other groups attacked OBE as a "dumbing down" approach to the curriculum. The state department of education as well as the state superintendent of schools, responded to the political pressure by abandoning support for OBE, leaving many school districts in precarious positions with their communities. The Lake School District and its superintendent were among the casualties.

By the end of the school year, OBE had been rejected, ostensibly, by the majority of schools in the state. In fact, the concept of OBE was removed by the legislature from all reform laws and policies. This hostility toward OBE contributed to the failure of the bond issue in the Lake district. Some citizens saw a vote of "no" on the bond issue as a way to send a message to school district leaders. The fiasco left many continuing rifts within the community.

CRITICAL PERSONNEL INCIDENTS

A series of incidents relating to personnel were also troublesome for Hank. One of these involved an employment discrimination grievance and subsequent litigation filed by a 48-year-old woman, who had been rejected for a position as an elementary school teacher. The district hired all first-year teachers to fill vacancies. The complainant, an experienced teacher, alleged that she had not been chosen because of her age. Although this complaint was eventually dismissed, it required Hank to expend considerable time and energy to properly respond to the charges. In fact, he felt that the individual involved abused the intent of federal guidelines in order to financially hurt the district. The complaint did, however, motivate the district to develop and implement new hiring and interviewing procedures.

A second personnel issue surfaced when a coach borrowed a driver education car and drove it to another town without the superintendent's knowledge. The coach had an accident that totaled the vehicle. When questioned as to why he took the car, he said that the previous superintendent allowed him to drive the vehicle as a job reward. Upon checking with the previous superintendent, who was retired but still living the community, Hank discovered that this was indeed the case. He also discovered that the previous superintendent made other special deals with coaches, teachers, and administrators. For example, in one case, because the district was unable to provide an adequate salary increase, the previous superintendent provided an administrator additional vacation time without the board's consent.

A third incident related to personnel involved the behavior of coaches during athletic events, which prompted a number of complaints from parents. Waters described the problem as inappropriate "bench decorum" on the part of several coaches, but in particular the head football coach. Hank carved out his territory on this issue and refused to accept what he considered to be an increasing level of "verbal abuse of athletes." His coaching values were crystal clear when he discussed this situation, and it was his most emotional response to any issue. He met with the head football coach several times, and, although there was some improvement, the coach eventually left the district to take a principalship elsewhere.

Finally, Hank's expectation that principals would be instructional leaders was particularly difficult for the high school principal to accept. This individual simply refused to change or improve. Hank helped this employee to find a superintendency in a nearby district, thereby expediting his departure.

LEGAL AND FISCAL CONCERNS

The third category of critical incidents involved legal and fiscal concerns. Early in his first year, Hank Waters discovered that virtually no records were kept on district purchases or bids. This mismanagement cost the district over $80,000, because monies paid to vendors had not been properly encumbered. The previous superintendent had a cavalier attitude toward money, and Waters was appalled at the absence of accountability. This negatively impacted the amount of carryover dollars for Hank's second year in the district. Hank also determined that many items had been purchased without any administrative oversight. To rectify the situation, he initiated new purchasing policies and hired an additional secretary to keep track of financial matters and perform other necessary duties.

Even after Hank had taken steps to rectify previous fiscal mismanagement, he was amazed one day when a woman came to his office and asked him for the vehicle registration to a school bus. She declared that she had been given the bus by the previous superintendent in return for a load of gravel. The trading of school district property for gravel, or anything else, is unlawful, and it took some time to resolve the situation. Dr. Waters further discovered, in early April, that the high school principal, who was leaving to become a superintendent elsewhere, had failed to conduct teacher evaluations as required by law. This meant that, although teachers had to be notified of reemployment for the next school year under the state's continuing contract law, the district was not able to do so based on appropriate instructional evaluations. Instead the district was forced to rehire all teachers because of the absence of appropriate documentation. All teachers, whether excellent, marginal, or terrible, were rehired by the school district.

LEARNING FROM EXPERIENCE

Critical incidents in the categories of global school board or district issues, personnel matters, and legal and fiscal concerns underscored the need to draft and implement new board policies and to establish internal organizational controls. Clearly, Hank Waters was obliged to spend much time solving problems he either inherited or had little control over because of his lack of knowledge of the district. The Lake School District was able to successfully address each area because of Hank's years of experience in another district and expertise in the areas of personnel and school finance. The new policies and structures were intended to help keep critical incidents from recurring.

When Hank Waters was asked to discuss any other lessons he learned from the first year of his superintendency and to identify areas where he believed his university preparation was inadequate, he quickly indicated that he was not as effective a communicator as he had thought. He identified the bond issue as a prime example, lamenting that he had spoken "to so many people and yet the issue was still defeated."

He also cited the incident where he denied the band director permission for the band to march downtown prior to a football game. He complained that his directive had been blown completely out of proportion. Hank had continually crafted his statements carefully, whether speaking one-on-one or in public. Nevertheless, these incidents occurred, as well as others.

In regard to his university preparation for the superintendency, Hank Waters identified a greater need to understand fundamental activities such as "designing a board agenda" and "developing policy." He also indicated the need to have more knowledge regarding school finance. He stated there was a need for "a better understanding of the county assessor's office and the treasurer's office, and . . . how do they assess, when do the taxes start on the properties, what and how do they change for revaluation." In fact, at one point during the year, Waters had to threaten to sue the county treasurer in order to receive some documents that by law were public information.

Another area of inadequate preparation he identified was school law, particularly as it related to issues such as the open meeting law and school board rights. He also believed there was a greater need for knowledge of how the total educational system functions.

The final area Hank mentioned reflected the need to know how to keep better records and to gather data that would prove useful to school management and decision making. On the whole, his suggestions about university preparation for superintendents focused on day-to-day operational concerns and not on issues such as curriculum development.

FINAL THOUGHTS

Although Hank Waters had considerable administrative experience in another district, when he finally began his first superintendency, he discovered that his past experience had not provided the skills and perceptions necessary to be fully successful. For instance, Hank expressed unrealistic perceptions of the time demands of the superintendency when he said in a November interview, "It seems like I spend more than my 8-hour day here, and I don't get it all done. I take it home sometimes, and I know that's not good."

One reason that Hank was surprised by the demands of the superintendency was that he had moved from a large district to a small one. In his previous role, he had been an assistant superintendent with several subordinates. In the Lake School District, he had no assistant and, initially, only one secretary. Eventually he was able to add an assistant superintendent, another secretary, and a part-time computer data entry person.

Other reasons Hank found the superintendent's job to be so demanding involved problems with personnel and finance and problems resulting from illegal or unethical acts by his predecessors. Gaining knowledge and control of the school system took him longer than he expected.

Hank's plans for the district often took a back seat to reality and the continuing problems besetting the school district. He also was never able to fully use his espoused participatory leadership style but instead was often forced into a more directive autocratic style. Some of the reasons for this situation relate to the laissez faire leadership of previous superintendents, as well as Hank's desire to gain "control" over several district factions.

Another area of dissonance between perception and reality was Hank's initial belief that he was highly knowledgeable of the community because he had once taught and coached there. He thought that this history and living in a nearby community provided him both longitudinal and current knowledge of the school district. Hank's conviction that he was, in many ways, an insider proved to be only partially true and often with a negative result. He was astonished to discover that his difficult relationship with one board member was the product of advice given some 20 years before. Additionally, many teachers believed he had been hired to "clean up" the system, a belief that was reflected in their mistrust of him and in a series of miscommunications with him. The fact that he took away their "freedom" during their planning periods and limited their use of professional leave seemed to corroborate their views. This perspective was underscored by Hank's termination of private deals struck by employees with the previous superintendent, such as the use of the driver's education vehicle and extra vacation time. His directive leadership style further reinforced this view. If Hank had better practiced what he espoused—participatory leadership—some of these miscommunications might have been alleviated.

Hank's ambitious attempt to pass a $3.5 million bond issue was also a result of viewing himself as an insider. However, his failure to involve teachers and administrators in the planning process combined with his attempt to implement an outcome-based curriculum doomed the bond proposal. Although Waters worked very hard to pass the bond measure, either he exhibited a sense of naivete or was unrealistic about his leadership and communication skills. That the issue received a positive vote of only 35% was a strong message from the community. The failure of the bond measure impacted Hank throughout the remainder of his first year and influenced his interactions with others. In fact, he began to behave and act more like an outsider. Waters often referred to the bond defeat and how it depressed him. He had difficulty understanding why people, especially some educators, failed to support the bond election.

As Hank began to match his supervisory style to the readiness and maturity of his staff, he became more productive and focused in his activities. His termination of an ineffective support staff member was supported by the teachers. His efforts to improve instruction and the learning climate were also greeted with community and district support. These efforts included emphasizing time-on-task, replacing an abusive coach, and helping an ineffective principal to find another position, thus making room for an instructional principal. Allowing teachers to contribute sick leave to a colleague with a heart condition, and other similar acts, were seen as examples of a superintendent who cared. Negotiations conducted toward the end of his first year progressed smoothly even though the teachers were granted few of their requests.

Hank Waters ended his first year as superintendent with a solvent district, with a fairly supportive school board, and with teacher negotiations behind him. He looked forward to a new assistant superintendent who would provide him support and a new principal who would focus on instruction. Finally, he had a new football coach with a past record of building winning football teams. He had a new home under construction and only five years to go until retirement. "What more could a superintendent want?" he asked!

QUESTIONS FOR REFLECTION AND DISCUSSION

1. How did discrepancies between expectations and reality impact Hank's superintendency?

2. What similarities do you see between the first-year experiences of Hank Waters and those of Jackie West (described in Chapter 3)?

3. What factors might account for Jackie's greater success in keeping focused on her vision for the school district?

4. How did the absence of clear and consistently followed policies and procedures impact the Vista and the Lake School Districts?

5. What were the advantages and the liabilities of Hank's becoming more autocratic as the year progressed? What kind of a leader or manager do you think Hank will be in his second year as superintendent?

REFERENCES

Hersey, P., & Blanchard, K. H. (1988). *Management of organizational behavior.* Englewood Cliffs, NJ: Prentice-Hall.

Manasse, A. L. (1985). Vision and leadership: Paying attention to intention. *Peabody Journal of Education, 63*(1), 150–173.

Reddin, W. J. (1970). *Managerial effectiveness.* New York: McGraw-Hill.

Sergiovanni, T. J. (1992). *Moral leadership: Getting to the heart of school improvement.* San Francisco: Jossey Bass.

5

CHAD
System Entry Sets the Stage

C. M. Achilles, Eastern Michigan University

*ABSTRACT.   First impressions count. A new leader's entry into an education system paves the way for success or failure. Recognizing this, Chad Chi conscientiously followed the detailed plans provided in the book **Entry** (Jentz et al., 1982), which included initiating a program of careful listening throughout the system and involving diverse groups. Dr. Chi came to the system with the intention of being as open and communicative as possible. His early entry work was followed by building inclusive structures and focusing on staff development. These steps were so important to Dr. Chi that he built into his contract the provision that he follow a detailed entry plan for nearly half of his first year.*

This chapter highlights a new superintendent of a small New York school district designated by the Greek letter Chi (X), suggesting a crossroads. I've called the new superintendent of the Chi District Dr. Chad Chi because this first superintendency is a crossroads in his own career.

Dr. Chad Chi, a 39-nine-year-old white male, has a doctorate in administration, planning, and social policy from Harvard; a master's in curriculum and instruction; and a bachelor's degree in biology from Cornell. Before coming to the Chi District, he was a director of an alternative school, a principal in two high schools, and an assistant superintendent. He also held a variety of teaching positions including some adjunct responsibilities in higher education.

During the study, Dr. Chi continuously displayed confidence, candor, concern, and courtesy. He offered me his private direct phone number and his home phone number for convenience. He responded promptly to all requests for information and for meetings.

Although much of Chad's first year focused on instruction, a clear lesson can be learned from his careful attention to entry into the new system, including his attention to building support, processes, and systems to advance his leadership role. Early in the year, it became clear that a key element of success or failure would involve his entry into the system. His style of openness contrasted sharply with that of the previous superintendent, whose style was much more "close to the vest."

THE DISTRICT AND COMMUNITY

Though the area appears rural, the Chi District is about 20 miles from a major eastern city and is classified as suburban because it is within a metropolitan statistical area (Johnson, 1989). According to Dr. Chi, the community is "blue-collar, middle-income, and mostly white." Only about 5% of the students are minorities; about 25% of the pupils qualify for federal lunch support, and district finances seem "healthy."

Observation showed well-maintained facilities and modern equipment, the products of recent extensive bond-supported renovation. There are five schools in a total of five buildings. One large building houses both a primary school and the Chi District Central Office, which includes central services providing functions such as transportation and buildings and grounds. This building is conveniently located close to the center of Chi Village.

The district is governed by a seven-person board of education. The members are elected annually to staggered 3-year terms at the school-district budget election each May.

The Chi District is served by the area Board of Cooperative Educational Services (BOCES), a New York State Education Agency "arm." Each BOCES provides a variety of services to its constituents, usually fairly small school districts, on a regional basis.

A drive through the district shows lots of open spaces, plenty of farm land, and an encroaching edge of suburbanism. Most of the Chi District's activities are in a cluster of buildings in the Village of Chi. The school system spreads across parts of four towns. Each town has its own governance structure, and there are varying tax rates and assessment levels. Although none of the towns are totally within the school district, centrally located Chi Village is totally within the Chi School District.

The Chi District had been growing slowly and included about 23,000 people. The enrollment of 4,100 students, when Chad became superintendent, marked the first time in 11 years that the district exceeded 4,000 in the public schools. Chi District bussed 4,500 students, including about 400 attending private schools.

The district is located close to important higher education sites, as well as to several other villages, towns, and small cities in the metropolitan area. Chi Village residents may work in the city, but Chi Village is a bedroom community that does not have the sprawl of suburbia. This pleasant upstate village is in a rural area that is likely to become more suburban because of outward expansion of firms in the nearby city. The schools seem to be a source of community interest and even pride.

The small town atmosphere of Chi Village and District is highlighted by some of the school district's community relations procedures. For example, district senior citizens over age 55 can receive passes allowing free admission to district events and continuing education programs. Facilities are available to public groups free of charge, with priority given to instruction or educational events. School volunteers can earn free passes to school activities by accumulating hours of service. The community benefits from invitations to school events, such as band, chorus, drama, and athletics.

Although Chi Village is not culturally diverse, the metropolitan area provides outstanding activities and cultural events. Dr. Chi lives in a neighboring community somewhat larger than Chi Village, a community that has considerable cultural diversity and many activities generated by a growing state university.

SELECTING THE NEW SUPERINTENDENT

After the retirement of the long-term prior superintendent, the job was widely advertised. However, the local scuttlebutt was that a district assistant superintendent had the *inside track* for the job. Dr. Chi heard about the opening and saw the advertisement in professional publications. In spite of the indications of an inside favorite, Dr. Chi applied. After screening and interviews, six members of the seven-member board visited Dr. Chi in his former district. Based on an employment vote of seven to zero, an agreement was reached in January that Dr. Chi should be the new superintendent. Formal employment began six months later in July.

Dr. Chi was probably chosen primarily for his low-key style and practice of involving others in decisions. The district seemed ready for a change in administrative styles, and Dr. Chi's style was much different from that of his predecessor, who operated in more of a top-down, micro-management mode. It is not unusual to hire an outsider when there is interest in district-wide change.

Dr. Chi was seeking several key elements in his first superintendency, including what he called "a good superintendency," proximity to a major university so his wife could work on her doctorate, some flexibility, and cultural diversity. He moved to the Chi District from a small, rural New England setting where he was an assistant superintendent.

SETTING THE STAGE: ENTRY

Because he was an outsider, Dr. Chi negotiated a structured and detailed 150-day entry plan with the school board. This plan provided direction for getting to know the district and allowed Dr. Chi to obtain data and opinions that would help him set an agenda for action. The community and educators received this plan well and seemed to appreciate Dr. Chi's genuine willingness to learn about them and their schools.

Dr. Chi emphasized that he brought with him no predetermined agenda other than to provide outstanding educational opportunities for the pupils, parents, and patrons of the district. This approach offered an opportunity to heal old wounds, develop trust, and build on the strengths of people in the district. Dr. Chi felt that the board members had already recognized that they were too deeply involved in day-to-day operations and personnel management issues. Dr. Chi planned to develop an agenda for action and for school improvement as he worked through the entry plan.

Dr. Chi followed closely ideas set forth in the book *Entry* (Jentz et al., 1982) as his way to learn about the Chi District. He began with plans to build long-term trust and to establish a strong administrative team that would seek involvement and commitment. Some direction had already been set by the New York State Education Agency through a planning document entitled *Compact for Learning* (1991). The *Compact* included such ideas as decentralized, school-based plans; site-based administration; shared decisions; and alternative assessment methods. The Chi District had already organized "effective schools" teams to facilitate school-improvement processes.

THE BOARD, ADMINISTRATORS, AND TEACHERS

Dr. Chi started work in July, and a board election was held in May of the next year, with two of the seven seats contested. The first part of this section includes information obtained during the period that Dr. Chi worked with the original seven-member board that had hired him; the latter part of this section includes information obtained after the election of a new board member. Interviews and visits to Dr. Chi lasted from early August of one year to late October of the next.

Most of the seven board members were between the ages of 35 and 46 years. They included five males and two females, elected for 3-year staggered terms. The former president, who had served for 8 years, was replaced by a new president, a business person who took over in July when Dr. Chi began.

Dr. Chi worked closely with the board to focus their activities more on policy and planning, in contrast to prior involvement in administration. This began during a board workshop session conducted soon after he came to the new job.

Two assistant superintendents had responsibilities for curriculum and for administration. Dr. Chi was able to hire two new principals from outside the Chi District to fill openings before the beginning of the school year. He sponsored a leadership development seminar for all administrators soon after he arrived in the Chi District. He considered principals, central office administrators, and directors as the administrative team. Early attention to staff development with the board, with this team, and later, with the teachers set the stage for Dr. Chi's continuing emphasis on staff improvement as a key to success.

The Chi District teachers were represented by the American Federation of Teachers as a bargaining unit. In fact, one unit bargained for teachers and another for administrators—including directors, principals, and assistant principals. This structure proved unwieldy at times; for example, the directors and principals both had supervision and evaluation responsibility for assistant principals.

The teachers' organization was firm but not unreasonable in its dealings with Chad, but seemed to be taking a "wait and see" attitude. Although there had not always been a contract in force, teachers and administrators seemed to get along well. The next contract negotiations were due in one year, when, it was rumored, teachers would try for a substantial raise. Yet, recent budget elections in the area did not bode well for a large raise. In the face of this contradiction, Dr. Chi hoped to increase trust and involvement. Because negotiations were to be a crucial test, he hoped the process would proceed amicably.

Several personnel issues arose early in Chad's superintendency, including some that he handled personally. These were issues related to teacher tenure, teacher discipline, and administrator discipline. Each issue, of course, brought Dr. Chi into a formal relationship with union representatives.

The prior administration's emphasis on unilateral and top-down operations had blocked open communications and trust to some degree. The new superintendent, following his entry plan, stated his intention to open communications, to listen, to build trust, to seek involvement, and to provide a quality education system for the Chi District. He repeated this at each opportunity.

THE STRUCTURES FOR CHANGE

Dr. Chi followed his carefully crafted entry plan, as stipulated in his contract. Jentz's book (1982) notes the need for "structured collaborative inquiry" and "activity mapping," for example, and recommends that the best time for a leader to establish the structures for change is early in the new job. In line with this entry strategy, Dr. Chi accepted the challenge early in his tenure to create a structure for collaborative action, not for control.

Some structure for collaboration was already in place. The Chi District had School Improvement Teams (SIT) at each building and a District Improvement Team (DIT) to consider district-wide issues. These groups had developed improvement ideas built on "effective schools" concepts. One challenge was to adjust these plans to fit the state's *Compact for Learning* (1991), which emphasized outcomes for students and for the district and required diverse representation on site and on district teams. Even though decision-making structures met at least the minimums required in the *Compact*, Dr. Chi planned to expand membership of SIT and DIT groups. The October school newsletter advertised for volunteers, and the November newsletter reported progress and again invited folks to volunteer:

Team Building Creates Atmosphere for Change as School Improvement Teams Recruit Parent Representation

Two years into its School and District Improvement Team process, the Chi School District has zeroed in on creating the open communication needed between parents, teachers, administrators, and office, bus, and custodial staff members to take blueprints for improvement off the drawing board and into action. The Village Elementary School, with six Action Teams reporting to a central School Improvement Team, has taken steps to bring school personnel and parents together. "The biggest factor has been the very high percentage of faculty, parents, and staff participating on these teams," said a Village principal. "Things happen because everyone is involved. It's their school, and what happens directly involves them and makes a difference to them." Supported by summer workshops in communication and consensus-building, School Improvement Teams at each school have taken the goals developed by the District Improvement Team and have translated these goals into action: academic mastery, with a goal of 95% of all students reaching this level; positive social development, with a decline in disciplinary actions and the dropout rate; lifelong learning as evidenced by surveying graduates as to postsecondary education; caring and productive citizenry leading toward community service and critical, self-directed, and creative thinking.

Surveys of staff and parents, standardized test results, discipline, and attendance data have been brought to the teams. According to the assistant superintendent, "This information helped teams develop plans based on data that revealed areas of strength and areas of concern. The teams have addressed school climate and are now paying more attention to student achievement issues."

There is an ongoing need for parent volunteers on each school's team as well as the District Improvement Team. Please contact your child's principal if you are interested in becoming a part of this exciting process.

This invitation to become involved and to participate expressed Dr. Chi's style and his pursuit of the goal of involvement and open communications in the Chi District. He continued to use the monthly district newsletter to inform district residents of plans, progress, and opportunities.

A second example of the move toward openness was Dr. Chi's plan for a new budget process and his calendar for preparing and presenting the budget. This process included 11 committees, 5 for school sites and 6 for departments, with representation from various levels of interest, such as school board, principal, department head or director, staff, parents, and community. The budgets would be developed in accordance with projected fiscal growth by providing site allocations for expenditure decisions to be recommended by the appropriate committee. Individual budgets would be compiled for board action into the total budget. And, finally, the budget would be presented for a vote by the community. Dr. Chi recognized that board involvement on committees would be time consuming, but believed that the involvement would keep board members aware of plans and make it easier for them to respond to questions raised by the community. The initial working budget for the coming year was based on a per-pupil allocation and/or on a sum determined by expenditures for the prior year.

The budget committees were to help decide allocations for predetermined activities. Although budget decisions did not determine new directions for the district, they provided operating support for directions already decided upon. To assure that committees understood their role, Dr. Chi orchestrated a large training and information session for about 100 people. There was a presentation of the budget and of major budget issues. The expectations for committee responsibilities in the budget process were clearly delineated.

One key point, explained to the entire group, was that approximately 80% of the budget was "untouchable"—it was locked in for personnel and related costs. Thus, although it was important, only 20% of the budget was flexible. Training for the committee provided direction and set the limits of the committees' tasks. The committees were not to address program issues but to determine the allocation of funds, answering the question, What kind of system can we afford? The budget committee process reflected the structures-for-change idea of the entry plan. The new budget process illuminated the fact that there were no definitive district goals. Hence, the budget process could be used for setting goals that would be implemented through the SIT and DIT structures.

Recognizing the need for a shared vision, Dr. Chi worked with the District Improvement Team and the school board to develop a mission and five belief statements intended to guide decisions. He disseminated the document, shown in Figure 5-1, with the following explanation:

> The Board of Education has adopted the following mission and belief statement with the intent that it will guide our practice and decision making in the Chi School District. We believe that everything we do should be aligned with this mission in order to make it a reality. This statement of mission and beliefs will be prominently displayed throughout the district.

FIGURE 5-1
Mission of the Chi District

OUR MISSION

We of the Chi District will engage and support all students academically and socially in becoming self-directed, lifelong learners who think critically and creatively, and function as caring, productive citizens. We believe the following:

- Learning is an unending, ongoing process, and extends beyond the limit of the classroom to include school, family/home, and community.

- Learning requires active, productive, and meaningful student engagement.

- We learn best when treated and respected as individuals.

- We learn best through our strengths and in a variety of ways and in different environments.

- We learn best when the needs of power, freedom, fun, and sense of belonging are an integral part of the learning environment.

The statement of mission and beliefs was widely distributed and was the basis for two day-long board work sessions. In establishing the process of working with the mission and belief statement, Dr. Chi provided the board with a credo explaining much about his leadership philosophy and style. He said, "I wanted to have a very different experience both for them—the board—and for myself." The process of sharing this "credo" with the board was characteristic of Dr. Chi's way of expressing his ideas about key issues. The credo, reproduced here, provided a context for the board work sessions:

> *The significant problems we face cannot be solved at the same level of thinking we were at when we created them.*
>
> *Albert Einstein*

This quotation has profound meaning for how we all should pursue our roles in public education. It strongly influences what I do and how I do it. As I have related to several of you, how I choose to perform my role as superintendent is not modeled after anyone I know. In fact, my focus and style are more or less derived from what I have **not** seen in my former superintendents and in many of my colleagues. This is not intended as an indictment of any individual or any group of people. It is only meant to underscore the fact that the challenge to significantly improve the educational quality of any school district remains enormous, despite the sincere efforts of those who have previously sat in our seats.

In terms of leadership style, I try to push and not to pull as I attempt to move the district. Instead of using a charismatic or dictatorial approach, I am working toward a shared vision that encourages commitment rather than compliance. I do not see myself as a knight in shining armor who can do it all by himself. The best metaphor I have for myself in this role is that of an orchestra conductor: making sure everyone is on the same page, encouraging, cajoling, and pushing them to produce their best—**in harmony.**

One of my primary goals this year has been to develop a thoughtful, collaborative, and supportive administrative team (including the principals, directors, and assistant superintendents). (A group aligned around a common purpose, open, inclusive, and thinking together.) We have spent hours in this effort, and I believe that we are getting there. Our group is more cohesive, supportive, and open with each other than any other such group I have ever experienced. The individuals themselves are vibrant, thoughtful, talented, and experienced. The Chi District is very fortunate.

Our overriding goal must be to improve the school district. I believe that all children initially come to school wanting to learn. Look at those kindergartners! They are ready. And they are eager. Our challenge is how to maintain that motivation. When children fail to learn, we automatically look for the culprits—the students, their parents, mediocre teachers—when the real problem is the system itself. It is very easy to become distracted by efforts to remove the incompetent teacher, the incorrigible student, or that mechanical gorilla. But we cannot lose sight of the big picture. Every problem we seek to solve and every question we seek to answer must be in the context of improving our school system.

How do we significantly improve our school district and build successful schools? We can begin by creating an environment built by leaders who see the system as a whole; an environment where people truly want to be, doing what they love to do; a place where everyone affiliated with the organization can learn.

What is my vision, my hope, for this school district? **It is to create such an environment.**

Dr. Chi proceeded to describe two projects already underway in the district as examples of an environment dedicated to improvement: the ninth grade language arts initiative and a proposed alternative elementary program. He spoke of the energy, excitement, and enthusiasm teachers were investing in these projects. He made it clear that he was talking about more than programs and activities, that he was concerned about outcomes for students:

On our way to establishing this environment, we, you and I, must aggressively support higher expectations and standards across this community and this district. No matter how much we spend per student, if we and the community have low expectations, very few students will rise above them.

Dr. Chi proposed a new decision-making structure for the board of education. The new structure called for board members, school employees, and community members to work together on committees and forums that would encourage open and thoughtful communication. He described the tasks and composition of each of the proposed committees, asking board members to assign themselves to the various groups. Committees and forums for communication and deliberation included the school board budget subcommittee, school building and department budget committees, a school board negotiations subcommittee, the District Improvement Team, and a policy committee.

EVALUATION PROCESS

As part of the entry plan, Dr. Chi established a continuous communication and evaluation process so that both he and the board could have open discussions of his effectiveness and of the board's progress toward a new planning and policy role. This process was designed to enable board members to be informed and act as a board rather than as individuals, so they would not be subject to special interest brokering and pressures. The ongoing process involved written goals, questionnaires, discussions, and evidence.

Throughout his first year, Dr. Chi showed progress toward the goals, and the board demonstrated continuing strong support for the superintendent and his plans. There was continuing board progress toward policy and planning and away from day-to-day administrative efforts. The first evaluation session went well. It opened areas for future work and showed that Dr. Chi was operating "above expectations." Subsequent quarterly evaluations continued to show the same results. These steps fed information into contract decisions. Dr. Chi had an "evergreen" contract with a rolling 1-year extension, thus keeping a 3-year contract, given continuing satisfactory performance.

SOME EARLY RESULTS OF FOLLOWING THE ENTRY PLAN

As he followed the plans provided in the book *Entry* (Jentz et al., 1982), Dr. Chi compiled results of the community and school meetings and of needs assessments. Key targets for change, or areas to conserve and improve upon, were open communications, trust building, emphasis on excellence in education, and staff development. The invitation for volunteers to work with the DIT brought over 50 people into that process, with 40 to 45 attending regularly. The budget process had 11 active working committees. The superintendent remained readily accessible to community groups and presented school information to all who would listen. In this capacity, he was the agent of the board and the "keeper of the philosophy" that he articulated at each opportunity.

Part of the articulation of philosophy was through staff development. The staff development director coordinated key staff development events that were part of the entry plan, such as a district-sponsored regional workshop with Steven Covey, author of *Seven Habits of Highly Effective People* (1989). The following year, the district continued this initiative of hosting well-known keynote presenters with Peter Senge, author of *The Fifth Discipline* (1990).

Dr. Chi used questionnaires and surveys with high school seniors to get feedback about the system. He also established some cooperation and sharing with a neighboring and slightly smaller district. He initiated ways to get the Chi District students involved in a 3-1-3 option at a nearby state university, a plan to help students make the transition from high school to higher education. He challenged the Chi District people by calling the Chi District "an average district in a below-average nation," in terms of educational outcomes.

The budget committee, the calendar committee, and the SIT/DIT processes were major structures for change and communication established early in the new superintendent's tenure. Other elements that helped to get things moving in accordance with the entry plan were key new hires for administrative positions and training seminars for administrators and the school board to set the tone for leadership.

At the May 5 school election, two seats on the school board were contested. Two incumbents—the current president and the immediate past president—ran, as well as three others, including Ms. N., a woman recently retired after many years as secretary to the six prior superintendents in the Chi District. She received 1,324 votes; the current president received 752 votes. The two were elected to the board. The past president was third with 709 votes. The election drew 2,054 voters.

NOT EVERYTHING WAS WITHOUT TURMOIL

There were some first-year frustrations. The major one was fiscal. A headline in the major regional paper noted: "OLYMPIC HERO JOINS A PLEA IN CHI DISTRICT: Third vote today on school sports." The Chi District total annual budget had failed at both the first and second school elections. The budget lost each time by a few hundred votes, the first budget defeats in 8 years. Some potential reasons for the defeat were a recent release of property reassessment data and the large turnout of older voters who supported Ms. N. She "sort of" ran on a tax-conscious platform that would appeal to senior citizens. One must say "sort of" because Ms. N supported both the budget that was defeated and a school busing referendum that would have saved funds by making bus pickup mandatory only for pupils who lived more than 1.5 miles from school in contrast to the current 1-mile limit.

Ironically, the property reassessments were long overdue, as some were 20 years old or more. However, there was no parallel information on tax rate adjustments among the four towns and the one village in which the Chi District is located. This lack of good information hurt the budget vote, and the release of reassessment information just at election time did not help the budget vote! Dr. Chi believed that the budget would have passed without the assessment issue and the influential voter draw of older citizens. Fortunately, the budget was passed at the third vote.

The division in the district over more heterogeneous classes and a touchy personnel situation requiring removal of a principal were the other main frustrations of Dr. Chi's first year. Given the propensity for problems in a new superintendency, Dr. Chi felt relieved that the first year went so well.

The DIT continued to draw interest. Involvement was "pushing 50 folks." Each meeting lasted about four hours and focused on the mission and belief statement. This provided a structure for governance and community input built around the idea of improvement. The process was designed to guide the board, superintendent, and union in taking positive actions by conveying constituent wishes.

SOME MEMORABLE TASKS FOR FUTURE BENEFITS

The Education Outcomes Project—Identifying Exit Outcomes or What Kids Should Know—was a 3-day event scheduled for mid-June of Dr. Chi's first year. This event was related to DIT work and to the State Education Agency's *Compact*. Outcomes served as targets for improvement in the district and were subject to discussion and review through Dr. Chi's open communications processes. The teacher organization did not have free rein on all education decisions because of the "opening up" effect of the District Improvement Team. The DIT knew what was going on and had a sense of direction for the system.

The DIT worked on an "effective schools" platform, and the group moved these ideas along. Some active teachers pushed the idea of a "choice" school with different curricula and instructional strategies such as Multiple Intelligences.

During the summer, at the end of his first year on the job, Dr. Chi worked with the board to emphasize their policy role and to diminish their day-to-day involvement in administrative issues. He changed the prior twice-per-month regular board meetings to once a month, and then added a second meeting that featured two board subcommittees. Chad encouraged board members to be actively involved in DIT and other committees so they could hear substantive dialogue on change and improvement. In this way, board members could be informed by ideas of broad-based groups and open discussions rather than being subjected at board meetings to extended presentations by small but vocal special interest groups. In his work with teachers, administrators, and community members, as well as with the board of education, Dr. Chi used team building, open communications, and change process activities to energize positive involvement in schools.

A PERSONAL GLIMPSE

Dr. Chi is low key and derives considerable strength from his family. At the beginning of his first year, he established as part of his entry plan some personal or private time so that he could exercise and relax. Chad enjoyed bicycling, walking, and playing in a "pick-up" game of basketball. He usually reserved 1 to 1.5 hours daily, around the noon hour. Indeed, he was able to keep some time almost daily for his exercise and to protect "family time." When asked "What joys, successes, and frustrations are you experiencing?" Dr. Chi said, "Every day, a little of each."

SUMMARY COMMENT

At the end of the first year, Dr. Chi seemed well on his way to achieving his goals. He had followed carefully the ideas and directions set in the book *Entry* (Jentz et al., 1982). He had conducted several work and training sessions with the school board to share his ideas and vision. He had demonstrated his concern for professional growth by supporting staff-development efforts, and he carefully set up his structures for change that would keep things open.

He demonstrated his commitment to open communication, trust, and processes for change that he would follow through the structures that he established early in his tenure. These structures invited participation and openness in the Chi District education process that included the District Improvement Team, budget committees, budget calendar, and staff development. The superintendent spent nearly 150 days of focused energy on his "entry plan" to learn much about the Chi District and its education system. He established new or refined old communications approaches such as the *Newsletter*, *Board Briefs*, and *School Calendar*.

The new superintendent seemed to have aligned what he believes, says, and does. This was reflected in the visible structures and processes that he put in place, and in the ways that he spent his time. He worked hard at establishing team spirit and open communications. Dr. Chi seemed comfortable in the job, with himself, and with the processes and structures he established. This impression was reinforced by his wondering, at our last interview, if the processes and system that he had put into place would work in a substantially larger system.

Although the Chi District is not large, with just over 4,000 students, Dr. Chi worked to decentralize responsibility. He kept his finger on the district's pulse, but he had enough help that he was not swamped in details or solely responsible for all things. Though he had broad knowledge of events, he was not burdened by trivia and did not try to be a "jack of all trades" (Schmuck and Schmuck, 1992). This enabled him to maintain a generalist stance.

Dr. Chi was a "figurehead" and was visible (Mintzberg, 1973). He demonstrated open communications and trust in his talk and deeds. He attended meetings, demonstrating "visibility," even when he was not in charge. He embodied Mintzberg's "negotiator" role by taking a major hand in formal negotiations as he worked for guidelines and structures in pay negotiations with administrators. He was a more informal "negotiator" in that he kept the DIT and budget committees on schedule.

FIGURE 5-2
Mintzberg's Classification
of Managerial Work
Note: From *The Nature of
Managerial Work* (pp. 92–93)
by H. Mintzberg, 1973, New
York: Harper and Row.

I.   Interpersonal Roles
   A.   Figurehead
   B.   Leader
   C.   Liaison

II. Informational Roles
   A.   Monitor
   B.   Disseminator
   C.   Spokesperson

III. Decisional Roles
   A.   Entrepreneur
   B.   Disturbance Handler
   C.   Resource Allocator
   D.   Negotiator

These roles are determined by four sets of "nested" variables: (1) environment/context; (2) job/work itself; (3) person/personality; and (4) situation.

Dr. Chi believed that the approach he was trying was correct and would work. He described it as "trying" because he did not know of other places that were using the same approach. He took every opportunity to explain *what* he believed and *why* he believed that it would work. He *advocated* and *demonstrated* the ideas. He was not only the *keeper* of the philosophy; he constantly shared or expressed it, illustrating Mintzberg's "salesperson." Figure 5-2 summarizes Mintzberg's (1973) concepts. These concepts fit Chad's entry plan closely. During the study of Chad Chi's first year, each of Mintzberg's roles was visible, showing the blending of practice and theory.

QUESTIONS FOR REFLECTION AND DISCUSSION

1. How do you think Jackie's and Hank's first years might have been different if they had followed an entry plan similar to Chad's?

2. Assume that you are moving to an administrative position in your current school system and can structure a formal entry plan. What ideas or elements will you include? How much time will you request? You may wish to consult the book *Entry* (Jentz et al., 1982) as you think through your responses.

3. Assume that you are moving to a new administrative position in a new district and can structure a formal entry plan. What ideas or elements will you include? How much time will you request?

4. Is an entry plan more important or less important in a new district than for a current district? Why or why not?

5. Dr. Chi was successful for numerous reasons. What were some effects of Dr. Chi's careful application of research and theory? What are some examples of substantive research results that he applied, and what are the theories that you believe guided his decisions?

REFERENCES

Covey, S. R. (1989). *The seven habits of highly effective people: Restoring the character ethic.* New York: Simon & Schuster.

Jentz, B., Cheever, D. S., Jr., Fisher, S. B., Jones, M. H., Kelleher, P., & Wofford, J. W. (1982). *Entry: The hiring, start-up, and supervision of administrators.* New York: McGraw-Hill.

Johnson, F. (1989). *Assigning type of locale codes to the 1987-88 CCD public school universe.* Washington, DC: National Center for Education Statistics.

Mintzberg, H. (1973). *The nature of managerial work.* New York: Harper and Row.

New York State Education Department. (1991, March). *Compact for learning.* Albany, NY: Author.

Schmuck, R. A., & Schmuck, P. A. (1992). *Small districts, big problems: Making school everybody's house.* Newbury Park, CA: Corwin Press.

Senge, P. M. (1990). *The fifth discipline: The art and practice of the learning organization.* New York: Doubleday.

6

KATHLEEN
Whirlwind Courtship, Passionate Honeymoon, Quick Divorce?

Ira E. Bogotch, The University of New Orleans

ABSTRACT.   *Kathleen Connor's induction to the superintendency came with a sense of urgency: an inherited sales tax referendum. Her impassioned campaign took Kathleen to the legislature, the bond commission, every elected official in the district, and all the people she thought were interested in public education. To each, she spoke about children and our country's need for public education. Her "up front and out there" style was highly successful not only in winning passage of the referendum but also in getting the school board to pass most of the dedicated items during her first year. Yet, as board elections approached, some members viewed the newly passed agenda and its spokeswoman as political liabilities with their constituents. Among those most critical was the young board president with whom Kathleen had formed a strong personal relationship.*

T he urgency that permeated Kathleen Connor's entry into the superintendency was a desperate need for Madison County's Public School System of 82 schools, 7,000 employees, and about 60,000 students to pass a sales tax referendum—only 6 months away! Passage could bring in $22 million a year for 10 years. Residents of this southern district had not passed any new school tax increases since 1979. Still, it was not difficult to see that the needs of public schools were greater now than ever before.

Madison County's population of mostly white, middle- and working-class families had grown in two decades to almost the size of its neighboring city, which was the center of the metropolitan statistical area. This burgeoning suburb was plagued by many of the same social problems, including poverty and violence, from which families had sought refuge by white flight.

Geographically, Madison County is so large and diverse that within its borders are rural schools accessible by only one road, urban schools surrounded by subsidized housing projects, and vast stretches of look-alike streets of the working class. Today, it is a cauldron where traditional American values are challenged daily by social change and resistance.

Economically, the district is the second largest employer in the county. Yet, through long-term neglect and historical support of Catholic schools, Madison County's public schools were over $6 million in debt, with its teachers earning less than those in any of the surrounding school districts.

The previous superintendent quit shortly after one central office administrator pulled the trigger of a gun that was pointed at his head; it misfired. Guns were not all that had misfired in Madison County. The school board had been deadlocked over two candidates after a 4-month national search for a new superintendent. Their compromise candidate was the assistant superintendent of finance, who had absolutely no experience as a teacher or building administrator. Because it was committed to passing the sales tax referendum, the district desperately needed someone who knew finance. However, the state board of education disagreed with Madison's County's choice and rejected the non-educator candidate for the superintendency.

In the midst of this crisis situation, Kathleen Connor, on a sabbatical leave at her second home in the Far West, received a telephone call from a school board member, asking her if she would be willing to become a candidate for the superintendency. Before giving her answer, she asked for an hour to think about it.

I thought about the commitment involved, the amount of time, effort, energy, and the amount of spirit. You have to be devoted to this job if it is going to be done right. And, I thought about whether I have the desire to do it and if I have the capacity for it.

She also thought that she did not want to go into the job without some sense of unanimity from the board. Of course, after seven months and two interim superintendents, there could be no illusions that she was their unanimous first choice. Still,

I think they felt comfortable with my level of professionalism; they knew I was a fair [person] . . . and that I wasn't interested in the politics of the board. I think there were board members who wanted somebody else and there were board members who did

not want somebody in particular. I wound up being the person that everybody could agree on, not necessarily everyone's first choice, but most assuredly, not anyone's last choice.

So, with a seven to zero vote and two abstentions, Kathleen Connor was officially appointed superintendent of the Madison County Public Schools.

No one seemed to question, at least publicly, that the district had made an outstanding choice, a quality human being who was also qualified to be superintendent. What was questioned, however, was the propriety with which the school board had acted in naming Ms. Connor, who had not even filed a formal application for the position.

KATHLEEN'S BACKGROUND

Kathleen Connor's professional and educational background were not typical of most superintendents (Glass, 1994). Her resume listed only one year of self-contained classroom teaching experience in an out-of-state school and no experience as a principal. Instead, she worked as a gifted and talented consultant, a special education director in the Madison County central office, and, most recently, an assistant superintendent for personnel. At the age of 51, fully vested in the retirement system, she contemplated retirement with her husband, a former state senator, at their mountain home in the West.

Her previous tenure in the central office gave her a working relationship with eight of the nine members on the school board, and as the top personnel officer, she knew many of the district's 7,000 employees.

The two jobs [director of special education and central office personnel administrator] had prepared me better than anything else one could have possibly done. Those two were the worst jobs in the school system in terms of complaints, problem solving, balancing job responsibilities, nighttime work, weekend work, legal aspects, and the giant load.

Similarly atypical was her educational background, which was primarily in counseling, school psychology, and special education. Although she held an administrative certificate, the state, at the time, did not require any more than two administration courses for certification. Not surprisingly, when asked about the value of educational administration courses, she stated that it is "not what you studied, but that you studied something and demonstrated self-discipline to study that is important." What she valued most was her special education perspective applied to all children and her background in personnel. What she came to value in her first year as superintendent were matters of finance

because that was never something that I had to have any particular responsibilities for beyond setting up the budget for whatever particular aspect of the school system I was responsible for at the time; never did I have the universal responsibility for the entire school system.

AN INHERITED SALES TAX REFERENDUM

Once named to the superintendency, Ms. Connor immediately faced the challenge of passing a sales tax referendum.

*Certainly the night the board directed me to go out with a half-cent sales tax proposi-
tion . . . really has set the focus and tone for several months. . . . I had to go to the
capital and petition the legislature for the passage of a bill to allow us to actually seek
a revenue measure on the ballot. Then I had to go before the bond commission and
have it approved. There was an amazing amount of very complicated work that had to
be done when I first got here, and it really was a challenge.*

To address the issues convincingly, Ms. Connor had to learn the intricacies of bond financing.

*I have a new found relationship [with] the superintendent for administration and finance.
We get along extremely well, and he has been a very patient tutor in teaching me a
great deal about the intricacy of the school system finances in a very short period of
time. And I have been a very willing student. I am a person who will keep my mouth
shut and listen. I know what I don't know, and I didn't know anything about the
finances.*

There were two aspects to the referendum that influenced the results of the election: the dedicated agenda on the ballot and her "up front and out there" leadership style. The sales tax referendum included a dedicated agenda with a 10 year sunset provision—a strategy deliberately different from previous school district efforts. It told the public exactly how the monies would be spent; they were to go for salaries, instructional materials, maintenance, compliance with the Americans with Disabilities Act, in-school suspension, counselors, and debt service.

With a set agenda in hand, Ms. Connor went directly, and often, to the public. Complicating the campaign, however, was the fact that many business and political leaders could not and would not forget how Ms. Connor had been selected and how this bond issue had been introduced—without their consultation and input. A number of associations, including the chamber of commerce and the prestigious metropolitan area committee, chose to remind the school board of these slights by refusing to support the sales tax referendum. Undeterred, Ms. Connor built her support outward from the children to parents, to the school system, to the larger community. Her descriptions of how she approached these groups reflect her intense energy and commitment.

Building Parent Support

*I think there is something about the body politic that when people collectively get
together as a group that it is sometimes easy to lose that focus [that children are
important]. But I think as individuals they truly do believe in the importance of the*

child. . . . I look to parents. . . . I think we sometimes take them for granted or we just sometimes forget about them. But to me the biggest power I've got is the power of the parent, the support of the parent. . . . I think you marshal [parent power] by making the parents realize that the one thing that is the most important, the one thing that is the Achilles' heel for most parents, is that child. That's their one area of vulnerability. And that by working together and taking our vulnerability for our children, we can turn it into a strength. We can make people recognize that those children are powerful messages we are sending out into the future. . . . I asked the parents to work with me. . . . I stand up in front of them and make an impassioned plea to work with me.

Building Support of Business and Government

I have been to see every elected official in the district; I have gone to see and speak before every body, every board. . . . I have spoken before all of these groups of people introducing myself, telling them what my hopes and aspirations are for this school system, pledging the cooperation of the school board, asking them to work with us so that we don't necessarily have to spend more money, but that when we pool our resources, this synergy takes place. . . . We can get a whole lot more for our dollars by working together than we can by working as a separate entity. I have been to see all the people I think are interested in schools. I have gone to speak to the chamber of commerce, the sheriff, the assessor, with all the people I think have any kind of ability to work with the public at large and also work with the school system. . . . It made me get out into the public, and it focused my energies on developing an agenda for children. . . . If I'm going to be pilloried for something, I'd just as soon be hung up on a cross for children as for anything else I could think of.

"Flabbergasted"

Less than three weeks before the voters went to the polls, Ms. Connor woke up to read in the morning papers that united school board support for the sales tax proposal had been publicly shattered. The lone African-American member on the school board spoke out against the tax, because it failed to restore personnel such as reading teachers and librarians and a career center. These areas had been cut during the previous two years of retrenchment and most directly affected his minority constituency. This board member had initially objected to Ms. Connor's selection, but had supported the board's decision.

Ms. Connor voiced her reaction: "I'm flabbergasted. He certainly didn't discuss it with me. Not having had the opportunity to talk with him, or discuss the issue, I don't know what effect it will have." The board member responded:

I wasn't consulted in formulating this proposal, and it was presented to me as "take it or leave it." Vocational education is of a higher priority than some of the items listed on the proposal. The career center will have to be addressed on any ballot. I've got a responsibility to my constituents to look out for them.

He also claimed that the dedicated agenda on the ballot did not provide any funds for long-range planning, an issue that he knew would align him with at least one other board member who consistently voiced opposition to the superintendent.

Behind the scenes, Ms. Connor worked to win his support. Publicly, she explained how the alternative proposal could not work, given mandates in state and local financing. One week later, the board member reconsidered his position stating that, "A dedicated agenda, however faulty, is better than no agenda at all." Kathleen had successfully weathered her first political conflict.

ELECTION RESULTS AND POSTELECTION ACTIONS

One week before the election, the editorial board of the largest, most influential newspaper serving the metropolitan area surprisingly urged voters to vote "yes" and stop the further deterioration of the public school system. The editorial decision was strongly influenced by the dedicated agenda for public schools and its adherence to fiscal responsibility. On election day, 35% of the voters went to the polls. Of them, 51% cast ballots in support of the public school sales tax, a margin of 1,800 voters.

As soon as the election results were announced, Kathleen publicly stated that "no one person can take credit for this; the parents came out in droves to support it." Most public sentiment, however, credited Kathleen Connor personally for the victory. The following sample comments reflect their feelings:

- Every time I turned on the TV or radio, or heard about meetings, you showed up or sent someone. You went the *extra mile*!
- We feel that the sales tax passage was due to your leadership and untiring efforts.
- You are certainly a powerful image-building component of our educational process.
- Our superintendent cares for public education and is not afraid to stand by her beliefs.
- We owe its passing to your devotion to young people and your personal wholesomeness and integrity. You *are* what you represent and your sincerity shows!
- I believe that your detailed presentation of exactly how the money from the half-cent sales tax would be used and the good feeling about Madison County Schools contributed to the victory.

The victory and postelection comments all expressed unprecedented confidence in the new superintendent. Even while her office overflowed with congratulatory flowers and gifts, Kathleen took immediate steps to build on the business-government-schools coalition she had used so successfully in the sales tax campaign. She pushed for continued business-education collaborations, such as data processing, libraries, and recreation. She strengthened the school district's public relations program to communicate successes of the school system. She urged increased parental involvement to provide for meaningful participation by parents in the decision-making process of the school system. She helped to create a climate for collaborative effort among educational agencies, educators, and those interested in public education to provide relevant and valid information about what works in schools. Kathleen addressed her rationale for these actions saying, "I think it's very important that the school system have somebody who's speaking about all the good things that are going on out there."

At the same time, the academic package that Ms. Connor put in front of the school board and the public represented a not so subtle shift toward introducing social change realities into the mainstream values of suburban middle America. She injected programs responding caringly to the challenge of social problems (Beck, 1992; Starratt, 1991) while continuing to support the values of competency and efficiency, cultural literacy, student achievement, which included a strong "pass to play" board policy, and the implementation of character and values education.

Changes Kathleen proposed included increased support of a drug free school program, development and implementation of programs that identify and target at-risk student populations, and implementation of a mentoring program for minority youth, featuring prominent Black professionals such as judges and politicians. She supported an elementary social work and counselor program, in-school suspension in the middle and high schools, and implementation of a new promotion policy of no retention. In short, she argued in social terms for a broad curriculum "that meets the ever changing educational needs of the individuals, the community, the state, and the nation."

In her first year, she won passage of most of her program, but not without conflicts. She expressed a political perspective, however, not usually found in novice superintendents:

I don't get emotionally involved in issues . . . that I bring to the board. If it [a proposal] passes, fine; if it doesn't, I go back and start over again. I don't take that personally. What I do get very emotional about is when I go out talking to parents and working with kids. . . . I guess maybe I have just learned how to divorce myself from issues, but I can't divorce myself from people.

Unfortunately, as her first year progressed, that pragmatic line between program and people would become harder to distinguish.

ACCOMPLISHMENTS

One local television personality introduced Kathleen Connor on her show as a "delight" and a "gift" to Madison County. Staff said she restored "dignity and quiet" to the central office. Throughout the school system, there was more pride expressed among administrators, teachers, and staff than in a long time, as reflected in comments such as, "You're the best superintendent we've had during my 22 years." The compliments were not only about the new social programs but also about a new image, a human image with a sense of caring (Beck, 1992; Starratt, 1991; Gilligan, 1982; Gilligan, Ward, Taylor, & Bardige, 1988). Part of that caring meant that new voices were being heard. This feeling of inclusion extended toward minority candidates, primarily African-Americans for administrative positions. She reached out often to individuals, from principals to custodians, who were involved daily in "saving lost souls" (Lightfoot, 1983, cited in Beck, 1992).

Midway through her first year, Kathleen assessed her relationship with the school board:

They are beginning to coalesce as a board; they act by consensus across districts, not independent by political districts. You may not want to go spend your spare time with them when you get off in the afternoons, but there has to be a sense of professional respect and I think that they are very interested in pursuing that. . . . Our life experience has been such that we become rather cynical or perhaps even sardonic. Most assuredly some people become paranoid, and it is because life has taught you to be that way. . . . I think if we learn to develop a sense of trust and respect that you can deal with that in a professional arena and have that be the parameter around which you develop the decision-making process of the board.

Her early, personal assessment of individual board members was that most tried very hard to do a good job and were sincerely concerned about improving the system. In fact, she seemed to genuinely like working with all but two of the nine. Although there was consistent opposition from these two board members, only one of these relationships ossified: "I don't perceive there is anything I can do about it at this point. . . . The real issue for me is that we have to have some common ground, some common goals."

During Ms. Connor's first year, the school board elected a new president and vice president. Kathleen's described the new president as follows:

She is young, energetic, and has a lot going for her in terms of what she thinks the school system can accomplish. So I think it is going to be a really good year and am looking forward to it. . . . I call her a lot. I really like her. She is an attorney and is very bright, and I very much like gifted people. She is funny, decisive, can be sarcastic, but I just like working with her and I also call her and bounce something off of her, which is probably kind of strange because she is the same age as my daughter. I obviously could be her mother, but we have a very nice working relationship.

She described her working relationship with the board as follows:

I feel very autonomous. I don't ever feel, "Oh gee, well no matter how great an idea that is, I better check with people first." I don't feel I have to pick up the phone and call and say, "May I." I often pick up the phone and call and say, "You know, I think this is really a great idea, and I would like to bounce it off of you. What do you think about it? How do you feel about it?" I talk to board members, but I don't ever call them up and say, "Do I have your permission to do it?" My management style is that you hired me and you pay me a lot of money to tell you, to make recommendations to you, about the running of the school system. Now let me do it. However, I do let board members know before something happens so they will know about it. I am a person who feels that information is power, and so if you get as much information as possible, then you have empowered everybody. So I always keep everybody informed, and I send out lots of FYI's. If one board member asks for information, then I send it to all board members. I don't want anybody to feel that there are games being played, that one board member is getting more attention or more information than another.

Ms. Connor's energy, commitment, and accomplishments also extended far beyond the boundaries of Madison County public schools. Prior to her superintendency, the governor had appointed her chairperson of the state board of trustees of higher education. She often wore both her public school and higher education hats in reminding him that "leaders from business, government, higher education, and public schools are ready to discuss common problems and perhaps more importantly to arrive at some common policies to improve the quality of life in our state." One colleague, a school superintendent whose district included the state capital, wrote that "your eloquent comments at the meeting held with the governor . . . the cogent, clearly delineated remarks were very impressive."

Additionally, as superintendent, Ms. Connor was appointed to the steering committee of a powerful business alliance for school reform, and the state superintendent appointed her to his advisory committee. Kathleen initiated a meeting among the major school districts in the state, as well as cooperative arrangements between the county government and the school system and between Madison County and her neighboring school districts. Ms. Connor found that she was comfortable being in the midst of power, and as superintendent, she now could choose to do with her time as she wished.

I don't have any small children and I have a wonderful husband and I can spend time [with him] . . . doing whatever it is we want to do. So, I think that it's a very wise use of my time to be constantly the spokesperson for public education.

FRUSTRATIONS

Kathleen's list of frustrations was not surprising: lack of time, lack of staffing, lack of money, and school board relationships. She described how these liabilities affected her.

Time

It's just a very frustrating job because there's never enough hours in the day. I'm always running; there's always something that I haven't done; always something that I want to do. . . . It's just an extremely demanding job, requiring a high level of energy, and you've really got to have your internal self straight because if not, you can just get to feeling real down about things.

Staffing

Although Madison County has received national prominence for its very efficient ratio of administrators to students, its effect on Ms. Connor was evident.

There isn't much central office left anymore. We kind of have staff development everyday because there are so few of us, we see each other every single day, and we often have little 5 or 10 minutes of discussions on issues we really think are important. I could get in this room right here every person who works in the central office in an administrative position.

Ms. Connor had neither a deputy, an assistant, nor even her own full-time secretary. For clerical assistance, she shared a secretary with the school board.

[There is] nobody who works directly with me to whom I can say, here, go write this letter or go take care of this problem or you go cut this ribbon today; there's really nobody else to do it. . . . I would certainly recommend [that the next superintendent] needs someone to help. . . . The volume of mail and telephone calls by itself . . . you would never get out of your office and I like being out of my office. I often get the visual image of myself as the man on Ed Sullivan spinning the plates. You know that by the time I get the last plate spinning, I've got to rush back to the first plate to keep it spinning, and I'm always fearful I'm going to break one.

Additionally, Ms. Connor and the staff had to adapt to each other after having worked together in Madison County for 14 years.

I didn't choose the staff; the staff already existed. And, there can be some natural resentment, particularly towards somebody who has risen through the ranks and used to be considered at this level with everybody else and now has moved into the position of the chief executive officer.

Money

Within a few short years, the fiscal benefits reaped from collecting the sales tax will ease the system's ability to service its debt and fund new programs. However, the state's current minimum foundation plan will not provide Madison County with any additional funds even as its needs increase. Fortunately, for Madison County, the state did pass a "hold harmless" provision in its school finance plan preventing the state from decreasing its contribution. Although this eased some of the financial burden, it did not address the problem of expense increases. One area that is unlikely to be fully funded is some needed staff development on diversity.

We don't have money for consultants. I very much would love to be able to pay for someone to come to Madison County, and over the course of this next year work with the staff on cultural relationships, not just Black-white relations. We have a lot of Hispanic populations, Vietnamese, East Indian. . . . We have a lot of cultural differences. I just would like someone to come and start to work with the administrators in the schools and school system in central office to help them understand one another's diversities, because I find that very frustrating. I hear an awful lot of jokes, things bandied about, disparaging remarks. . . . My personal plan is to address ethnic differences, to begin to deal more with the at-risk child, and to really deal with community issues [such as safety].

Board Relations

At first, only one board member, the lone minority representing the single minority district, had, in Ms. Connor's view, tried to micromanage the school system.

Yeah, he does that. I like to believe that there is hope that he will eventually realize that's not necessary and, indeed, probably is inappropriate or he'll begin to get enough confidence that things are being done right without his having to super micromanage. . . . A lot of it reverts back to how many Black females and males are in administrative positions.

Throughout her tenure, superintendent-board communications, especially written communications, were characterized by a tone quite different from other superintendent communications. The office of the superintendent in itself elicited little respect from board members. Internal memos, letters, notes, and faxes were often devoid of the usual, even cursory pleasantries found in other business or government written communications. Rarely did a board member provide a reasoned explanation for why he or she was requesting specific information, even when the gathering of that information would require the superintendent's staff to spend many hours to complete the task. For example, a fax to the director of personnel requested, "Please send me a list of positions that require a master's degree, and let me know, by positions, if it is a state requirement and/or this school system's requirement." Another letter requested "a review of all central office positions take place so that a determination can be made regarding which should be 12-month positions . . . [and which] have been converted to eleven months or less."

On more than one occasion, Ms. Connor's responses also departed from her usual polite manner and tone. For example, she wrote:

In spite of the confusion that existed around your request . . . and the opposition to it from other board members, I began to put together the information you requested. . . . [However] the greater question here is that the superintendent cannot serve all nine board members unless the majority agree on priorities. . . . I am proceeding with gathering the information requested, but this is an example of a situation where the superintendent's judgment should prevail on how quickly the information can be provided. It will simply take time.

When the information was not forthcoming in the agreed upon time frame, the board member wrote back to Ms. Connor:

Please be reminded that I am still waiting . . . I am not impressed that a department that spends over a million dollars per year is not adequately computerized that its expenditures can be reviewed in a multiplicity of ways by a stroke of a finger.

In addition to being directive, superintendent-board written communications could be characterized as defensive, sarcastic, and petulant. The following are three examples of memos crossing the superintendent's desk:

Defensive

It happens to all of us [that we cannot make all meetings]. I never take it personally if my calendar cannot be accommodated. . . . I never think of it as a conspiracy; no slight was intended to you personally.

Sarcastic

I cannot believe, knowing what I know about your belief in fair play and equal opportunity, that you will allow this type of unfair treatment to continue.

Petulant

I was surprised, disappointed, and disgusted to receive and read your notice on Friday evening that there is a special executive session scheduled for Monday. . . . Give me a reference that says that board members must publicize all meetings during which educational matters are discussed. . . . While I am indeed the "new kid on the block," I have not observed a practice of this type by other board members.

A VULNERABLE LEADERSHIP STYLE

Ms. Connor described her leadership style as "up front and out there." Although she accepted and emphasized the public role of the superintendency, she was also aware of the personal price one pays.

It's a whole lot easier not to let people see you as vulnerable, not to let people see what's important to you, not to let people know you as a person. Because if they knew all those things, then they could hurt you in some kind of a way, or they can take advantage of you. I think that superintendents, particularly in large public school systems, have a very difficult job.

You're under a microscope 24 hours a day. . . . I literally cannot even go to the grocery store without somebody walking up to me and talking to me about an issue. I find that I have lost a lot of my privacy. I have to always look nice when I go out. If I were to go out on the weekend in my cutoff blue jeans and my flip flops or whatever, you know the kind of things most people feel very comfortable about wearing down to the store to pick up a carton of milk, people would probably think, "Would you believe? Look how she dresses."

Your life has become one big public book for everybody to slip a page in, to make a comment about, and it's real easy to begin to hide behind either layers of administrators or to hide behind layers of statistics and facts and figures. I guess I'm still fresh enough and naive enough and optimistic enough that I believe you make more of a difference when you are vulnerable. . . . It may be more painful for you, but you definitely can make more of a difference. I tend toward believing that people usually function from an emotional base, and they usually function from a life experience base that teaches them to either believe or not believe in people. [By what I say and do] it makes people feel like there's a human being sitting in the superintendent's chair.

But if you get out there, it means that you are going from early morning to late at night, and I do not know how long a person can keep it up without beginning to feel either physical reaction to it or maybe even an emotional reaction to it, beginning to feel resentful that you never have time for yourself and do the things you want to do. So, there has to be somehow a balance in all that to where you do not give 100% of your time.

What gave Kathleen the strength to be vulnerable as a school system leader were (1) her belief in children's education and (2) the support she received from her husband.

We really touch the life of the child every day. When I talk to people, parent groups, civic groups, I can get so emotional on the subject that I literally almost end up in tears because I am so intense on the subject. I don't speak from notes, ever. I just stand up and talk to people, and I look in their faces and look in their eyes. I get very emotional about things like students looking fresh and hopeful and just full of excitement and anticipation. I am making life better for them, trying to help them.

My biggest booster, my biggest fan is my husband. He continues to be extremely supportive of me, and I think that makes a real big difference in your ability to concentrate on what you have to get done every day. If your personal life is in order, I wouldn't denigrate the role your personal life plays in your success in your professional world.

QUICK EXIT

About nine months into her first year as superintendent, Ms. Connor described her feelings about the job as follows:

I like my job. I am happy. I get up every morning with a spring in my step. I am very glad to wake up in the morning. . . . I am enjoying it very much. If there are criticisms, I don't know about them. . . . This is a job in which people are only too pleased to tell you about criticisms, and I don't hear that. . . . I work too hard. . . . I work so hard that people appreciate that and that overcomes a lot of criticisms, because they don't see me sitting back and taking it easy.

Even in terms of job frustrations, she said:

I've never had to sit down and have a good cry over anything. . . . Nothing has ever made me feel frustrated to that point. I've gotten aggravated; I've even gotten angry, bewildered, hurt; but never have I felt that there was a situation that I just wanted to turn around and walk off from it or just keep driving and not bother to come back. I have never been at home at night gnashing my teeth or wanting to burst into tears; I have never had that happen.

These positive, upbeat statements make it difficult to comprehend why Kathleen Connor decided to resign at the end of her 2-year contract. Publicly, Ms. Connor stated she wanted to devote more time to family and church; the 12-hour days were just too long to sustain. Politically and structurally, the door remained open to her staying. In fact, the school board voted seven to two to extend her contract. Even after she announced her decision to leave, behind the scenes efforts conveyed higher salary offers. Parents and citizen groups made impassioned pleas for her to stay. Even the usually hostile press wondered in print if she might reconsider. Although deeply moved by these outpourings of affection, Kathleen's decision to leave never wavered.

EXIT ANALYSIS

After observing Ms. Connor for an entire year, it still puzzles me why she left. Although I have spoken with many people in and around Madison County, I don't believe anyone has the whole story, perhaps not even Kathleen herself. Although it is true that the average tenure of superintendents in large school districts is short, the research literature reveals very little about superintendents' feelings and emotions about the job, an exception to this being Cody (1993). The literature certainly fails to offer any insights into why someone as popular as Kathleen Connor, with seven of nine board members urging her to stay, would leave.

In trying to better understand her reasons, I compared what Ms. Connor said about her leadership style, accomplishments, and frustrations with descriptions of writers who have used similar terms to picture school administration. The language and leadership of caring, along with its complement, vulnerability, were clearly evident in Kathleen's words—as they are in the writings of Starratt (1991) and Beck (1992). Morality and interpersonal relationships, too, were dominant themes during her short tenure. Here, the feminist writings of Gilligan and her colleagues (1982; 1988) may be insightful. I found congruence between Kathleen's words and actions and aspects of the three theories, perhaps through omissions and even distortions of these theories as a whole. Therefore, what follows is more my own speculation than rigorous application of the theories themselves to actual events.

In defining her own leadership style as "up front and out there," Kathleen made relationships a central tenet of her superintendency. Many of these relationships were interpersonal, both inside and outside of the school system. In speeches and private meetings, she publicly cared about her audience, revealing herself through personal anecdotes, ribald stories and jokes, tears, and hugs. She sought connections, declared her support and commitment, and asked others to join her in educating all the children of Madison County. She recognized, too, that these actions made her vulnerable to supporters and enemies alike. Kathleen's commitment and responsiveness to others epitomized her morality of leadership (Gilligan et al., 1988). Everyday, before coming to the office, she would attend 6 A.M. mass "to put the day's work into perspective." She combined her faith in God with what education could do for all children.

Breaches of Faith

With her silver tongue and political acumen, Kathleen successfully communicated her faith in public schooling to others. However, in two instances near the end of her contract, others breached that faith, or exhibited "conflicts of loyalty" (Gilligan et al., 1988, p. 6). The first breach of faith occurred during discussions to extend her contract. The person closest to her, whom she had nurtured in the role of new board president, acted in terms of what Kathleen saw as self-interest. This was in conflict with Kathleen's perception of their relationship (Gilligan et al., 1988) and social responsibility (Beck, 1992) toward public education. It clearly violated Kathleen's administrative ethic of caring (Beck, 1992) and morality (Gilligan, 1982). The ethic of caring requires fidelity and loyalty to another: "Isolated individuals functioning only for themselves are but half persons. One becomes whole when one is in relationship with another and many others" (Starratt, 1991, p. 195).

The second breach of faith, while less personal, was also seen as relational. Regardless of the success Kathleen achieved in the sales tax referendum, the passage of her social program, and as a statewide spokesperson for public education, she came to realize that the political culture of Madison County remained essentially the same.

In trying to change "the way things are," Kathleen confronted the "preservation of powerful groups' hegemony over . . . the political process" (Starratt, 1991, p. 189). She was at a loss as to what more she could do. The voice with which she spoke of connection and care (Gilligan, 1982), captured the imagination of voters, parents, and teachers alike, but was not heard by the dominant political forces in the district represented by school board members. Thus, despite a seven to two vote, representing perhaps, in Gilligan's terms, a detached, pragmatic contractual arrangement for the majority on the board, the psychological pain of not being connected and understood—a forced silence—belied Kathleen's ability to detach issues from people. Essentially, the two merged as relational.

Of the two votes against Kathleen, one was cast by a board member with whom no relationship had ever developed or was likely to develop. Ms. Connor defined the relationship as "ossified" and "irrelevant as that hat rack in the corner." Yet, however irrelevant the relationship and the vote seemed to Kathleen, it represented a different view of governance and mission to others, one that upholds more traditional notions of student academic achievement and standards. It took aim directly at the so-called nonacademic direction of Kathleen's social programs. Even though others on the board may not have been willing to publicly challenge the popular superintendent, this opposing perspective defined the academic-social agenda debate. However fallacious the debate may have been, it left enough space for board members to distance themselves from the superintendent.

The debate climaxed in public opposition from one particular board member: the young, energetic new president. Specifically, she objected to Ms. Connor's placing emphasis on a social agenda ahead of the school system's academic mission. The two, in Kathleen's own words, had formed a close working and personal, even mother-daughter like, relationship. The young president of the board told the newspapers that her opposition to Ms. Connor was not personal; rather, it was based on a difference in educational philosophy.

In the past, when Ms. Connor viewed a vote as a political educational issue, she said she would accept the necessity to refine and renegotiate her position. Time and again controversial issues facing the board had been handled that way. Using this political strategy, as the record shows, Ms. Connor was very successful. Rarely were items passed that did not eventually have consensus.

The dynamics around the board president's negative vote, however, were different. To Kathleen, it crossed the line between programmatic and personal, between public and private (Gilligan, 1988). Previously, Kathleen made a distinction between the two processes, divorcing herself from issues but not from personal attacks. She once said, "Now, if someone tries to attack me or my family on a personal level, that is a different situation. But no one has done that." No one, that is, until this one vote, cast by someone very special to her.

The distinction between what is political and what is personal was central to Ms. Connor's leadership. For the board president, the vote reflected a fear that her white, middle-class constituency would not reelect her if she supported the social agenda of the superintendent. This young board member sought to differentiate her personal support and liking of the superintendent from her "principled" opposition to social programs. Although Kathleen never publicly labelled the opposition in relational terms, the ruptured relationship meant more than a difference of opinion on educational purposes; it was a violation of trust. I would go so far as to say that Kathleen's relationship to the board president symbolized her failure to create new meanings among those responsible for education in Madison County.

Ms. Connor was perhaps naive to assume that interpersonal relationships and social issues could, in one short year, change the political culture of appealing to political districts instead of working for consensus across districts. As board elections approached, Ms. Connor viewed criticisms and board opposition as stemming more from political decisions based on reelection, than on the needs of children. Although she achieved political consensus on individual items, she sought deeper changes reflected in new attitudes within Madison County's political culture. She may have even misinterpreted her winning support from the lone African-American board member who had become one of Ms. Connor's strongest supporters. That, too, represented the old political culture more than any change.

For Madison County officials to embrace personal development and community growth (Beck, 1992) over political alliances and individual success, Ms. Connor would have had to remain in office longer. This might have enabled others to see change along the lines she advocated, but, it is not certain that she would have succeeded.

Although changing political cultures is a long, difficult process (Deal & Peterson, 1991), Ms. Connor's leadership was primarily symbolic and embracing. Neither her interview statements nor her public speeches were succinct treatises on educational or management theories or classroom pedagogy. She did not talk or write in letters and memos about "educational stuff" such as cooperative learning, whole language, and constructivist teaching. What she did was to create an environment that enhanced other peoples' ability to do the "stuff" of learning and teaching. Lacking the "stuff" necessary for transformational leadership (Leithwood, Begley, & Cousins, 1994), and perhaps not seeing that capacity in those around her, Kathleen chose to exit.

In educational terms, it was not always clear how Ms. Connor's program consistently favored children. This was evident during protracted debates over, for example, personnel decisions, the need for vocational education, and restoring librarians and middle school extracurricular activities. However, it was clear that children were the centerpiece of her leadership style. What every audience heard from Ms. Connor were emotional messages on the importance of public education and of the many wonderful things happening to children in Madison County Schools.

The greatest challenge is keeping children as the focus. There are so many extraneous aspects to the superintendency . . . to get everyone to agree that children are the reason we are here. . . . If really what we're trying to do is produce a finished product, in terms of a moral human being who can then go out there and do whatever it is he or she has to do, we've got the thing [testing and test scores] all upside down and backwards, because the majority of children in public schools, particularly in the South, are not going on to college.

Ms. Connor put children and public education on a pedestal—as she, herself, had been placed on a pedestal after the sales tax victory. But the image of a "feminine pedestal" was not about one strong individual picking it up to hit others over the head. Even in private, there were no explicit or sexist statements of power. Rather, she used the pedestal to encourage others to step up their work, to reach higher, to expect more of themselves and children, and to essentially join her on the pedestal (Beck, 1992; Gilligan, 1982).

A LEGACY AND OPTIONS

Without question, under Ms. Connor's leadership there were significant gains in public education for Madison County. The passage of the bond issue added needed dollars for the system. Each item in the dedicated agenda had a program life of 10 years or more to effect change, regardless of who sits in the superintendent's office. In addition, the new monies could be used to restore previous cuts in the vocational, library, and athletic budgets.

Behind the new social agenda was the movement to open the district to new voices within the system: Vietnamese, Hispanic, and African-American. The demographics of Madison County have changed faster than either the educational programs or the political culture of the district. The coming years will be difficult in Madison County as new voices come head-to-head with the power structure that reflects a system closed and fearful of change. Ms. Connor's multicultural efforts on behalf of at-risk students and parents and her coalition building strategies threatened the entrenched power structure. As her agenda moved along a broader social path, board members who represented white middle- and working-class residents viewed such changes as not beneficial to students in their constituencies.

As for the future of Madison County Public Schools, they retrenched immediately, naming a sitting board member as an interim replacement for Ms. Connor. The question of a superintendent search was deferred until after the next election, in which it was unlikely that any incumbent would lose.

As for Ms. Connor,

I think that there is no such thing as fate. I think you make your own fate, and I think that you either decide to deal with whatever the dilemma is in a professional fashion and get the best that can be gotten from it or you just capitulate and say, "Oh it was me" and start wearing a hair shirt and start beating yourself with a cat-o'-nine tails. I'm not a masochistic person; **I do not believe in beating myself up over something I can't control;** *I know what I can and cannot control [my emphasis added].*

Both personally and professionally, Kathleen Connor had options other than being a superintendent. Although other superintendents might be happy to stay under these same conditions, Kathleen was not. She decided to leave while her image was still on the pedestal. Although it was unlikely that she would take another superintendency, there were other educational and political arenas open to this dedicated career educator. Kathleen chose to get off the "odd, emotional roller coaster" called the superintendency.

QUESTIONS FOR REFLECTION AND DISCUSSION

1. How did increasing economic and social problems impact suburban Madison County, whose traditional culture embraced the core values of middle America?

2. How did the superintendent's political agenda address these dynamic tensions?

3. Kathleen Connor was clearly a compromise choice for this superintendency. How do you think her leadership reflected this political reality?

4. What are some ways that Kathleen's energy and intensity impacted her work as superintendent? How were they both assets and liabilities?

5. What personal qualities or background characteristics contributed to Ms. Connor's leaving the superintendency in spite of having the support of a majority of the school board? What other factors might have led to her resignation?

REFERENCES

Beck, L. (1992, August). Meeting the challenges of the future: The place of a caring ethic in educational administration. *American Journal of Education, 100,* 454–496.

Cody, C. (1993, November 17). Requiem for the superintendency. *Education Week,* pp. 33–34.

Deal, T., & Peterson, K. (1991). *The principal's role in shaping school culture.* Washington, DC: U.S. Department of Education.

Gilligan, C. (1982). *In a different voice: Psychological theory and woman's development.* Cambridge, MA: Harvard University Press.

Gilligan, C., Ward, J., & Taylor, J. (Eds.), with Bardige, B. (1988). *Mapping the moral domain.* Cambridge, MA: Center For the Study of Gender, Education, and Human Development, Harvard University Graduate School of Education.

Glass, T. E. (1994, February). *A profile of first-year superintendents.* Paper presented at the Annual Meeting of the American Association of School Administrators. San Francisco.

Leithwood, K., Begley, P., & Cousins, J. B. (1994). *Developing expert leadership for future schools.* London: Falmer Press.

Lightfoot, S. L. (1983). *The good high school: Portraits of character and culture.* New York: Basic Books.

Starratt, R. (1991, May). Building an ethical school: A theory for practice in educational leadership. *Educational Administration Quarterly, 27,* 185–202.

7

JEENA
Out of the Peace Corps, Into the Fire for an Elected Superintendent

Joan L. Curcio, Virginia Tech University

ABSTRACT.   Jeena made a quantum leap from her role as a teacher in a high school dropout prevention program to the position of superintendent. She had become disgruntled with the district's leadership and saw winning the superintendency election as a means to initiate change. Her purpose was to raise issues; her motto was "Children First." She proudly acknowledged that she was motivated by idealism, which early in her life had taken her to the mud huts of Africa as a member of the Peace Corps.

This is Jeena's story of developing "on the job" and coping with her lack of administrative experience by a direct and energetic approach to the awesome task of making instruction a priority in this community of high violence, poverty, alcoholism, and abuse. She soon came to understand that good intentions, starry-eyed idealism, and unpopular stands had to be tempered by the practicalities of building trust, forging relationships, and opening communications, especially and foremost with the school board she served.

Elements of the past can play a powerful role in examining present behaviors and actions, and be a key to understanding them.

(Kofodimos, 1990, p. 6)

Jeena was unique among the participants in the Beginning Superintendent Study in that she won the office of the superintendency through a hard-fought campaign and election, a tradition that still persists in some of the nation's southeastern states. The requirements for the position are no less than those expected of any county candidate. Before her election to the superintendency, Jeena taught in a school in the district. It may never have occurred to her to seek the chief executive office if a lifelong idealism for how things could be had not spurred her to take action. Her own words best describe her motivation: "It's almost a moral imperative, this mandate to move forward to reach all children. . . . I see the big picture. . . . We don't have a choice."

Strongly held convictions, purpose, caring, and determination—character elements from her youthful past—brought this 42-year-old from the teaching ranks to the top position of a school system. The story of her first year is one of external conflict resulting from the change she represented within her district and community, and unresolved internal conflict that she honestly disclosed:

It's a delicate balance—of toughening up yet retaining a certain vulnerability. I need to be open to the pain in the system and can't toughen up to that point where you don't see the face of the child. You're no good to anybody if you're hurting.

In November, following her election in the early fall, Jeena assumed the "office" of the superintendency. The school district she leads is a high-minority, economically poor district with 13,000 students—5% Hispanic, 30% African-American, and 65% Caucasian. Of the students, 60% percent are identified as low socioeconomic status and there is a high dropout rate. This community, where the school system is the second largest employer, has a high incidence of violence, domestic abuse, and alcoholism. The district is classified by the Office of Educational Research and Improvement of the National Center for Educational Statistics as a town district—districts "in communities whose population equals or exceeds 2,500 people," but are neither cities nor suburbs (Chapman, 1995). Although that is an apt description of the largest town in Jeena's school district, the district actually encompasses a county of 60,000 people.

The superintendent is white, married to a well-known and respected professional in the community, a mother, and an "insider" to the school district. Winning the superintendency election catapulted Jeena from a district classroom into the school district CEO's chair. The chair did not immediately appear to fit this petite woman—a runner by avocation, a teacher by choice, a learner by inclination, and perhaps most relevant to this case study, a former member of the Peace Corps.

RESEARCH METHOD AND THEORETICAL FRAMEWORK

Grounded theory methodology was clearly the appropriate approach for a research study where the purpose was to investigate the developing professional identity of a first-time female superintendent and to seek emerging patterns, practices, and themes that characterize the shaping of her professional identity. Grounded research procedures make use of the researcher's ability to be sensitized to what is going on with the phenomenon being studied. This ability to understand, referred to as theoretical sensitivity in naturalistic inquiry, gives meaning to data and separates the relevant from what is not. Such sensitivity "allows one to develop a theory that is grounded, conceptually dense, and well-integrated" (Strauss & Corbin, 1990, p. 42).

Theoretical sensitivity comes from a number of sources, including professional and personal experience. This case study, then, represents an interplay between a focus on a woman's experiences entering the superintendency and a scientific mode of inquiry designed to provide rich insight and understanding into that phenomenon. The perspective is enlightened by the theoretical sensitivity of a researcher whose personal and professional experiences include years of public school administration, working with superintendents and as an assistant superintendent, often as the first female in a particular position.

The theoretical framework from which to interpret the patterns, practices, and themes that emerged from the study of Jeena was derived from several sources representing current perspectives of leadership (Sergiovanni, 1992; Shakeshaft; 1987; Greenleaf, 1977), as well as philosophical and psychological perspectives, particularly feminist (Noddings, 1992; Belenky, Clinchy, Goldberger, & Tarule, 1986; and Gilligan, 1982). Gilligan's psychological theories of woman's development and Noddings' philosophically grounded "ethic of caring," with its moral orientation to schooling, constituted a particularly cogent lens through which to view the entry of a female superintendent who saw herself as an activist and who expressed herself in language that clearly reflected a concern for caring relationships with students.

JEENA

I first met Jeena early in her term of office at a luncheon for four newly elected female superintendents in that southeastern state. The luncheon was designed to bring them together with two female consultant/trainers who wanted to create a support system for these women to facilitate their success in their new role as superintendent. At that early point, they were already able to swap stories of challenges to their entry into the office, some of which were incredible! One of these superintendents, during her election campaign, found that a long snake had been hidden in her car while she was in a store—whether to frighten, intimidate, discourage, or embarrass her, she did not know. She discovered it as it slithered over her shoulder as she started the car!

Jeena listened quietly to these stories, but shared none of her own. She was intent on finding out how the consultants could assist her in making a successful entry. Among the four superintendents, Jeena gave the appearance of being more confident, more focused, and perhaps more determined. She seemed articulate, bright, energetic, professional in manner, and slightly aloof or self-contained. She did not on first impression divulge the idealistic side that emerged in her interviews. Among the four superintendents, Jeena seemed the most likely to succeed. Shortly thereafter, she agreed to be the subject of a case study, and our first interview took place in a city about 35 miles from her district, early in the morning, prior to a workshop.

RUNNING FOR ELECTION

Jeena had been "in and out of education" since 1972 when she went to Africa to be a Peace Corps teacher, living in a mud hut, and teaching 5th through 10th grades in one class. Five years ago, she and her family moved south to the county where she is now superintendent of schools. Her first position with the school system was teaching in the dropout prevention program. What happened there sowed the seeds for Jeena's eventual candidacy for the superintendency. She was frustrated by the apparent lack of support from the district, without which "the teacher couldn't really make progress." She felt powerless to be effective with potential dropouts. Perceiving the problem to come from the superintendent's office, and thinking about the prospects of these children against those of her "own bright kids," who had been nurtured and encouraged from birth, she shared her perceptions with a colleague, a principal in the system. "I was disgruntled," this younger-day activist said, and she thought the principal could identify a candidate whom they could jointly support to run against the deeply ensconced and apparently politically powerful incumbent superintendent. There appeared to be no one. "It will have to be you," her colleague said.

So Jeena decided to declare for election, not with the thought of winning but with the purpose of raising issues. "I'm a Peace Corps idealist," she told me, referring to her early experiences, adding, "It's part of my personality." Several district teachers and some administrators expressed their support to her secretly and from a distance—apparently afraid of the consequences of speaking out. According to Jeena, her opponent used "somewhat reprehensible" campaign methods, to assure Jeena's loss. Yet when the election was over, Jeena was the new superintendent of schools.

What happened? Jeena's explanation came not from the political present but from an older core set of beliefs and values: "I won because I ran on the basis of 'Children First,' and I think people are idealistic really." School patrons had experienced 12 years with the old superintendent and were ready for a change, she believed. But was Jeena ready? She had some doubts. She didn't feel entirely qualified because she had not followed the traditional steps, learning administrative skills along the way. She knew it would be a full-time job, and she had a family of three young children. Nevertheless, she stepped energetically into her role, optimistic about what could be accomplished. She was determined to be above all an instructional leader.

EDUCATIONAL PLATFORM

Somewhere along the line, educators usually develop and live by an internalized educational philosophy or platform. In preparing to win an election to secure the county's top educational job, Jeena had to put her platform before the public. It had four planks. The first was a commitment to developing appropriate programs and alternatives to reduce the number of students dropping out. The second plank addressed bringing students and parents into the mainstream to reduce violence in schools. The third addressed the quality of education in the district, and the fourth involved decreasing administrative costs in order to funnel dollars back into the local schools where education takes place. As she addressed these planks, she hoped to eliminate corporal punishment as a disciplinary measure, reduce the expulsion rate, and involve parents every step of the way.

ENTRY STRATEGY

Although Jeena lacked prior top level administrative experience, she intuitively recognized the importance of an entry that was well-considered and successfully executed. As a first step, she assembled her staff and "holed away" for 2 days in an administrative retreat with a consultant/facilitator. The issues addressed concisely defined her focus and goals for her first year as superintendent. Among the issues were how to encourage excellence, support risk taking, and open communications. Seeking input and commitment to her early goals from her administrative cadre, a number of task forces were started to address the issues. She saw staff training as one key to the goals. Being practical, she also perceived constraining forces such as modest fiscal resources and the time it takes for task forces to struggle through the process. What she did not anticipate, however, was the critical need to develop relationships with staff, community, and above all, the school board, before the "real work" of schooling could be done.

DEVELOPING RELATIONSHIPS

The Teachers' Union

Relationships emerged as a common theme throughout the study as the new superintendent reflected on her entry. From the beginning, Jeena believed her relationships with the teachers' union to be good, stemming from the fact that she had risen from their ranks. However, initial relations with the union president were not as clear. About to go into negotiations early in her tenure, Jeena admitted she did not fully trust the union president because the president had supported the defeated superintendent in the election. However, it was not long before they found themselves on the same side, when Jeena made it clear that she supported substantial increments in teachers' salaries.

First-year negotiations went well, giving Jeena confidence that she enjoyed a good working relationship with the teaching staff. It was interesting, as well as foreboding, that she noted her need to keep and build upon a teacher/union relationship before she saw an urgency to have close communication with the board.

The Administrative Staff

From the beginning, her relationships with her assistant superintendents were comfortable, although reserved. "I know they are not going to undermine me, but they're still holding back. They're hearing a lot of talk, but are still not sure of my walk."

The school principals, however, were another story. One of Jeena's first actions had been to reveal her intention to do away with the district's provision that administrators could "cash in" their accumulated sick leave upon retirement. She planned to retrieve funds through this action and consequently spend them directly on the schools and instruction. The principals "felt as though they had been slapped by my proposal. . . . I'm not quite sure it was worth it. . . . It was a lose/lose situation and affected staff morale negatively, including teachers who would not have been affected [directly]." Jeena finally turned the incident into more of a win/win situation when a compromise was crafted, one that would not take away previously committed benefits but would provide future savings. As she discussed her relationship with administrators in the light of this experience, Jeena noted:

Even my principals said that they didn't take it personally. I'm a starry-eyed idealist, and they know I'm not attacking them. I'm not adverse to taking an unpopular stand, and I am going to do it, if I have to.

Jeena admitted that the school board was not behind her original action. The situation, in fact, had been her first skirmish with board members, who had been quick to recognize the political implications of taking away a perk that it had given to the administrative staff. However, according to Jeena, the business community strongly supported her on this issue, and it improved her standing with them. The newspaper also supported her and encouraged the board to reconsider its position.

As Jeena went for more change, without always having developed the necessary trust level, she began to experience retaliatory blows—beginning with the board.

The School Board

Jeena described her relationship with the board as a struggle, "perhaps the greatest" she faced. At least two board members had campaigned for the past superintendent, and it took some time to break the ice. Further, Jeena did not have the benefit of a "honeymoon" or "grace" period by virtue of being selected and appointed by a school board, as the majority of superintendents are throughout the country.

The board and I are still a little uneasy from the campaign. When I say we need this [a budget increase], they don't have enough faith in me yet to trust that we really need these things . . . maybe in a year.

Jeena had much to do to gain open support from the school board as a body—primarily to establish a working relationship to replace the one it had for 12 years with the former superintendent. She saw the members slowly coming around, as she began to work at never embarrassing them and at trying to follow up on their concerns. She understood that board members were susceptible to being lobbied, but when the board did not support her fully on her decision to discontinue the reimbursement of administrators' accumulated sick leave upon retirement, she felt publicly beaten.

Reflecting on wanting respect whether or not the board agreed with her stands, she said: "People have to see me as having a deep commitment to education." Yet, from her failure to work with the board to solve a political dilemma, she learned the importance of listening:

I need to get a lot more input from the board AND teachers. . . . The board meeting made me realize that I had assumed that one conversation with a board member is enough, but that's not true when it's so controversial. I learned, listen to the old timers who have seen other such things. I was seeing black and white. . . . Communications were not what they should be with the board. I had been extremely busy working on programs and working with the community. I neglected involving the board, and they let me know that in not particularly kind ways.

COMMUNICATION

It was becoming clear that communication needed to be firmly established between the superintendent and the board, and other key groups as well. In fact, it emerged early as the goal necessary to attain all the others she had for the district. Jeena's first response to the need for improved communications was a monthly newsletter that reflected her current thinking, where the district was headed, and other priority issues.

I created the newsletter for the board, but then I decided that all administrators needed it too. So I'm sending it out, and in it is a recap of the work of the task forces and the goals.

Another insight led her to seek even stronger communication, especially with her staff. In preparation for CEO training she would undergo near the end of her first year, Jeena had the staff fill out information sheets about her leadership, which were to be processed during the training. In the training session, it "hit" her that she was sitting in another state getting feedback from her staff, when she needed to be doing that at home. When she returned to find that the district principals had been "jawing" at a meeting in her absence, she took advantage of the opportunity:

It alarmed me. . . . I was angry and needed to clear the air. I met only with principals, told them I'd heard rumors that people were disgruntled. It didn't show a whole lot of respect for the office. I started out a bit negative . . . but gave them file cards on which they were to answer the question, What kind of support do you need from the superintendent, from the central office? I read the cards aloud. I didn't try to be defensive. Some signed the cards; some came to see me later.

She took quotes from each card and developed a survey to gather more information. The principals were candid in their replies, saying, among other things, that there were too many layers of authority to pass through. Some said they were intimidated by her. They liked the direction she was headed, but they wanted to meet with her directly on a regular basis. Jeena shared the results with them, and she proceeded to set up regular meetings. "Principals need to hear from me how important they are to the mission . . . and to know that I'm not going to tolerate any yammering."

Jeena then went through a similar process with the central office staff. They spent a morning sorting out concerns and doing team building activities, "so that we are caring about each other. You know, it sounds funny, but I do come from that orientation."

Jeena's immediate determination was to confront the undermining and somewhat conspiratorial behavior of the district's building level administrators, and to do so in a manner that reflected caring leadership. This process called for personal strength and courage that won her time and the opportunity to face the real issues.

THE REAL ISSUES

Numerous issues and needs lay heavily on this relatively poor district. When budget crises struck other districts in the state, Jeena's district was no exception. Getting the board and the community to support local tax increases to meet educational needs was unlikely. There were many needs such as school buses, asbestos abatement, and alternative programs. However, it seemed probable that no additional monies, beyond present operating funds, would be available to accomplish them. The possibility of grant money, particularly from the state, appeared to be the only source of assistance, however little.

In addition, the district, like others throughout the nation, struggled with violence in the schools. In Jeena's first year, she said that there were incidents

that used to be thought of as pranks. There was a situation of boys chasing girls to stick them with hypodermic needles. It resulted in an 11-hour expulsion hearing, and lots of publicity.

In another incident, students put chemicals in a teacher's soft drink with the intention to harm. Without discounting the seriousness of these events, Jeena reflected on how juvenile crime in schools had become a major focus for boards and school staffs.

There were also all the usual tough personnel issues—being careful not to harbor incompetence while taking legal requirements into consideration, and being sensitive to the human needs of employees who had served well in the past. Jeena began to confront situations such as inducing an elderly employee to seek immediate retirement: "It made me feel bad," she said.

PERSONAL AND PROFESSIONAL PROGRESS BY YEAR'S END

As the end of Jeena's first year approached, changes representing progress appeared everywhere. The superintendent, who in earlier months spoke of weariness and needing time for herself, had found ways to take what she needed. She resumed jogging three or four times a week, and stopped spending her weekends at the office. She found more time for her children, and decreased the time she was away for training. She did, however, participate in CEO training out of state that appeared to play a part in accelerating her progress.

After the leadership training, she refined the broad goals crafted at her entry retreat to make them tighter, more focused goals that "will directly impact the district and be much more useful." Although the goals were really action plans, there was a crispness and clarity to her decisions. They included (1) developing a long-range facility plan and getting funding for it through a bond referendum, (2) studying administrative staffing patterns for effectiveness, and (3) creating a vehicle to award schools of excellence.

As though experiencing a spring thaw, she described project after project that was being started in her school district. These projects included an incentive program for schools of excellence based on the National Blue Ribbon Schools and effective schools research; a grant for after-school programs for middle school students that involved community agencies; and the possibility of seeking a full service school grant despite political backlash. "Some people have real reservations. People don't take the larger view of a child who has lice, AIDS, etc., and that child is not going to be a good learner."

Jeena planned also to include a full-blown alternative school in the bond referendum in order to curtail wholesale expulsions. Although seeking alternatives for troubled students, she saw herself as "taking a strong stand on fighting." She even supported a new principal who created a school regulation calling for the arrest of students found fighting on the premises. "We haven't had any fights worth looking into at the school since," she explained with some pride, exposing her ongoing dilemma between toughening up and remaining open to the pain in the system, between setting a consistent and caring direction for her staff to follow and supporting them in their individual approaches to common problems.

She consistently tried to move toward effective schooling. She steeped herself in the literature, formed a district-wide community group to set criteria, and created task forces.

I came back from a workshop with Larry Lezotte on fire—and with the idea that all children can learn. . . . Next fall, we'll have a number of forums, with both educators and non-educators facilitating. We're just going to head out into the community for several months. It ties in with what we've started with schools of excellence. We need to begin disaggregating data scores, and see why some aren't succeeding. . . . We don't have a mechanism in place to reach all, and when you think of the consequences for children, we just can't afford that as a society any longer.

Jeena reported a happening concurrent with all the activity she was describing: better relations with her board. She attributed the occurrence to being relaxed and not so defensive. Her energy was being rekindled by the activity and participation she was witnessing. "I feel good. It's a tremendous lot of work. We have to think long range. I plan to run for reelection, in the middle of all these programs. . . . I need eight years."

CONCLUSIONS AND IMPRESSIONS

Jeena's emerging professional identity as a superintendent has roots in her Peace Corps experiences and the motivating factors that pushed her into "climbing aboard" a plane 20 years ago to head for West Africa. In her words, "It was a wonderful, watershed experience—this superintendency may rival it, but nothing before has."

Her concept of herself as a "rabid idealist" at that time, defines her and motivates her still. In her own words, she had always been strongly pushed internally to "make a difference." Although missionary zeal and an ethic of care (Gilligan, 1982) inspired her to again become an activist in running for the superintendency, the independence and single-mindedness that distinguished her in the Peace Corps appears to have worked against her in her early months of office. In the Corps, her resourcefulness quickly built her self-esteem, leading to an administrative position and the opportunity to work on national governmental curriculum projects. However, upon entry into her district, her purposiveness and focus on the task impeded her natural inclination for caring and building relationships. Working to exhaustion exacerbated the situation. Finally, she broke the cycle through her own insights:

I keep going back to the book you gave me, **The Female Advantage,** *and the idea of the spider web as an organizational pattern with the leader being in the center and not at the top. That is much more an apt description of how I see myself, in the center, with lots of little threads reaching out all throughout the system. I see it as all very interconnected. The image of family always raises its head with me also. As in the family, until relationships have been built and people are valued and know they are, things will not work well. And I didn't think it would be that way when I ran for superintendent. I thought I would be more of an instructional leader, that the academic would be my thrust. But what I'm seeing is that relationships are absolutely critical.*

Several characteristics and actions played into breaking the cycle. There were those willing to give her a chance and not mistrust her motives. She was honest and wanted to do the right thing. She came from the teaching ranks and had support there. But two things played more significantly than others. First, she was intelligent and had intuitive insights that allowed her to learn what was happening quickly and to take action. She would go out to learn more, then quickly return to test and apply what she learned. In that way, she absorbed the responsibility of the superintendent to stay in close communication with the school board and to appreciate their positions and pressures. The second factor was her instinct to be angered by the disloyal "yammering" of her "officers," and to be willing to deal with it directly and sensitively.

She was beginning to get in touch with her own way of knowing (Belenky et al., 1986) and leading. Whether or not she could continue to stay in touch would depend on how much she valued it. There remained, in her words, dynamic tension between her determination and ethic of care, her idealism and the political realities that had yet to be resolved. Jeena's story of becoming a superintendent described her emerging professional identity and her struggle to stay with a natural inclination to lead through caring.

QUESTIONS FOR REFLECTION AND DISCUSSION

1. What are some ways the challenges of an elected superintendent might be different from those of an appointed superintendent?

2. What similarities do you see between the roles of Peace Corps worker and school superintendent?

3. How can superintendents balance idealism and realism as they seek to improve schools?

4. What similarities in motivation and leadership style do you see between Jeena and Kathleen?

5. What indicators do you see in Jeena that are consistent with the caring and vulnerability described (in chapter 6) as typical of women leaders?

REFERENCES

Belenky, M. F., Clinchy, B. M., Goldberger, N. R., & Tarule, J. M. (1986). *Women's ways of knowing: The development of self, voice, and mind.* New York: Basic Books, Inc.

Chapman, C. H. (1995, Fall/Winter). A study of beginning superintendents: Preliminary implications for leading and learning. *Record in Educational Leadership 15,* 74–82.

Greenleaf, R. K. (1977). *Servant leadership: A journey into the nature of legitimate power and greatness.* New York: Paulist Press.

Gilligan, C. (1982). *In a different voice.* Cambridge, MA: Harvard University Press.

Helgesen, S. (1990). *The female advantage: Women's ways of leadership.* New York: Doubleday Currency.

Kofodimos, J. R. (1990). *Using biographical methods to understand managerial behavior and personality.* Greensboro, NC: Manus Associates and Center for Creative Leadership.

Noddings, N. (1992). The challenge to care in schools. New York: Teachers College Press.

Sergiovanni, T. J. (1992). *Moral leadership: Getting to the heart of school improvement.* San Francisco: Jossey-Bass Publishers.

Shakeshaft, C. (1987). *Women in Educational Administration.* Newbury Park, CA: Sage.

Strauss, A. L., & Corbin, J. (1990). *Basics of qualitative research: Grounded theory procedures and techniques.* Newbury Park, CA: Sage.

8

EUGENE AND KEITH
A Tale of Two Suburbs

Freddie A. Banks, Jr., Eastern Illinois University, Charleston

ABSTRACT.   Two suburban districts of a large metropolitan area each employed males in their 40s as first-time superintendents. One was African-American and one was Caucasian; each had a doctoral degree and more than 10 years of administrative experience. One district served 4,400 high school students, 84% of whom were minority and nearly a quarter of whom met federal guidelines for free-lunch eligibility. The other district served 1,500 elementary students from very affluent homes, only 7% of whom were minority.

The elementary district superintendent's goals included implementation of a middle school plan and outcome-based education. Critical issues in the high school district were student achievement and providing a safe school environment. Though challenges facing the two superintendents were different, both set out to increase staff involvement in decision making and move from the authoritative, top-down management approaches of their predecessors to more collaborative, site-based management.

WENDELL, A MINORITY SUBURB

The Wendell High School District was comprised of two high schools. Located in the suburbs of a large metropolitan area, the 25 square-mile district enrolled 4,400 students. The two high schools, located in adjoining communities, served a student body that was predominantly minority, including 68% African-Americans and 16% Hispanics. The two communities within the district were culturally, racially, and socioeconomically diverse. Residents in both communities were in the lower- to middle-income levels, as reflected in the 23.5% of students eligible for free or reduced-price lunches.

The Wendell High School District provided educational programs that had been designed to meet the needs of its diverse student population. Three curriculum options were offered; students could pursue general, vocational, or college preparatory interests.

Although one high school was constructed in the 1950s and the other in the early 1990s, both were quality facilities, equipped with modern laboratories for reading, writing, science, foreign language, vocational education, and computer literacy. In addition, the district took pride in its wide variety of extracurricular activities, including athletics, student government, debate, and musical performing groups, as well as 30 clubs that provided outlets for students with diverse interests and abilities.

The district's administrative council was comprised of 2 principals, 2 assistant principals, 3 deans, and 14 department chairs. Support services included a registered nurse, a social worker, a speech therapist, a counselor, and a work study coordinator.

Of the 300 teachers for both schools, 90% had earned master's degrees. Even with an almost 95% minority student body, the teaching faculty was predominately white; fewer than 10% were people of color. The percentage of minority faculty had remained relatively consistent over the past 5 years, notwithstanding the resignation of a few each year.

Four males and three females were elected to the seven-member board of education, including three African-Americans, three Anglos, and one Hispanic. They represented diverse political, racial, and religious interests in educational issues that came before the board. Both the board of education and the administration were committed to an emphasis on excellence.

However, students in the district performed well below national and state averages on standardized achievement tests. Although 52% opted to pursue the college preparatory program, only 32% entered junior colleges or universities. Unfortunately, both schools were plagued by violence and gang related activities, and parental involvement was almost nonexistent. These were the challenges facing Dr. Eugene Brown if he left a highly recognized school district in the West to become the first African-American superintendent of the Wendell High School District.

COINCIDENCE OR PROVIDENCE?

Flying to Washington, D.C., for a professional conference, Dr. Eugene Brown sat beside a legislator from his state. By the time they landed at National Airport, the state senator, an African-American, had told him about a school district near the senator's boyhood home that was seeking a new superintendent. Through this chance meeting, Dr. Brown learned about the suburban Wendell district and began to wonder if it might be a good place to work.

At the conference, two days later, Eugene met another African-American whose name tag identified him as from the Wendell area. Eugene asked what he knew about the district and was surprised to learn that he was the person responsible for conducting the superintendent search. He gave an enthusiastic account of the district and urged Eugene to apply.

Almost as if it were preordained, Dr. Brown had heard from two different sources in two days about a superintendency opening in a distant state. Accordingly, Eugene, whose interest was piqued, submitted an application and found himself invited to the first round of interviews. Within a few weeks he was invited back for a second interview with the board of education. On his own, but with the board's assistance and consent, Eugene arrived on site a few days early and met with Wendell administrators, teachers, parents, and people representing support service and staff.

When asked why he was selected for the position, Dr. Brown said, "I'm not sure," adding that "there was some dissatisfaction, by at least a majority of the board of education, with the way some things had gone in the past." Eugene knew the board was looking for a person with administrative experience who could reorganize the district and bring about change. He was confident he had both the vision and experience the position required.

The 47-year-old Brown was one of two finalists; the other was from within the district. The board considered factors of which Eugene was unaware. The insider had professional baggage, having been terminated by a neighboring district before his employment in Wendell. In addition, there was some sentiment that a qualified African-American should be hired as superintendent. After evaluating each candidate, the board offered the position to Dr. Eugene Brown.

Upon receiving the offer, Brown had to decide if he wanted to leave a familiar, comfortable position where he was well respected and move across the country to an unfamiliar area where none of his family, friends, or relatives lived. Moreover, it would be the first time he would be away from his daughter, who was in college and lived with her mother. Additionally, Eugene had been a member of a very competitive, talented tennis foursome who had played together every Saturday for nearly two decades. Leaving such rich, close associations would be hard.

However, after 18 years as an administrator in the district, Eugene was not committed to staying there for the rest of his life. What appealed most to Eugene about the Wendell opportunity was that it offered enormous potential for educational growth. "I felt as though I could really make a difference working in a place with a large African-American population and with students who were not performing to their highest level of academic achievement." Though Eugene knew the district was not a wealthy one, its annual per pupil expenditure far exceeded that of his nationally recognized school district in the West. He said, "It is my belief that with the people, the board, and the faculty working together, the district would provide better educational programs for the students." Dr. Eugene Brown accepted the challenge.

URGENT PRIORITIES

Eugene quickly found that people in a small suburban district with a majority of African-American students expected its new African-American superintendent to undo within months the conditions created by years of neglect and, in many cases, mismanagement. Although neither the timetable nor the expectations were realistic, Dr. Brown set about confronting the challenges and enlarging on the opportunities.

The district had a lot of traditions and past successes, but was not currently serving its students well, as reflected in declining scores on achievement and ACT tests. Improving academic performance was an immediate challenge. An urgently needed first step was to provide and maintain a safe and orderly environment, so students could be free to learn without the threat of physical harm. Policies and procedures needed to be developed and implemented to improve discipline and allow teachers to provide instruction without disruptions.

Dr. Brown believed that, in the past, the district had been under a stifling bureaucracy that had negatively impacted the schools and inhibited student achievement. He also found that building administrators and central office personnel were not working cohesively because of the previous superintendent's heavy-handed, top-down management. He believed a more collaborative, site-based management would foster better educational programs, enhance academic performance, and provide a safer and more positive learning environment for students.

Though most board members favored greater community involvement, problems of student achievement, registration, and safety were not being addressed collaboratively at either high school. And community involvement did not center around areas of educational significance such as improving instruction and curriculum programs, graduation requirements, school climate, and opportunities for student-community partnerships. Eugene observed that "people feel pretty uninvited to participate in school matters." Though a parent teacher association meeting at one school drew 65 people, including students, parents, and teachers, the other high school had not even had a PTA for 10 years.

AN EARLY VICTORY

One of the first challenges Dr. Brown faced was student registration. He learned that in the past only 60% of the student body attended classes on the opening day of school. Eugene addressed this problem by calling together the superintendent's advisory council to plan a preopening registration campaign strategy.

Superintendent Brown met with the community's council of ministers, the village council members, and the central office staff to wage a war on poor attendance rates. County and local social services supported the effort by arranging for free physical exams. Eugene's efforts were rewarded by an attendance of 88% on the first day of school and 95% by the end of the first week.

SHARED DECISION MAKING LEADS TO RESTRUCTURING

Dr. Brown began immediately to involve faculty in school district decision making. He soon learned that staff members saw finance as a major constraint. He had been warned of fiscal constraints during his interviews and found that Wendell's high salaries and the high cost of business in this metropolitan area left surprisingly little in the way of discretionary budget. Refusing to be discouraged by the financial constraints, he declared:

I feel that the staff was poorer in spirit than in pocket. A vast majority of the staff feel that improvements cannot be made in the educational program because of the lack of funds. Many people feel that there is not enough money to even think about improvements, so why bother.

Determined to turn the ship around, Eugene involved staff in designing a transition plan providing for regular staff interaction with management. Dr. Brown had his biggest opportunity, if not his greatest challenge, when he revealed his working objectives for his first year and beyond. These objectives included reaffirmation and implementation of the Wendell High School District's mission statement. Though the statement was in place when Brown was hired, its intent needed to be clarified. To support planning for shared decision making, Dr. Brown began a formal process of organizational renewal, characterized by progressive implementation of school-based management.

Dr. Brown presented to the school board a philosophy and set of recommended practices that placed authority, decision making, implementation, and accountability at the school level. In other words, his proposal was to empower his staff to move away from a high degree of centralization and toward a more democratic type of leadership.

Eugene realized that this plan called for complete restructuring of district procedures to support the implementation of school-based management. Most importantly, it featured Total Quality Management (TQM), which empowers people, focusing on the system and reducing barriers to generate a quality product (Deming, 1986). According to Dr. Brown, "TQM must be applied to every district educational program in an effort to continuously make improvements." For this approach to be successful, he would have to implement an ongoing staff development program, focusing on developing human relations and technical skills, including the areas of communication, teaching techniques, working with diversity, problem solving, and dealing with change. Eugene's vision called for Wendell to begin implementing the TQM philosophy described by Bonstingl (1992, p. 5):

> . . . helping educators view themselves as supporters rather than judges, as mentors and coaches rather than as lecturers, as partners with parents, students, administrators, businesses, and entire communities rather than isolated workers within the walls of the classroom. We now understand that the only way we can ensure our own growth is by helping others to grow; the only way to maximize our own potentials is by helping others to improve little by little, day by day.

Consistent with his desire for site-based decision making, but requiring an accelerated time line, Dr. Brown faced the immediate challenge of developing a school improvement plan for each high school. This challenge was initiated by the state board of education. The state board changed its accreditation system to focus on improvement at individual school sites and required plans for improved student performance as a part of the process.

UNTRACKING TO IMPROVE ACHIEVEMENT

Student achievement was a major concern in the district; in particular, African-American students were not performing well. Addressing this issue uncovered the fact that students needed to take more challenging courses in English, mathematics, social studies, science, and foreign languages.

Dr. Brown believed that student performance was being inhibited by tracking. Feeling the urgency of student needs and the pressure of time, Eugene did not wait for shared decision making to address this issue. Instead, he began to systematically reduce tracking so that all students would have access to the full range of knowledge, skills, and program options available in the curriculum. Many faculty members rebelled against this part of his agenda because the changes meant that they would teach different students than they had in the past. A petition drive, with some union backing, was initiated, calling for continued tracking of students into nonacademic courses. Slowly and deliberately, Eugene revealed his philosophy of tracking to the group.

Brown's approach to this issue resembled those of the critical humanist leader described by Marshall (1995) as one "who engages in a constant search for equality and oppression, questioning assumptions that governments set up institutions (like schools) to guarantee equal opportunity" (p. 489).

In Brown's opinion, tracking came in many forms, but fundamentally he believed that it locked students into decisions that limited their opportunities and separated them. At its worst, tracking divided students into different groups on the basis of perceived ability, past performance, and expectations of the students by others. Students were generally locked into a determined track by the design of the curriculum and the operation of the school system, depriving some students of access to certain courses or programs.

Brown's ideas were consistent with the conclusions of Slavin and Braddock (1993), who reported research showing that low achieving secondary students in tracked schools performed substantially lower on achievement tests of reading, math, social studies, and science than did their matched counterparts in untracked schools. They noted, "One of the most consistent effects of ability grouping is to create classes that have disproportionate numbers of students from the same racial or social groups" (p. 14). Not surprisingly, Braddock's research also found "students in the low track to have significantly lower self-esteem than low achievers in mixed-ability classes" (p. 14). Dr. Brown was eventually able to convince a number of parents, faculty, and administrators to support his program to eliminate tracking, though some opposition continued.

In addition to eliminating tracking, Eugene recognized a need to review graduation requirements. He challenged the tradition of awarding units of credit based on time spent in class and a passing grade of A, B, C, or D. He suggested the implementation of a system of mastery outcomes as an approach to both instruction and accountability.

The vertical articulation between grade levels was another area in need of improvement. The curriculum needed to allow students to make a smooth transition from one grade level to the next. The staff was challenged to work together on the design of a curriculum that would build upon previously learned skills instead of repeating them.

Finally, there was a need to develop a multiyear financial plan for the district. This was important to support plans for enhanced educational programs. However, the district was not wealthy, and its per pupil expenditure was $1,100 less than the average for high school districts in the county. The need for planning was intensified by the fact that the district was saddled with retiring a long-term debt that had resulted from a deficit of almost $4 million in the educational fund.

Eugene realized that financial planning would need to consider two possibilities. The first would be increased revenue that might result from a successful referendum in the spring of his second year as superintendent. The second eventuality would require contingency plans if voters did not approve the referendum, because this would ultimately lead to significant reductions in programs and personnel. The idea of increasing taxes brought mixed reactions from faculty, the board, and parent groups, and financial pressures continued to mount.

IMPROVING SCHOOL CLIMATE

When Dr. Brown assumed his superintendency, it became evident that morale was lower than one would expect. To reverse this situation, certain problems and issues needed to be addressed immediately. For example, student discipline at one high school was out of control and needed to be tightened to provide a safe learning environment.

Eugene's strategy was to involve those previously not involved. He hoped to make many changes and to communicate frequently. Brown developed weekly board packets, separate from the agendas, with an intent to keep the board up to date on what was happening in the district. He planned to communicate and meet with faculty and with the board president on a consistent basis. He also planned to meet regularly with the administrative advisory council to discuss building level issues and problems, as well as to address district-wide problems.

Eugene found that staff development needs in the district were enormous. Though previously staff had not responded positively to staff development programs, the new superintendent convinced 80 of the district's teachers to sign up for a 4-day workshop. This helped to create a positive environment and greatly improved staff morale.

The activation of the advisory council also made the faculty feel wanted and appreciated. The council provided the faculty with the opportunity to discuss their needs with their principals, who took them before the council. That principals were afforded a free hand to run their buildings added positively to the school climate.

With gang activity impacting both high school campuses, the district needed not only to improve climate but also to provide a safe and orderly learning environment. Prior to Dr. Brown's arrival, the district had used punitive approaches to the gang and fighting problems. These included lock-down control, suspension and expulsion, and other measures that compromise a positive school environment. Dr. Brown and the district addressed the gang issue by developing a hard-line policy on fighting. Consequently, during December of Brown's first year, about 25 students were expelled, most of them for fighting.

In addition, a dozen staff members were sent to discipline workshops to learn intervention and preventive strategies to combat student misconduct. Finally, besides taking a hard line on discipline, the district worked with the state board of education on operational procedures for a student code of conduct.

ETHICAL AND LEGAL DILEMMAS

Any school climate is affected by the board members' reactions to issues, problems, and concerns in their respective communities. Getting to know who board members listened to became a priority for the new superintendent. Although the superintendent recognized that school board members had sharply variant opinions on particular issues, he refused to allow himself to become a puppet. Working with a very diverse board, Eugene found ways to pull his own strings, especially when ethical and legal standards were at risk.

As a person of high integrity, Eugene refused to allow political patronage to run the district. For example, when a board member approached him asking that, as a favor, a friend of his be hired, Dr. Brown quickly asserted himself as someone who would not give in to the corrupt system. He firmly told the board member that all candidates for employment must be processed through the district's hiring procedures administered by the personnel office and that appointments would be made on the basis of merit. In another instance, some board members wanted to go on golf outings at district expense. He was able to persuade them that this was not a proper expenditure of educational funds.

In late August, soon after he became the Wendell superintendent, Eugene was faced with allegations that a male teacher was sexually harassing a male student. He placed the teacher on administrative leave with pay, pending investigation, and advised both the local police and department of child and family services. The police investigation was expanded to the nearby county where the teacher actually resided. Authorities there took over the case, removing it from the district's jurisdiction.

Eugene was also confronted in late August with a situation in which a payroll employee was suspected of embezzling money by writing herself checks. His investigation verified the suspicions. Furthermore, he discovered that the district's procedures were not precise enough to prevent similar incidents in the future. Eugene reported, "I was able to successfully convince our board that this is not only a criminal offense but also one that we ought to treat that way. So we have filed charges with the state's attorneys." He went on to describe procedural changes:

We brought in our auditors to advise us, and now there is a check on the work of the payroll person. I think we've got that loophole covered, but frankly, it should not have been there. It's probably good that it happened. It gave us an opportunity to get some attention to it before it was $75 million and the person was in Afghanistan.

These incidents are illustrative of how Eugene Brown responded when his integrity was tested at the very beginning of his superintendency. He demonstrated commitment and credibility, identified as keys to leadership by Bennis and Nanus (1985). Choosing to do the right thing as well as to do things right enabled Brown to model moral leadership, positively influencing the district climate.

OTHER POLITICAL CHALLENGES

One issue that Dr. Brown had to face early in his superintendency was the proposed deannexation of two communities from the district. The board had informed the district's attorney that it did not want to allow the two communities to deannex, because the district would lose revenue from its already strapped budget. The reason given in support of deannexation was that parents wanted their children to go to a smaller high school where friends from their elementary school district went. However, there were reasons to believe that the petition was racially motivated. Consequently, having been in the district less than two months, Eugene found himself spending three long, hot August nights appearing before the county board of school trustees. After hearing the petitioners and the defense of the Wendell district, the county board found in favor of the district.

In another issue, three appointments made before Eugene became superintendent presented political and diplomatic challenges. The former superintendent, upon stepping down at his own request, had been named to do life safety work for the district; the retired principal of one high school had been appointed as the hearing officer for the district; and an unsuccessful building administrator had been placed in central office as the personnel director.

Other difficulties concerned loyalties to the former superintendent that created problems for the organization's governance. Moreover, relationships with certain board members were both strong and influential in policy and personnel matters. Dr. Brown had to develop a strategic plan to deactivate, or at least neutralize, these relationships. The development of a personnel manual and job descriptions helped to alleviate some of these problems.

A concurrent problem Eugene faced was that several board members not only promoted but also attempted to implement pet ideas and programs. In the past, end runs such as these may have occurred because issues, problems, and concerns were not being adequately addressed administratively. The board members had been in the habit of telling the former superintendent just what to do, and he complied.

Eugene Brown tried to create an ideal arrangement between himself and the board. He asserted that the board should make policy while allowing him to administer the district. The fact that board members pushed certain agendas created an obstacle to this arrangement. Through the process of establishing better communications with board members, in-service workshops on board roles and responsibilities, and constant interactions with the board, Eugene saw some progress in board functioning.

Dr. Brown quickly learned about the special bonds that form between board members, school employees, and other influential groups in the community. He found that custodial maintenance persons were fiercely loyal to board members who got them their positions. Eugene observed that, "This tended to be our white employees." These individuals were tied to the democratic political machine in one of the district's communities.

Eugene also noted that there were a small number of Black noncertified employees who got their jobs through the grace of certain African-American board members. These individuals were perceived to be protected and, hence, beyond the control of the new superintendent. Sinecures such as these made Eugene guarded as to what he could share and with whom. Unfortunately, it also made for a pervasive mood of distrust in the district.

RACE AND THE SUPERINTENDENCY

One of the pressures that Eugene Brown faced every day was being the first Black superintendent of the district. He declared, "I feel like we certainly are in a difficult situation from several respects," adding, "There are people who believe that all of the problems and concerns that were not addressed or solved [earlier] are automatically going to be solved." He further explained, "There are those people that really cannot be counted upon because [they see it as] a racial issue and do not feel or think they can buy into the leadership."

There were also Black community leaders who expressed concern that the district had too few teachers of color and had not been able to retain the ones they had employed. This problem was certainly not unique to Wendell but reflected a national trend for talented African-American students to go into fields other than education.

On another front, and yet related to race, Eugene reported:

There are those who seek special favors. For example, a Black female faculty member who is working toward a school business manager degree expects the district to subsidize her internship at the same time she normally teaches classes. She became angry because she was not granted special privileges. To this day the teacher does not speak [to me].

She claimed that white people do this and asked why it was not all right for Black people to do so, regardless of policy. The superintendent responded, "We are running a $4 million deficit, and I cannot see having an intern at the district's expense." He added, "You kind of catch it from all ends and sides of various situations."

Dr. Brown explained that a source of constant strife in the community was concern among historical and political factions as to whose agenda was of most importance. He reported that running the organization became very complicated when he was faced daily with the nuances of Black-White agendas that came from board members, faculty, staff, and the community.

Perhaps indicative of past practices, when Dr. Brown came to the school district, many students mistakenly identified him as a paraprofessional or a security person, because most of "these" people tended to be African-Americans. Eugene said, "You are faced with people in the district who do not like to take orders from women or people of color, and this certainly presents problems as you begin to put forth new programs."

SIGNS OF PROGRESS

In spite of dealing with many difficult issues, Eugene experienced some satisfying successes. For example, an African-American female who was appointed as principal of one of the high schools proved to be an excellent leader and was innovative in turning the school around.

In addition, the athletic department proved to be a source of pride. Basketball was the premier sport and football was a minor sport in both schools. Eugene reported, "Ironically, our most successful and highly viable sport programs are not headed by Black coaches."

Eugene also reported with pride, "We certainly have made progress clearing up the discipline problems on both high school campuses. At least they are safer environments and are more conducive to learning than they were six months ago."

NEIGHBORING SUBURBS, A STUDY IN CONTRASTS

Eugene Brown shared with Keith Young, another new superintendent, in a nearby suburban district, the strategic objective of developing collaborative, site-based management. Both districts made significant progress on this objective. Understanding that progress will be enhanced by comparing the two districts and their superintendents. Keith and Eugene came to different suburban districts in the metropolitan area as new superintendents at the same time. Comparisons of the men and their districts are summarized in Table 8-1.

TABLE 8-1
Comparison of Two Districts and Their Superintendents.

	Eugene's District	Keith's District
District	Wendell	Moemonie
Population	29,000	35,000
Level	High School (9–12)	Elementary (K–8)
Enrollment	4,400	1,500
Minority Students	84%	7%
Free-Lunch Eligibility	23.5%	0.003%
School Board Composition	4 males, 3 females; 3 black, 3 white, 1 hispanic	4 males, 3 females; 7 white
Per Pupil Expenditure in Relation to That in Similar Districts in the County	$1,000 per pupil *less* than the average for high school districts	$1,700 per pupil *more* than the average for elementary districts
Superintendent's Prior Position	Assistant Superintendent for Curriculum and Instruction	Associate Superintendent for Curriculum and Instruction
Education	Doctorate	Doctorate
Age	47	40
Gender and Race	Black male	White male
Age at First Administrative Position	25–30	25–30
Experience	Teacher, Principal, Central Office	Teacher, Principal, Central Office
Salary	$100,000	$100,000
Search Process	Professional search firm	Professional search firm

The appearance of affluence was the most striking characteristic of the Moemonie School District when I first visited its new superintendent. Dr. Keith Young's elegant office was equipped with modern, utilitarian, professional furniture and the latest in computer technology. The quarters presented an aura of graceful authority and efficiency.

In contrast to the lower middle-class Wendell community, the racial composition of this old, and quaint, but highly affluent community was predominantly white. The 35,000 citizens of Moemonie were distinguished by their strong religious affiliations; 70% were Jewish, 15% Catholic, and the rest a mixture of Protestant and other religious groups. Though at first apprehensive about the impact of this religious environment on his family, Keith found the board to be sympathetic with his desire to live near his children's church activities. Though industries dominated the Wendell landscape, Moemonie was characterized by business parks and shopping centers. The school district was the community's largest employer.

The Moemonie School District served 1,500 students in two primary schools for kindergarten through Grade 3, one intermediate school for Grades 4 and 5, and one middle school for Grades 6 through 8. Achievement on standardized tests was well above national norms, and the average class size was 19 students. Only 7% of the students were Asian-American, and the rest were white.

AFTER MORE THAN TWO DECADES, A NEW SUPERINTENDENT

Dr. Keith Young, the Moemonie School District's first new superintendent in 23 years, was 40 years old when appointed. Prior to joining the district, Keith was an associate superintendent for curriculum and instruction in a neighboring school district. In addition, he was directly involved in professional negotiations, facilities management, support services, student enrollment projections, scheduling, and hiring of personnel. He had financial experience thanks to working with the district's business manager in developing the school budget.

Keith applied for the Moemonie position through the consulting firm overseeing the search. In his letter of application, he described his comprehensive experiences in all areas of district leadership. Moreover, he cited his productive and collaborative relationship with his board of education, parents in the community, administrators, teachers, and noncertified staff. Keith was attracted by the Moemonie district's excellent reputation for outstanding educational programs.

The deciding factor in accepting the position was the board's willingness to compromise their desire that the superintendent live in the district. Keith explained that moving to Moemonie would disrupt his family, especially the lives of four of his five children who attended church at differing times during each week. A compromise was reached that gave the superintendent a 10-mile radius in his contract. The Young family would still need to sell and to purchase a residence, but Keith and his wife would be able to live near a church of their choice.

Dr. Young was seen as ideal for the Moemonie superintendency. According to one board member, "His diverse background made him the perfect candidate for the job." When queried about why he accepted the appointment, Keith said he had been "looking for a superintendency that would be receptive to his talents, skills, and abilities in the development of an educational program to meet the needs of the children." He also sought a district that wanted to aggressively move its program toward the twenty-first century and would prepare children not only for the present but also for the future. Young saw the Moemonie School District's program as congruent with his own professional objectives; it was a good fit.

After being named superintendent, Keith outlined his major goals, which included, among other things, the implementation of a middle school educational plan and the development of a curriculum model that included outcome-based education. Like Eugene, he also wanted to develop and implement a plan to involve staff members in decision making in order to develop a collaborative environment. He observed, "My personal goal is to begin by building trust and integrity with the staff and community." Once trust was established, Keith stated that he wanted to address issues pertaining to the needs of the four individual buildings, for it was his belief that school site personnel must be involved in decisions impacting individual building needs.

SETTING THE STAGE

Like Eugene Brown's predecessor in the Wendell district, Moemonie's previous superintendent had maintained a top-down, authoritarian leadership style during his 23 years in the district. He wanted to personally address all problems, concerns, and issues; so no other administrators made any decisions without first clearing them with the superintendent.

Keith realized that he had to cast aside the rigid rules of his predecessor in order to establish his own style. His first task was to create an environment that would move his faculty and staff from a highly controlled, centralized approach to a more decentralized and collaborative orientation. In other words, like Eugene, Keith wanted to empower his staff and strive for a more democratic decision-making model. Keith's vision for the district had been shaped by extensive reading of authors such as Deming (1986), Fullan (1991), Juran (1988), and Vaill (1989).

Young, who takes pride in his communication skills, began this task by meeting with the board, central office staff, administration, teachers, and influential community members to explain the new goals for the district. Concurrently, he sought input from all segments of the school community. He also met with the central office staff with whom he knew he must inspire loyalty and respect if he were to be successful in building his administrative team.

After establishing himself with the central office, Dr. Young focused on the teachers' association. He decided to address the entire group and told them of his open door policy, encouraging groups or individuals to take advantage of it. Next, he set up regular meetings with the president of the teachers' association so that emerging issues, problems, and concerns of teachers could be aired.

Externally, Keith made a concerted effort to garner as much parental support as he could in the larger community. Realizing the close connection that the staff members have with the board of education, he sought to gain support of the board. Throughout his early months, he was trying to learn about both large and small issues and to seek means for resolving them.

Dr. Young sought to familiarize himself with the school community and its culture. He described the process he used:

The superintendent who was here was wonderful! He put together planning packets for me. I've been reading the local papers, number one. I've been reading the newsletters from all the schools. . . . I went through their budget; I went through the planning guide; I went through their staffing and enrollment patterns. I've begun looking at the curriculum. . . . I've tried to look at the processes that they used to make decisions and the people they work with. . . . Whether I like it or not, I'm coming into a very well-established culture, and I am not intending to come in and change the culture. I'm intending to come in and get to know it, and see what has been so successful in that culture. And then, from there, I'll try to maneuver to these new areas [I think are important.]

Looking back on his beginning, Keith credited open communication for allowing him to quickly become familiar with every aspect of the district's programs. An advocate of a proactive approach to administration, he spent the first few months listening, internalizing problems and issues, responding, and making efforts to correct problems and mend fences.

BUILDING ON STRONG FOUNDATIONS

Dr. Young found that the district had a strong curriculum. High student achievement in Moemonie allowed him to concentrate on enhancing curriculum rather than on improving achievement, as Eugene needed to do. He worked collaboratively with the middle school planning committee as it developed an implementation plan, including block and flexible scheduling to allow time for special projects and events for the students. He also appointed committees to study the district's staff evaluation program and outcome-based education models.

Dr. Young also identified other goals for his first year as superintendent, including development of a shared decision-making model and an effective administrative team including principals and central office staff. He sought ways to strengthen board-superintendent relationships while reducing time spent with board members, so that he could increase time spent out in the buildings with administrators, teachers, and students.

Dr. Young began his tenure just as the Moemonie School District was in the midst of professional negotiations. He scrupulously avoided influencing the proceedings, allowing the board team and the faculty alliance to work out the items being negotiated. Keith stated, "A low profile this year would give me an opportunity to start off new next year."

Labor peace came about after the board approved a 3-year contract with the Moemonie faculty association. Their accord, reached several months after Dr. Young's employment, called for attractive increases in teacher salaries over each of three years. The accord also called for a committee composed of representatives of the board and the faculty association to study escalating health insurance costs and to recommend methods of cost containment.

The faculty association and the board also agreed on new retirement provisions. These provisions created complex negotiation dilemmas for Keith and the board. For example, eligible teachers in the district wanted to take advantage of a new state law offering attractive early retirement benefits while still claiming the retirement incentives that the district previously offered.

COLLABORATION FOR CHANGE

When the faculty alliance representatives met with Keith, they said that teachers wanted to move away from the autocratic relationship they had experienced with the previous superintendent. Their desire for participatory decision making was consistent with Young's goal of changing traditional approaches to school district operations. Though the board of education may not have fully understood the changes contemplated, Keith described them as supportive:

I can honestly say that the board and I are of a single mind, and that they want to see me develop a collaborative, consensus-making organizational approach and implement it by the end of the school year.

The board agreed to send several teachers, administrators, and board members to professional workshops, including one that focused on enhancing student learning by bringing together teachers, administrators, and board members to stimulate and promote changes in school structure and relationships. This approach was similar to the TQM model being developed in the Wendell district. When implemented in Moemonie, the fruits of this workshop could enable them to look at their own district's culture, the shared decision-making process, and the impact on the school's curriculum and district personnel.

Keith worked to increase building administrator autonomy. His goal was for principals to be able to deal with unique, specific contractual variables that surfaced in each school. In essence, Young wanted a system in place that allowed building administrators the flexibility they needed to run their respective buildings and, yet, that allowed the superintendent to assist in issues and acquisitions of importance.

Even as he worked at refining the roles and responsibilities of principals, Keith Young recognized a need for the board of education to perform its duties without interfering in the day-to-day operations of the district that are properly the province of the superintendent. As in the Wendell district, it took Keith several months to develop a working relationship with the Moemonie board. The most complex challenge was stopping the boards from micromanaging the districts as they had done in the past. To assist in sharpening the focus of board efforts, Keith organized board seminars and provided professional resources such as the book entitled *The Twenty-First Century Board of Education* (Flinchbaugh, 1993).

By the end of the year, Keith was generally pleased with the relationship he developed with the board. He respected the varied expertise of board members, and gave them credit for their skills. He inspired confidence and self-esteem in board members as they went about their roles. However, the need for continuing board development was evidenced by some of the political fires they started.

FIRE FIGHTING

Dr. Young spent much of his time putting out brush fires that had been kindled under the previous administration. As in Eugene Brown's district, the former Moemonie superintendent was still employed in the district. Keith described some of the transition pains early in the school year:

I've been placed in an awkward position in many situations where promises have been made by the old superintendent and I'm trying to smooth over the rough waters. I can tell you every single day I have dealt with at least one situation where someone says, "Dr. Former promised me that this was going to happen." I've heard that more times in the past 3 weeks than I can shake a stick at.

As tactfully as possible, Keith explained that he could not change what had happened in the past but that things were going to be different. He won his administrative territory with comparatively little pain, but with great patience, even though the former superintendent still worked for the district. Keith's predecessor was generally more helpful and supportive than was the situation for Eugene.

Other political fires were kindled by board members. In May, Keith described two kinds of board member behaviors that were creating problems for the whole board: (1) discussing privileged communications with community members or with staff members who were personal friends and (2) asking teachers to give special preferences to their own children. For example, one board member told a group of teachers that they gave in too early on the salary settlement and settled too low. Teacher determination to hold out on the retirement issue was fueled by feeling they had settled too low on salaries. Keith added, "I am convinced, beyond any shadow of a doubt, that one of the board members feeds private information to other community members who like to have a less than positive influence on the community."

Illustrative of the other kind of problem was a phone call Keith received from a mother asking if he was aware of board members asking for "special favors to get their children into special programs or to get special privileges like a part in a play, or the lead part in a play or sports team." Then the caller said, "Well, do not repeat this, but I heard from one of your board members that this is going on."

Keith worked very closely with the board president on this matter. She communicated to fellow board members, both in open session and in private, that they had to be aware of the negative effects their actions were having on other aspects of the district. Given this foundation, Keith called individual board members when such issues arose. He described how he handled these calls and the risk that he took:

I know you may be mad at me, but I am going to tell you that you cannot do that because you and the district are going to get hurt. I have had to say that and I realize that there is job security [to consider] and that they could get ticked off at me and say something in the community and I could be gone. Those things happen. . . . I could always go out and pump gas, and I would be very happy doing that. Seriously, it is sort of like when you have been in the fire and it does not bother you the next time around.

Working through such territorial and emotional issues without incurring parental or board rancor proved a never-ending challenge for Keith as a new superintendent.

Another extraordinarily sensitive issue confronted Dr. Young when a coach was alleged to have displayed inappropriate sexual behavior toward female students. The issue had never been brought before the board of education, yet it was the former superintendent who brought it to Keith's attention. After investigation, Keith decided that the entire board should be informed of the issue and should participate in its resolution.

This approach meant that any resulting criticism would be shared rather than fall on the superintendent exclusively. The situation was complicated by the fact that memos and letters had been written and given to people no longer employed in the district. Despite opposition from one board member, they unanimously decided that the man would not be allowed to continue as coach and ordered that a letter of reprimand be placed in his personnel file.

In an unrelated incident, the board gave another basketball coach a letter of reprimand after a due process hearing in which the coach admitted having used foul language and inappropriate humor in front of students. These incidents, like the ethical stands that Eugene Brown took, enabled Keith Young to demonstrate his commitment to doing what was right as leader of the district.

BURNING THE MIDNIGHT OIL IN THE SUBURBS

Both Eugene Brown and Keith Young reported major frustrations in the area of time management. Keith, who had not been able to sell his former home and move closer to Moemonie, said:

I'm putting in 18 hours a day, and I guess no one wants to say that an 18-hour day is normal. . . . That is more than 80 hours a week. When you live an hour away from the district, you're on the road 2 hours a day. I have five children, but I virtually don't see the family at all. So . . . there aren't enough hours in the day. The other side of that is that you have to get the work done, so you do it.

Eugene lamented that he had insufficient time to keep up with all the required paper work. He got some relief when a student from a vocational office class was assigned to assist him. He liked working with the student; however, he continued to feel that there needed to be more help, reporting that he spent from 70 to 80 hours a week staying on top of the work. He reported that his work was infringing on his personal time at home "and not for good reasons." Near the end of his first year as superintendent, the Wendell board agreed to hire an assistant superintendent, though the district had not had one for a few years. Eugene believed that an assistant superintendent would lessen his work load and make it easier to meet with students, parents, and teachers.

COLLABORATIVE APPROACHES BEGIN TO MAKE A DIFFERENCE

Dr. Young's goal of developing a collaborative environment that provided for consensus-based decision making proved highly successful. In addition, there was an increase in instructional retreats, illustrative of how his superintendency had taken hold. Moreover, movement from a centralized form of administration to site-based management was rapidly taking place, but not without training the key individuals in their new or expanded roles.

Likewise, in the Wendell district, the implementation of a collaborative site-based management approach to administration was on its way to becoming a reality. Dr. Brown reported proudly, "The board adopted and endorsed this approach, the administrative team is partially supportive, and there is a great deal of support from teachers and the community."

Eugene was gratified by the enhanced organizational structure that had been implemented in the Wendell district during his first year. Improved board-superintendent relations and the manner in which the faculty, board, and community worked together helped to make the district a place where students can receive a quality education.

Strong inroads were made in building trust and integrity among administrators, board members, staff, and the community in Moemonie. Shared decision making paved the way for implementing a middle school education plan and an outcome-based curriculum.

All of this had been accomplished by the administration and staff developing goals and plans together. If a plan had everyone's input and commitment, it tended to be more thorough, and it had a better chance of success. Keith explained how he approached the development of a shared vision for the district:

I can't impose my vision on them. . . . We have to develop our vision together, but in the back of my mind, I am knocking it out, [trying to decide] where I want to go. I'm trying to raise the dialogue in those areas and get people to talk about them. I think that when you're dealing in the business of persuasion, shared commitment, and all that, [it] is a very slow process. . . . So . . . I think we are moving in a very reasonable time; . . . it's going to take some time.

The shared vision was evident when Moemonie faculty members designed several innovative programs that Keith recommended for implementation during his second year. These exciting proposals were the epitome of energizing persons subordinate to the superintendent to show their initiative and imagination and how innovations might enhance the students' experiences while studying in the Moemonie School District.

One such proposal called for a new computer technology program for sixth-grade students to reinforce the math processing skills taught earlier and challenge students to extend their computer knowledge. Another was an industrial technology program in which seventh-grade students expanded their computer skills and learned various underlined art processes. An economic education program provided a means for eighth-grade students to develop and run a manufacturing company where they designed a product, made decisions during its production, and then advertised and sold the product. And for first- through fifth-grade students, a new spelling program was developed, designed to produce competent independent spellers.

Dr. Young's vision for the future included considering new educational trends that might affect the district and seeking new approaches for developing curriculum and the implementation of promising instructional strategies. His vision also included continuing to strengthen site-based management and expanded use of technology in education. He hoped to enhance community and staff interest in the whole educational process, believing that, together, the entire educational community can integrate new directions with time-honored effective practices.

QUESTIONS FOR REFLECTION AND DISCUSSION

1. How did the different economic situations in their districts affect the challenges that Keith and Eugene faced?

2. What are the advantages and disadvantages of living in the school district where one is a superintendent? How might these factors be different if a superintendent has school-age children?

3. How do you think having a former superintendent working in the district would impact a beginning superintendent?

4. What do you think you would do to gain organizational support for changing procedures put in place by a popular previous superintendent?

REFERENCES

Bennis, W., & Nanus, B. (1985). *Leaders: The strategies for taking charge*. New York: Harper & Row.

Bonstingl, J. J. (1992).*Schools of quality: An introduction to total quality management in education*. Alexandria, VA: Association for Supervision and Curriculum Development.

Deming, W. E. (1986). *Out of the crisis*. Cambridge, MA: Massachusetts Institute of Technology.

Flinchbaugh, F. W. (1993). *The twenty-first century board of education: Planning, leading, transforming*. Lancaster, PA: Technomic.

Fullan, M. (1991). *The new meaning of educational change*. New York: Teachers College Press.

Juran, J. M. (1988). *Juran on planning for quality*. New York: The Free Press.

Marshall, C. (1995, August). Imagining leadership. *Educational Administration Quarterly, 31,* 484–492.

Slavin, R. E., & Braddock, J. H. (1993, Summer). Ability grouping: On the wrong track. *The College Board Review, 168,* 10–18.

Vaill, P. B. (1989). *Managing as a performing art: New ideas for a world of chaotic change*. San Francisco: Jossey-Bass.

9

SUSAN
Charm and Steel Facing a Public Mandate for Urban School Reform

Carolyn Hughes Chapman, The University of Nevada, Reno

ABSTRACT. Political discord and turmoil had complicated the functioning of the Renfield Board of Education for so long that the mayor of this urban metropolis led successful efforts to elect a "reform school board." Dr. Susan Oliver, a 50-year-old African-American, was hired from a distant state with the expectation that she would bring positive changes to the district of more than 70,000 students. White and middle-class flight following court-ordered desegregation had left a student population that was largely poor and minority. Though facing a budget deficit, an achievement deficit, and complex legal issues, Susan Oliver saw her most important priority as inspiring the people within the district to believe in themselves. Susan's past responsibilities had honed her skills of instructional leadership, but the unique context of this first superintendency would require her to refine skills of managerial, organizational, and political leadership as well.

The importance of the relationship between the context and the person of the superintendent was identified in a study of new superintendents and school reform (Johnson and Verre, 1993). Those researchers reported that individuals in school districts

> were well informed about their local schools, about educational practice, and about current proposals for reform. They considered whether those administrators had made a serious commitment to their district. They judged whether the superintendents respected them as individuals and professionals. They listened and watched the new superintendents to discern their values and assess their character. In the end, they asked themselves, "Does this person deserve my support?" Those in the central office and the schools know well how to passively resist the efforts of superintendents whom they doubt or distrust (p. 27).

Renfield is an urban district that serves 72,000 students in nearly 130 schools. The city is home to industries and businesses that provide the economic base for a metropolitan area of nearly 2 million people, of whom over 25% live within the core city. Approaching the city by automobile takes one past large, prosperous homes in the outer suburbs and through urban fringe suburbs of modest homes, closely spaced on small, well-tended lots. The city itself is typified by heavy industry, business and commercial areas, large older homes, apartments, and public housing areas.

The student population and the economic resources available to the Renfield Public School District have declined dramatically in the past 2 decades as a result of white and middle class flight following court-ordered desegregation. For 20 years, the goal of many young families has been to save enough to buy a house in the suburbs by the time their children reach school age. Although less than 20% of the metropolitan area population is African-American, almost 50% of the central city's population and approximately 70% of the district's student population is African-American. The rest of the population is a diverse group, including other minorities and many white families who came from central Europe in recent generations. A low tax base is one result of the out-migration of the economically able, as illustrated by the fact that 40% of the city's population is on public assistance. Over 70% of the district's students come from families that qualify for the free-lunch program. One half of the students entering Renfield's high schools do not graduate.

Far from giving up in despair, the city's recent efforts to bring a renaissance to Renfield's economic life have resulted in the investment of $5 billion in major downtown construction projects. Concurrently, business and civic leaders recognized that school improvement was vital to achieving their vision for the city. However, political discord and turmoil have long complicated the functioning of the Renfield Board of Education. Strong leadership by the mayor resulted in electing a "reform slate" of four new members to the seven-member board in the fall before a new superintendent was to be chosen. Their election was evidence of a populace eager for positive change in the school district. This board of education selected Dr. Susan Oliver as its new superintendent with the expectation that she would bring about major positive changes in the district. Susan, who had been an assistant superintendent in a distant state, was the ninth superintendent to lead the district in 16 years. She was the first female, but not the first African-American, to serve as superintendent. When asked why she was the person selected, Susan replied:

I think the district was ready for a superintendent that symbolized something different, because the city was very much believing that this was going to be a new day for the city and a new day for the school system. . . . I was indeed different . . . not only the fact that I was a woman, but my background was different in that I had spent most of my career in curriculum and instruction as opposed to the business side of schools.

Susan thought that public support was gained during her trips to the district for interviewing. She described days of visiting schools and meeting people: "I remember when I had to do a televised stand-up question and answer session with the press in the middle of a reception to which the whole public was invited."

Why would someone who was happy and successful in a significant professional role choose to take on the challenges of Renfield? Susan said:

It was almost an inspirational thing. After I visited the schools during the second inter-view, I decided I was really interested. And the keys were that, basically, this tapped into a mission that has always been buried deep within me, that I really believe in cities. I guess my heart strings are tied to poor urban children. . . . I grew up in the housing projects of Washington, D.C. There was that emotional tie, number one. Then, there was a civic spirit I detected in the city when I visited that made me believe it was possible.

The newly elected school board members strengthened Susan's belief that this troubled urban school district could be turned around. She described them as

just regular citizens, civic-minded citizens, interested in children and education. They had nothing to do with politics. They were not going to get on the board and try to hire people or give contracts; they were just regular citizens interested in schools. Everyone said they had absolutely no chance of being elected, but they all were—the slate won by a two-to-one margin.

Soon after coming to Renfield, Susan was asked: "What was hard about making the decision to accept the superintendency of the Renfield Public Schools?" She replied:

The hardest thing was leaving my major support system behind, and that's my husband. . . . The second hardest was, I have an excellent track record in every other position that I've held, and a good reputation. Anytime I've left, people have pleaded with me to stay. Yet, here I was coming into a situation where I realized I risked that track record. I risked coming into a situation where others hadn't succeeded. I wondered whether my record, my reputation and track record, would still be intact when I leave here. So that was a secondary concern.

FACING THE CHALLENGES OF RENFIELD

During her first month on the job, Dr. Oliver described her five most immediate challenges as (1) the budget deficit; (2) the achievement deficit; (3) shifting the staff and the board from total preoccupation with business issues to focus on the education program; (4) gaining permission of the federal court to reduce busing by proposing new educational initiatives; and (5) most important, inspiring the people within the district to believe in themselves and to be "proud to work for the Renfield Public Schools, because they've been bashed incessantly in the press and otherwise." In addition to these five immediate priorities, Dr. Oliver said, "Another big challenge will be to complete this year, a comprehensive, strategic education plan for the district that will show where we want to go over the next five years."

As the year progressed, Dr. Oliver discovered that the comprehensive education plan could be a tool for addressing the achievement deficit, focusing on the education program, and proposing educational initiatives to the federal court. Furthermore, the plan became a catalyst for inspiring people in the district to believe they could provide what the children of Renfield need.

Susan spent much of her first month in a series of briefings to enhance her understanding of the district. By early August, she had gained sufficient confidence to propose educational initiatives and reduced busing to the federal judge. Describing her preparation, she said, "I worked nonstop for 3 days at home. Because this was a last-ditch effort, this was not something I processed the way I would normally process things." Given only a few weeks before school would open in the fall, Susan proposed neighborhood attendance areas for a few elementary schools and reallocating transportation cost savings for educational expenditures. Susan's curriculum background had uniquely prepared her to craft ideas for educational changes that would enhance the learning of students while allowing children to attend neighborhood schools.

Reflecting on the results of her efforts, Susan said, "The judge ruled in our favor. . . . I think it won me a lot of credibility in the broader community." Though the plan approved by the judge allowed only about 1,000 children to attend schools nearer their homes, the board of education and many parents saw it as a promising first step. Parents quoted in the metropolitan newspaper voiced new willingness to consider sending children to public schools instead of to parochial or private schools. The school board president stated, "If the people in the city see us as moving forward, we will rebuild confidence. We know that the quality of the schools contributes to the growth of the city." However, the judge made it clear that his decision was a one-time event, declaring that future plans to reduce busing must be comprehensive rather than piecemeal measures.

SYSTEMIC CHANGE

By early October, in response to a board directive, Dr. Oliver proposed major organizational changes that would prepare the district for comprehensive planning. Her presentation to the board provided the rationale for her proposals as well as the changes themselves:

Although society has undergone rapid and dramatic changes over the past 100 years, schools and the organizations that support them remain virtually unchanged. These major societal changes have placed extraordinary demands on schools, yet schools have been unwilling or unable to change in ways that would make it possible for them to respond. As a consequence, school districts across the country now evidence major SYMPTOMS of a need for CHANGE. The Renfield City School District is certainly no exception and indeed displays every symptom of the need for major change (Gridley, 1990).

- It is unable to respond consistently and effectively to its customers' [children's] needs.
- Its top management is confused about priorities and direction and is often in disagreement with one another.
- Its ideas, when put forth, are often more of the same.
- There is evidence of much activity and even hard work, but there is seldom concerted and coordinated effort toward planned change efforts aimed at improved outcomes.
- There is low morale at the base of the organization.
- There is a wealth of study reports offering long lists of recommendations never implemented.
- Its performance has stabilized at a level below that which is required and expected.

These unanswered demands on the organization have prompted increased competition from outside organizations seeking to take over schools. Such demands and competition will increase as it becomes increasingly clear that strategies, approaches, and decision-making processes employed by schools and school districts are no longer effective. When it is no longer able to respond effectively and efficiently to its clients' needs, an organization is truly "endangered." In the case of schools, the situation can only be described as tragic because its customers are students.

Organizational Change Initiatives

Renfield Public Schools must find the courage, energy, and skill to reform itself from the inside, or it will be reformed from the outside (e.g., business takeovers, bankruptcies, receiverships, private school vouchers, exodus to private and parochial schools, and the like). The superintendent and board, therefore, must be prepared to undertake a series of Organizational Change Initiatives immediately. The first four organizational change initiatives are identified below:

1. Redesign of the entire central office administrative structure, beginning with the top level, and continuing over the next 12 months, with a redesign of the remaining levels.
2. A planned and concerted district-wide effort to change the organization's climate, culture, and thinking so that the Renfield City School District is, and is perceived

as, a caring and customer-centered organization focused on providing high quality services to meet its students' needs.

3. Design and implementation of a waste reduction plan to address the district's financial emergency and to target more resources to the classroom.

4. Development of a comprehensive education plan to guide the organization's attainment of its mission.

Susan Oliver's thoughtful analysis and preparation had gratifying results. In mid-October, she described what happened:

I had a very major victory! I had a six-zero vote on my reorganization. . . . The people in Renfield think it's quite, quite phenomenal. . . . The press was very positive. I like to think it was because it was a good plan. I also, for the first time ever, and very reluctantly, tried to orchestrate my press. And it worked. It worked a hundred percent. . . . I actually went to the newspaper and requested a meeting with the editorial board.

The effect of the meeting with the newspaper's editorial staff was evident in an editorial endorsing not only the reorganization plan but also the new superintendent. The editor asserted that

the Renfield School Board has put at the helm a superintendent who emphasizes she is an educator, not a politician. That is exactly what this district and this city need. Oliver has crafted a plan that ignores politics to focus on improving public education. And that, too, is exactly what this district and this city need.

HARSH FISCAL REALITIES

While putting her new organizational plan in place, Susan became increasingly aware that the district's financial crisis presented both immediate and long-term challenges. From the beginning of her superintendency, she had recognized fiscal concerns. By August 1, she had described the financial situation as "bleak." A projected $40 million deficit in operating funds underscored the need to pass a tax referendum, to gain state permission to borrow funds, or to do both. Even with the projected deficit and urgent fiscal needs, the board voted in mid-August to rescind its June decision to place a tax levy on the November ballot. If such a vote had been successful, it could have generated close to $50 million annually. The negative decision on the levy came as a result of advice from the mayor that the "time was not right to ask for money" and concern that the public would not support increased taxes.

The voters of Renfield had not approved an operating levy for nearly 10 years. Polls of voters during the summer had yielded inconclusive results. Although fewer than half of the respondents said they would support a levy, 85% said they would agree to pay more taxes if the money would result in better schools. As the year progressed, newspaper headlines added to public concern about the district's fiscal responsibility:

School Board Overspends on Legal Fees
Schools' Budget Chief to Lose Job
Loan Leaves Schools $35 Million Shortfall
Computing Bills Add Up to Trouble
Board Declines to Suspend Manager [who admitted ordering more
 than $4 million in goods and services without board approval]
Renfield Schools Losing $6 Million

Yet, two events brought hope to the district's budget planners. In December, the state approved a loan of close to $80 million, which would enable the district to get through the school year. Further encouragement came when the superintendent, the treasurer, and the board president visited Wall Street and were successful in securing an improved bond rating for the district. The issue of placing a tax referendum on the ballot continued to be debated. When the board president announced in March that the schools would not seek a levy that year, he stated the need to cut 10% from the district's budget by June 30. The newspaper reported that some school board members said privately that it would be difficult to spend time and effort selling a tax referendum to voters while campaigning for school board and mayoral elections.

The operations budget was not the only area of fiscal crisis. As the fall semester got underway, deterioration of school buildings in the district led parents and staff to air their concerns at board meetings. Leaky roofs and roach-infested buildings made headlines. Prior maintenance practice had been to "oil squeaky wheels" rather than repair structures systematically. However, in October, Susan persuaded the board to take a more comprehensive look at capital improvement needs before deciding how to spend limited funds. She asked, "How can you decide if you're going to fix those two schools before you know what all the emergency projects are?" At the board meeting a month later, Susan reported that the district had only $8 million in capital improvement funds to address $600 million worth of capital improvement needs, which had been identified in a 2-year-old assessment of the district's buildings by state officials. Susan, who had learned of the shortfall in the operations budget during her first weeks on the job, stated in November, "I've been surprised at the capital improvement part of the financial condition of the district. I go into these buildings and see floors torn apart, rooms condemned, auditoriums condemned, and gyms not usable."

Fiscal limitations also had personnel implications. Dr. Oliver felt fortunate that none of the employee unions were negotiating contracts during her first summer on the job. However, the need to reduce spending led to a controversial decision to lay off more than 40 maintenance workers in October. The political discord that had historically plagued the Renfield Board of Education again surfaced over this decision. The nature of the bitterness was seen when one of the second-term board members publicly charged the new board majority with being "cold, calculating, cruel, and corrupt" and "a band of political jackals intent on destroying people for a few dollars more." Immediately, one of the new board members shot back, "When my colleague speaks, I'm reminded of the inmates running the asylum." A newspaper columnist quipped, "Welcome to another Renfield school board meeting, known for years as one of the most action-packed shows in town."

Soon after that stormy session, the board had a retreat to discuss ways to make meetings more productive and less contentious. A news headline about the retreat reported: School Board Realizes Squabbling Must Stop. Though the board tried to become more businesslike, the persons attending board meetings failed to moderate their behavior. For example, a January board meeting had to be adjourned before any official business was conducted due to angry outbursts from the audience. The board president commented, "We have no choice. We can't conduct board business under these conditions." The next meeting also had to be adjourned because of rowdiness in the audience. Describing that meeting, Susan Oliver said, "Before the gavel ever hit, the people were yelling and screaming, and people charged up on the stage. I've just never seen anything like it. People were yelling and screaming, and TV cameras were going up in people's faces."

PUTTING FIRST THINGS FIRST

Though political, financial, and personnel issues had overshadowed educational issues in the past, Dr. Oliver established her priorities in October by initiating the comprehensive education planning process. She worked to build widespread involvement and to inspire visionary thinking. Parents and other citizens were invited to come to 1 of 15 schools scattered throughout the district. The invitation is shown in Figure 9-1.

Following the parent meetings at the 15 schools, a *Handbook for Work Teams* was developed. The handbook began by stating that "each work team has the charge to develop a viable action plan that will prepare our students to live and work harmoniously in a culturally diverse country. Students will be confident, competent, contributing members of a global society." A total of 26 work teams were appointed, comprised of principals, teachers, central office staff, parents, other community members, and experts in various fields. The work teams ranged in size from 15 to 50. Susan described the initial meeting for the combined work teams:

There were hundreds of people there, and I gave the charge and tried to get everybody up. It is kind of scary to have all those committees out there and not know what in the world they've got to come up with, or if this is going to be another kind of thing where the recommendations aren't specific enough. . . . We had to have a lot of faith they'd come through.

FIGURE 9-1
Invitation to Participate in Comprehensive Education Planning

The Superintendent, staff, and parent leaders are coming to **YOUR COMMUNITY** . . . .
You will be helping to design the future we want for **our children** . . . .
Superintendent Susan Oliver will be speaking via a live telecast.
Small group "dreaming" will begin immediately following the telecast.

The work teams began meeting in December and continued through March. To provide training and assistance for the planning groups, Susan Oliver contacted a local foundation and was successful in securing $100,000 to cover the ancillary costs of the work teams. This included having a consultant work 2 or 3 days a week to shepherd the process, meet with the committees, make sure they did not get off track, read what they produced, and coordinate their efforts.

In March, after she received the 26 reports, Susan worked with a small group to consolidate them into a comprehensive education plan. She spoke of the need to provide vision during this process:

There's a lot of work that this coordinating team is doing and that I'm personally doing to take more risks than the teams themselves took, to aim higher. For instance, I'm putting in a statement that says we will shift all of our priorities from remediation to prevention of early school failure, virtually guaranteeing that every youngster will read by the end of first grade. Now that's pretty risky, I realize.

As the plan took shape, Susan took time to recognize the vital contributions of principals to the planning process. She gave what she called "a small, kind of cozy dinner" for the 50 principals involved. She talked with each of the principals, giving opportunities to comment and make alternative suggestions. Though she had been meeting monthly with principals, she wanted to be sure principals were part of finalizing the plan. Susan recognized, "They're going to have to be strong enough to resist the other pressure they're getting not to change the schools."

Susan and her team presented the comprehensive education plan to a public meeting of 1,600 people on a Saturday in late April. The following Monday, a live telecast featured Susan Oliver presenting the plan and responding to questions from an invited audience. On Tuesday, Wednesday, and twice on Thursday, Susan personally chaired community forums in different parts of the city. At these sessions, anyone could come and ask any question and voice their concerns and objections.

In planning the public presentations and community forums, some of Susan's staff argued against her subjecting herself to night after night of attack. She reported:

The cabinet split right down the middle with half of them saying, "Yes, it's got to be you, because people identify with you. You're the one they can relate to. If you don't they'll feel like they haven't been heard." The other half said, "Absolutely not. Superintendents don't go out there and put themselves in a position to be attacked night after night on something. That's what you have us for, to be the buffers and to take some of this." The closer it got to the day, the more I intuitively knew it had to be me, and so I did it.

A newspaper reporter described the superintendent at these forums as "quintessential Oliver—defusing criticism by listening attentively, taking a personal approach, offering constructive suggestions." People interviewed at the forums commented about the process: "People seem tense before they question her, but you can see how she makes them relax. . . . She puts them at ease because she doesn't have a know-it-all attitude. She really does listen."

The city newspaper editor vigorously supported the comprehensive education plan. An editorial proclaimed:

The plan does not embrace piecemeal remedies that would leave the district looking like a rusted-out car held together by Bondo. If fully carried out, the plan could bring the kind of equity and improvements that fulfill the intent of the federal desegregation order.

After hearing four hours of spirited public debate, the school board voted six to one to approve the plan, thereby setting the stage for the district to move forward. The strategic plan included a comprehensive core program focused on improving teaching and learning and building equity by enhancing opportunity to learn, beginning in early childhood and extending through every content area. Special enhancement programs were developed to increase achievement of African-American students. Parental choice was to be expanded by implementing new magnet schools as well as community model schools based on a wide variety of nationally recognized, research-based models for school improvement. The comprehensive plan even gained the cautious support of plaintiffs in the desegregation suit, though their attorney expressed concern about the fiscal requirements to implement the plan.

SUSAN OLIVER, THE PERSON

Fifty-year-old Susan Oliver set priorities and approached tasks in ways that reflected her deep belief in people and her commitment to students. Her skillful presentations of the comprehensive education plan and sensitive responses to questions were widely recognized. However, few people knew that the personal cost of Susan's decision to lead these sessions had been escalated by an urgent need to be with her husband during his unanticipated cancer surgery. She returned to Renfield just in time for the presentations and forums.

Oliver's clear focus on education was evident early in her superintendency. In August, when the federal judge approved her plan for improving education while having students attend neighborhood schools, Susan described the public reaction: "I think they were impressed with my intent to move forward, focusing on the quality of education, and trying to diminish the emotionalism of the busing."

As time approached for the opening of school, Susan broke district precedent by inviting all 4,000 teachers to a continental breakfast on their first day of work. She described her strategy for the breakfast:

I'm not having a traditional program. In other words, there will be no one introducing me; there will not be a dais with all these people sitting on it; there is no one else invited. It's simply my walking up on the stage and saying, "Gee, I'm glad you came to breakfast."

Susan's speech to the teachers spelled out the leadership theory and her beliefs about education that grounded her approach to the superintendency:

I didn't invite you here this morning to dwell on the environments from whence children come. I want to talk with you, instead, about the schools to which they come. I want to talk with you this morning about BELIEVING, about ME believing in YOU, about YOU believing in ME, and about US believing in our children and in their "genius."

. . . I realize that many of you are already believers. But let's take our first step together today. There is POWER in our sheer numbers if we move forward together. Let's examine our belief system, the goals we see for our children, the beliefs we hold about them. This is where we must begin. If we see children come into our schools and classrooms tomorrow bearing the obvious scars of poverty, look beyond those scars to see a glimpse of their "genius." Believe me. It is there. I didn't say it would be easy. But it's our job! It's our moral obligation! . . . The most powerful act of caring is holding high expectations for students, then helping each and every one meet those expectations.

. . . Let me wrap up by talking about what you can expect from me, your super-intendent. . . . First and foremost, you can expect me to focus my energies on making things better for children, not for adults; but at the same time, you can expect me to show a great deal of love and respect and support for teachers. I am proud to be your superintendent. . . .

I will support teacher/principal empowerment whenever its purpose is to improve schooling and not "power grabbing." . . . Empowering teachers must become much more than a catch phrase. We must elevate the status of teaching, teacher access to new knowledge, and teacher access to decision making. . . .

I invite you to offer any constructive suggestions or ideas that you have for improv-ing our system. I encourage you to collaborate with colleagues and your building leadership and to move forward with reform in your classroom. . . . Begin tomorrow in your classroom. . . . Children can tell if we hold low expectations for them. Children don't care how much you know until they know how much you care.

The day after Susan Oliver's breakfast with the teachers, the newspaper reported that teachers responded enthusiastically: "She's different from past superin-tendents because she speaks from the heart and not from the point of politics." "There's a real strong sense of sincerity and toughness that comes across."

Throughout the year, Susan was asked to describe how she was spending her time. In August she said that, in addition to her work on educational initiatives, get-ting acquainted with the district, routine paperwork, and interviewing prospective principals,

the rest of my time is still being spent meeting with people from the outside who insist that it's necessary to meet with me. . . . That may have been very necessary in the beginning, but I'm coming to the conclusion that I'm just going to have to bring a moratorium to this. I'm doing all of my long-range planning on my own time at home, and I'm just not getting any personal time at all. . . .

As I look ahead to the next few months, I think I need to carve out more time for meeting with staff members inside and some personal time. Again, I don't mind it, because at this point I'm pretty energized. When I looked, though, I found that my cal-endar had expanded into meeting someone for breakfast, someone for lunch, and someone for dinner. . . . I think I need to back down from that so I can have maybe an hour alone. I do need to think about things like getting my clothes out of the cleaners.

Even when Susan crafted the plan to reorganize the administration of the dis-trict, she felt the time crunch. "This document is something that I had to write word for word myself. And I basically did it at four and five in the morning and then nine at night."

During an interview in mid-October, Susan commented further about the time pressures she was experiencing in her role as superintendent:

I guess it's hard for me to explain to you, Carolyn, the demands on my time and on me as a person. That's been the biggest surprise of this job for me. And I don't know whether that's Renfield, whether that's a big city, whether it's me, whether it's the first 6 months, or what. But it's just an unbelievable kind of thirst that everybody has got to see the superintendent; you've got to be everywhere doing everything. Legal cases, we have thousands of them going. That's why I have to get deputies in place. It took a tremendous amount of time to get the reorganization piece drafted, but at least it's done.

The only time I've taken off is when I've actually left the city. This is only the second weekend for doing that.

Though Susan had anticipated that the two new deputies would add significantly to her ability to get the job done and would relieve the time pressures she was experiencing, she was surprised to find how hard it was to recruit qualified deputy superintendents. In late November, she said:

I'm making absolutely no progress. . . . It's been a very frustrating experience, because I have pursued a number of people since we last spoke. Their story is always the same: their retirement. People say they're interested, and then they look into what it means for their retirement, and then they're not interested. . . . I thought, "Boy, if you had two plum jobs like this, people would be dying for them." . . . I did not think it would be so hard to recruit people.

Susan's anticipation that her superintendency would be closely scrutinized was realized in February when the city newspaper assigned a reporter to assess her first six months on the job. The reporter made it clear to Susan that she wanted to write a "balanced" article, one that presented both positive and negative aspects of the first six months. The only areas of criticism cited were the delay in hiring her deputies and people wishing she would be in schools more often. The headline for the article read: Oliver Says Schools Improving, But Critics Still Waiting for Results. The article was more positive than the headline would indicate. It also revealed a great deal about Susan Oliver as a person:

When it comes to speaking skills and poise, Oliver has few peers. Asked what they think of her after 6 months, descriptions from people inside and outside the school system invariably contain the same adjectives: articulate, inspirational, warm, gracious.

Charisma is something Oliver doesn't lack. After the . . . speech, indeed after nearly every appearance, people have clustered around Oliver, wanting to touch her, be near her, have her say a few words to them . . . In other words, the past 6 months have been better at showing Oliver's form than demonstrating substance.

Reflecting on this assessment, Susan commented, "I guess what bugs me about it is that somebody like that doesn't understand that inspiring teachers IS substance."

The reporter also told of comments by an elementary principal who said she liked Oliver's hands-on approach to dealing with a controversy about school bus services:

Some parents had complained about the route and the distance their children walked to the school. "So the second day of school she had her walking shoes on and walked the route herself. I respect that." Oliver walked the two miles and agreed it was too far for elementary school students to walk. . . . The board eventually voted to bus children who had to walk more than 1 mile.

Though time was a continuing concern for Oliver, she was able to realize some visible short-term successes even while leading the comprehensive planning process. One of these was a major effort to solve a long-standing textbook problem that had made headlines in October. Students, parents, teachers, and board members were upset about the lack of textbooks. Extensive news coverage identified ways that a lack of textbooks can affect student achievement and pointed out that suburban schools have one textbook for every student, in contrast to the Renfield students who must share class sets.

Susan took on the problem with her administrative team over a several month period. She explained that she told the team, "There is really absolutely no excuse for youngsters not having basic textbooks. . . . The students will have the books, and they will have them this year, not at the completion of the education plan, or next year, or any other time, but right now this year." After setting this goal, Susan proceeded systematically to review the ordering process, to determine a recommended formula for giving students books, to inventory needs, to make budget transfers, to order books, and to prepare a brochure for parents on what books their children could be expected to have. In early March, when the books had arrived in the schools and had been placed in students' hands, Susan decided to celebrate this short-term success. She did so by calling a press conference at a high school that had just received $75,000 worth of books. The city newspaper featured a large photo of Dr. Oliver surrounded by some of the books that were purchased for students at the school.

After nearly nine months on the job, Susan Oliver welcomed her long-awaited deputy superintendents to the district in early April. However, even with them on the job, Susan reported:

I think my main frustrations are still the time and politics. Time meaning seeing what needs to be done and not being able to do it. And I think that's partially my problem because I accepted an agenda that was maybe too ambitious. I think most new superintendents do that. And then the second frustration is to realize that a lot of what the board is thinking about, and maybe they have to be thinking about it, is reelection. But the truth of the matter is we should have a levy on the ballot, and we won't. But the children need it and the district needs it.

Following the board's six-to-one approval of the comprehensive education plan, Susan increased her efforts to raise awareness of the financial needs of the district. This issue would become a primary focus for her energies in the second year of her superintendency. Her personal commitment to the district and its students was underscored as she responded to criticism of the costs to implement the plan:

The district is not asking for luxuries but basic necessities to educate its children. . . . If anyone expects me to reduce this tension . . . by accepting less than our children are entitled to legally and morally, they're talking to the wrong superintendent.

Consistent with her recognition of the important leadership role of principals, Susan Oliver sent a memo to each building principal, thanking them for their role in developing the comprehensive plan. She also thanked them for spreading the word about the plan and provided an extensive set of transparencies for them "to use in presentations for community and civic organizations, ward or street club meetings, festivals, picnics, and churches."

Reflecting on the unique context of the Renfield Public School District and the personal characteristics of Susan Oliver, one is led to conclude that her energy, charisma, speaking ability, and commitment to education brought welcome change in the district. Her predecessors had concentrated on the business operations aspects of schooling. The public and school employees were weary of strife over finance, personnel, and politics while watching student achievement fall.

Dr. Oliver brought hope and enthusiasm as well as expertise on cutting-edge approaches for improving teaching and learning. One reporter portrayed Susan Oliver as "charm and steel," an apt picture of someone who is tough when student needs are at stake and yet inspires people to dream and work to make the dreams come true.

As a new superintendent, Susan Oliver applied the principles of transformational and moral leadership in a city where educators had long been subjected to widespread criticism. She helped employees to believe in themselves and their power to make a difference. She believed that educators and the public shared aspirations and values for their children. She crafted strategies to help people realize their shared aspirations and build consensus as to means for meeting the commonly recognized needs of students. She provided tools to help teachers, principals, parents, and community members determine and promote what is best for students.

Oliver's approach to leadership illustrates what Owens (1995, p. 135) calls "a pragmatic view of leadership":

Two major trends in understanding leadership have been expanding and accelerating with the passage of time in twentieth century America:

- Growing recognition of and acceptance of the perception that the members of an organization constitute extremely valuable resources—rich in ideas, knowledge, creativity, and an astonishing level of human energy—that are available to the organization in the pursuit of goals and purposes that the members accept as their own.

- Growing recognition of the relative ineffectiveness of command and coercion as forms of leadership, in contrast to the development of organizational environments that are motivating, caring, inclusionary, and empowering of members as forms of leadership.

QUESTIONS FOR REFLECTION AND DISCUSSION

1. How do you think the Renfield School District was impacted by selecting a new superintendent with strong interpersonal skills and a background in curriculum and instruction rather than in the business aspects of schools?

2. In what ways were the challenges facing Susan similar to those faced by other superintendents whose case studies you have read?

3. What factors influenced the time pressures Susan Oliver experienced? What steps might a superintendent take to cope with such pressures?

4. How did the mayor's role in the election of the reform school board influence the decisions of the school board members? If you were to become the superintendent of a district in which the mayor had taken a leadership role in calling for school reform, what kind of a relationship would you want to develop with the mayor? What strategies might you use to develop that relationship?

REFERENCES

Gridley, R. C. (1990, June). *The role of the CEO as a change leader.* Paper presented at The Planning Forum, Detroit Chapter. Cleveland: McKinsey & Co.

Johnson, S. M., & Verre, J. (1993, April). *New superintendents and school reform.* Paper presented at the Annual Meeting of the American Educational Research Association held in Atlanta, GA.

Owens, R. G. (1995). *Organizational Behavior in Education* (p. 135). Boston: Allyn & Bacon.

10

DON
Breaking the Mold by
Reading at Dawn

John L. Keedy, University of Louisville

*ABSTRACT.   Don Drake does not fit the traditional mold of beginning superin-
tendents. He had been acting deputy superintendent in a progressive, metropolitan district of 100,000 students, and his biggest problem as a candidate for
the Richmond County superintendency was convincing the local board of his
sincere interest in the position. Several members perceived the Richmond position as a potential "step down" for Drake. However, Drake had a mission to
improve the instructional services of a district, and he saw Richmond, with
6,100 students, as small enough to make an impact. Two other contextual factors explaining Drake's interest in this superintendency were community
pressure for economic development and the board's commitment to school
improvement rather than micromanagement. As we shall see, such a district
fit Drake's vision of himself as a change agent and culture builder.*

We need to shift our thinking about what it means to be a strong superintendent. . . . Superintendents need to pay more attention to the heroic dimensions of leadership if they are to promote local autonomy and professionalism. Superintendents must not only have personal vision, but they must also work with others to develop a shared vision and to find a common ground; they must not only have answers but also ask the right questions; they must not only persuade but also listen carefully and consult widely before making decisions; they must not only wield power but also depend upon others and develop caring relationships. . . . In this view, the real heroes are not only the highly visible superintendents at the top but also the less visible professionals and parents throughout the system who work directly with students.

(Murphy, 1989, p. 810)

Don Drake represents such a new breed superintendent. The themes of change agent and culture builder shaped the visions Don had formed about new directions for schooling in his district. His understanding of organizational change, the use of power, working with the public, and modeling collaborative interactions for principals and teachers grounded his administrative actions in a new definition of "strong superintendent," focusing on revitalizing schools for student academic and economic success. In this chapter, I shall describe the person and district before enumerating the contextual advantages for this first-year superintendent. Then I will analyze his managerial challenges and conclude by providing an account of how he developed his twin visions for school improvement as well as the strategies and tactics used to begin implementing these visions.

DON DRAKE: THE PERSON

Don Drake, a 47-year old white male, and a Pennsylvania native, resettled in a southeastern state after graduating with a degree in German from an academically elite private liberal arts college. He taught German for three years in a large metropolitan district before entering administration as an assistant principal for seven years. He then served one year as a middle school principal before a 7-year stint as a high school principal. In 1985, he became an area superintendent and for one year was acting deputy superintendent.

Drake married an elementary school teacher whom he met after college. They have two boys, ages 14 and 17. Don Drake earned a master's and a doctoral degree in educational administration from a major state university that provided a field-based cohort program. His dissertation focused on "mentors" within a career ladder program.

RICHMOND COUNTY PUBLIC SCHOOL DISTRICT

Rural Richmond County is located on the coastal plain with 34,000 people. It has significant economic growth potential with its large farms, a sizable Coast Guard base, a regional university enrolling 2,300, a community college, and the prospect for a large prison. The county seat, which has a population of 14,000, serves as a regional service center. This is also the location of the central office for the school district, classified as a town district according to the National Center for Educational Statistics. The Richmond County Public School District (RCPS) has 6,100 pupils enrolled, of whom 45% are minority and 55% receive free lunch. The 350 teachers and 109 classified employees worked in one high school, one junior high school, and eight elementary schools. When Don became superintendent, the central office staff was comprised of an assistant superintendent for administration and 13 other administrators. The district had recently spent $20 million on capital improvements. Don later realized that the district needed an additional $20 million for the renovation of older buildings.

The seven-member school board was comprised of professional people including a pediatrician, an engineer, a computer specialist, two college professors, a housewife, and a business woman. They wanted the new superintendent to bring about comprehensive school change and improvement. Soon after Don began his superintendency, Richmond Country Public School District received a state grant to pilot outcome-based education (OBE). The proposal, written prior to Drake's appointment, helped to shape his positive perception of the district. Don Drake saw RCPS as a small district on the move, with a supportive board focused on improvement, located in a high-growth area with a high quality of life provided by coastal waterways, temperate climate, industrial growth, and friendly people.

CONTEXTUAL ADVANTAGES

Don spent 25 years in progressively responsible roles in one district. However, because of profound philosophical differences with the recently appointed superintendent about management practices, he realized that it was time to move on. He sought a role where he could make an impact on a school district. Don interviewed for six superintendencies within the state; he received five offers. During his interview at Richmond, he laid out his game plan to improve RCPS. The board was so impressed with his experience and expertise that Don's biggest problem was convincing the board that he wanted the job. Board members asked, "Why leave a large, urban or suburban district to come to Richmond?" While still a candidate, he spent two days studying the district. Don was impressed with the potential to make a difference in Richmond County: "You can't make a difference in [my former] district; it's way too big."

He accepted the superintendency largely because of the seven-member board's commitment to changing and improving the local schools, and not to micromanagement. He believed that this was a district where he could be "the superintendent," free of external meddling. It was an attractive job.

Contextually, Don had four advantages in assuming the challenge of his first superintendency. First, his earlier central office experience as area superintendent and one year as acting deputy superintendent in a large, progressive metropolitan district with a nationally recognized career ladder program made his first superintendency equivalent to lateral entry. While area superintendent, he supervised more schools than when he became superintendent.

Second, the district had a local board unhesitatingly committed to change and school improvement, and not to micromanagement. The board, after all, had outdone itself to induce Don to assume the position. Several board members had grown up in Richmond County and were well connected to the political and economic infrastructure. Don made sure that he tapped their expertise and continually sought their advice as he contemplated managerial moves and leadership directions for the district. Several board members chaired crucial committees such as finance. Don was unwavering in his perception of solid, consistent board support.

Third, the district was in a relatively high growth area with pressure for economic development. Such an external pressure fit in with Drake's mission as change agent. Changing and improving schools and regional economic competitiveness were interrelated: Status quo school administration was not a norm at RCPS.

Fourth, the OBE grant provided needed money for staff development and consultants, as well as community focus for organizational change and instructional improvement. Collectively, these four advantages were to play a major role in Don's first-year leadership.

MAJOR MANAGERIAL CHALLENGES

Don spent the first two weeks collecting information and assessing the district's strengths and weaknesses. Board members, community leaders, parents, teachers, and most administrators forthrightly identified the problems as they perceived them with Drake. Two major problems emerged: personnel and fiscal concerns.

With the board's full support, Don created a second assistant superintendency and hired the new assistant superintendent for instruction from outside the district. The two assistant superintendents became solid partners in Don's effort to implement organizational change.

Don also informally set some norms for personnel behavior when he successfully induced the resignations of two teachers, two teacher assistants, and two classified employees. The two teachers, one a first-year teacher and one new to the district, had poor performance evaluations. The two teacher assistants were involved in questions of moral turpitude, although not so gross as to have attracted external notice. And the two classified employees were unwilling to meet expectations as to duty times and completion of delegated tasks.

Don's greatest managerial problem, however, was fiscal. RCPS had a $200,000 electrical utilities debt due to a 58% rate increase. Also, in the current budget were $500,000 in nonrecurring funds, which the schools would not have the following year. Third, RCPS needed another $20 million for renovation of existing buildings.

In December, Don realized that the schools would have to request $800,000 from the county commissioners for the next year's budget, in contrast to the $75,000 they had received for the current year. "If we are not careful, everything we are doing this year [school improvement] will fall by the wayside if we run out of money." In May, RCPS received a commitment of $5 million to convert an elementary school into a middle school and a budget increase of $575,000—the largest ever for this district.

Don and the board employed three tactics to gain this monetary support. First, Don gathered data to convince the commissioners of school needs: "We spent a lot of time with the county commissioners providing them and the general public with the information so no one would rattle their sabers saying that they did not know about our needs for more money." Second, Don saw to it that the various publics perceived the schools as a major game player within the Richmond County infrastructure: "We made sure that no organization gave more to United Way than the schools did." Third, Don was highly visible at meetings frequented by Richmond County politicians. "I'm aware of the reciprocity—I've got to be interested in what they're doing if they are going to support me." These included meetings with the Chamber of Commerce, the Lions Club, the Rotary Club, and school functions such as science fairs and PTA meetings.

Dr. Drake had an apt eye to see opportunities for collaboration with community organizations: "Can we plug in our OBE plans for students in community service and somehow meet some needs of the Chamber of Commerce?" He helped forge business partnerships with the Lions and Rotary clubs and made presentations defining OBE clearly and garnering support for the project. "I was on our TV channel to talk up our forum and exit outcomes."

Another managerial challenge was that of major board policy formulation, such as smoking in public places. By June, Don and the board were over halfway through this task. Last, but certainly not least, termites were discovered in the bus garage. With the cooperation of county commissioners, RCPS made a successful bid on a building, formerly owned by a bankrupt construction company, so that buses could be safely housed.

When Don was queried about the paucity of daily and weekly crises that usually confront first-year superintendents, he said: "We're all working together well. I also think that if something happened [an obvious case of neglect or incompetence], they know I'd nail their butts. I clearly communicated that expectation." Given his personnel moves, such a perception among RCPS personnel was certainly understandable.

CONCEPTUALIZING TWO VISIONS FOR SCHOOL IMPROVEMENT

The actions just described are *managerial* in nature: Don was responding to problems endemic to the district. The challenge of *leadership*, or providing direction for improvement, remained on the front burner. Don was hired to be a change agent in a district with great potential for improvement. He had realized during his doctoral program in the late 1980s that schools had to change. Having conceptualized the problem—that of the need for deep-seated organization change—Don continued to search for an answer.

As a new superintendent, he read widely, often beginning at five A.M. His favorite professional authors included Schlechty (1990, *Schools For the Twenty-First Century*), Covey (1989, *Seven Habits of Highly Effective People*), Lieberman (1988, *Building a Professional Culture in Schools*), and Senge (1990, *The Fifth Discipline*). His reading led him to conceptualize his ideas in writing. He did much of his writing as dawn broke into a new day.

Don developed, through his reflection on schooling, two strong visions about improving schools. First, schools could not change unilaterally; they needed pressure to change. And second, the school culture itself needed to change.

Don discovered that both internal and external pressure were needed to improve schools. An internal pressure developed when teachers and principals realized a discrepancy between the *now* and the *future:* Schools as presently organized could not prepare students for the Information Age. Teachers and principals, through exchange of views with community leaders, must be the major players in school organization redesign. An external pressure for improvement emanated from public education's consumers—the parents, students, and community leaders. When teachers and principals were confronted with standards of satisfying their own customers, this created a pressure more powerful than any mandate of a state education agency. Apparently Don had a clear understanding of the ecology of schooling, such as Goodlad (1984) expressed when he observed:

> Schools do not take on emphases unless they receive rather clear messages to the effect that these emphases are wanted. Then they respond, over time, with varying degrees of effectiveness. There is, at present, no strong pressure to change the ways schools conduct the business of schooling (p. 269).

Second, Don became convinced that the traditional school workplace culture in the school district was not conducive to teacher professional growth, customer accountability, and work redesign: "If we don't have the new culture, then programs become cyclical [they don't last and are replaced by new ones]. We're working hard to determine what needs to be done to institutionalize conditions for change." Assigning the decision making to personnel most directly affected by the decisions was interrelated to professionalizing work culture: "I don't have all the answers. I just have people around me who do. I'm not intimidated by bright, capable people." Don expected central office administrators, principals, and teachers to make most of the decisions, especially since they then would be accountable for those decisions. "I don't make many decisions; everyone else makes them. . . . People don't understand power, which they equate with decision making. I equate power with knowledge and helping people to make decisions."

During February, Don spent several days visiting in Louisville, Kentucky, with Phil Schlechty, one of the scholars he so respected. As a result, Don drew up a blueprint for action in the school district. The new culture he sought to shape had three elements: structural components, curriculum, and quality student work as identified by teacher work teams with the help of consultants.

The structural culture necessitated changing roles, rules, and relationships in schools, such as using staffers to free up classroom teachers for curriculum planning. At the high school, the administrators and teachers were experimenting with a new schedule. In the curriculum culture, specialists could begin with the exit outcomes developed through the OBE grant. This provided a foundation for task analysis and curriculum mapping.

To develop standards for quality student work, teachers used structured interviews with groups of 15 students. They could then identify indicators of quality work, breaking down the exit outcomes into operable student objectives. Instead of controlling students, "what we need to focus on is developing quality work that students will engage in." For example, from these qualitative data, teachers and administrators found that students are more apt to do the work when they have the ability to collaborate with others. This information provided a strong justification for teaching cooperative learning skills.

Don had two complementary visions: the need for pressure to change combined with a new school culture. Ultimately only teachers and principals in the schools can change the teaching and learning processes. Regardless of the pressures exerted on schooling, however, teachers and principals can only change within an established collaborative culture.

STRATEGIES TO IMPLEMENT DON'S VISIONS

When visions transform an administrator's mind-set and quality of decision making, organizational change takes place. Don employed two general strategies to act upon his visions for organizational change in the school district: He educated the public, and he supported and modeled collaborative patterns of interactions with his teachers and principals. Figure 10-1 presents excerpts from an end-of-year letter Don mailed to all Richmond County personnel on setting the stage for impending organizational change.

Dear Folks:

What I think we have been about this past year is significantly different from past initiatives [in Richmond County]. For the first time we have had the financial resources and the vision to build a system that will sustain change at the district level. . . . As we continue to work together over the next several years it is important that we continue to build this system of support, or this initiative, like all the rest, will collapse under its own weight.

I believe there are nine imperatives if a district is going to support change initiatives. The first is to develop a shared understanding of the problem. . . . Second, create a shared vision. . . . Third, focus all school activities on students. . . . Fourth, create a results-oriented management system. . . . Fifth, ensure a pattern of participatory leadership. . . . Sixth, foster flexibility in the use of time, people, space, knowledge, and technology. . . . Seventh, encourage innovation. . . . Eighth, provide for continuity. . . . Ninth, foster collaboration.

We have developed a planning process that, while allowing for schools to be different, ensures that we are all connected. . . . As a result we have made progress toward becoming a district-wide team focused on results. At the school level, conversations have begun across grades and disciplines. We need to continue to build our professionalism through sharing and expanding our knowledge and expertise in a collaborative setting. . . .

Sincerely,

Don Drake, Ed.D.
Superintendent

FIGURE 10-1
Excerpts From End-of-Year Letter

Educating the Public

When told of a superintendent friend who had been fired the night before, Don responded:

He [the former superintendent] had some great ideas, but he never learned how to deal with the public. . . . You have to educate the public. After all, they have kids in school and they are all "education experts." . . . We [educators] just can't do whatever we want to do. You find out early if they don't like what you want to do.

Because his biggest long-term challenge was to build a community-wide aware-ness of the need to change, the 4-year OBE project played into Don's hands. The OBE initiative could be used as a much-needed focus and attention getter. Building on the momentum established by the OBE project, Drake set up town forums in which teachers, parents, and business leaders developed exit outcomes:

We involved the community in our exit outcomes project to build a partnership between the schools and community. The town forum developed exit outcomes. This partnership has had several advantages. The exchange of views provided a subtle form of pressure. For example, school personnel began to sense that schools must become different organizations [if only because of community demands]. We provided various sources of information on why we need to change. We brought in an expert from the state department of education on changes in the workplace. This grant also helps us in the state-level accountability program, which appears to be shifting to a student outcomes driven model.

RCPS personnel also put together a video that portrayed administrators, board members, parents, and community leaders visiting a local plant whose operations had been streamlined by computers used to create a consolidated data base for prod-uct marketing. The video was intended to help Richmond citizens perceive the need to teach different skills in schools because of the rapid acceleration of change in the world around us.

Don also was aware of the importance of communicating clearly with the various publics: "We always set up forums and task forces to get the citizens to understand why changes in public education are needed. They then begin saying the same things we believe in, and yet it's now theirs."

Don's priority for clear communication was revealed when he and the researcher visited an elementary school whose principal had designed an innovative master schedule in which classroom teachers had extended blocks of time for collab-orative planning with specialists and with other teachers. While eating lunch, Don asked the principal to explain her schedule. Later, Don reflected on her explanation: "That was the third time I heard this innovative scheduling and I still don't under-stand it. How are the parents going to understand it?"

The potential for miscommunication increased as more decision making devolved to the schools. Don was observed receiving a phone call from a parent upset with the program objectives of the high school wellness center. "I'll bet the letter sent home [describing the program] wasn't clear enough. The parent probably thought teachers were distributing condoms." Other examples included Don receiving a phone call from a middle school principal who had complaints made by parents stating that teachers were teaching science without textbooks. "We didn't educate the public enough about the need to change how we teach [toward student self-directed learning]." In still another instance, Don received a phone call from an elementary school principal whose teachers were without math texts. Don explained, "Now that schools are responsible for textbook ordering, she has to set up her own system so she knows what's going on."

Educating the community, partly through clear, simple communication, was an essential tool for a change agent and collaborative culture builder in a small town district in a largely rural county in the Southeast. Careful use of such tools prevented Don from getting too far ahead of the pack. This strategy was useful in building a supportive, aware, and receptive culture in the RCPS external environment.

Supporting and Modeling Collaborative Interaction Patterns

Building a collaborative culture within the school district required different strategies. Several tactics were used to begin transforming the school work culture from an hierarchical to a collegial model. Don and the assistant superintendent for instruction started a reading group of about 50 people, including teachers, administrators, board members, and community leaders. They read Covey, Schlechty, and other authorities and began asking questions about the need to transform work culture.

A second strategy supporting collaboration entailed helping principals establish school planning and shared decision-making teams, providing the necessary autonomy from the central office to encourage site-based management. Don and the assistant superintendent conducted 2-day workshops on changing expectations among central office administrators, principals, and teachers. Schools were given large chunks of money, from sources such as OBE and federal grants, to make their own decisions free of central office control.

Central office administrators also encouraged specialists to collaborate with classroom teachers. In elementary schools, for example, teachers and principals were examining ways for music, physical education, art, and Spanish teachers to plan integrated curricular units with classroom teachers.

RCPS personnel were linking staff development to the district goal of site-based management. They established a technology center and provided competitive mini-grants to encourage teacher innovation.

Don set and modeled expectations both with district and building level administrators and with teachers. He established an annual, reciprocal evaluation process because he believed that teachers should have the opportunity to evaluate their principals. Moreover, he thought that principals should have an opportunity to evaluate their supervisors, including the superintendent. In setting a new value structure for eventual site-based management implementation, Don began moving toward a growth orientation and a model for empowering teachers.

Drake also brought in consultants to help develop a district-wide maintenance plan that included community teams rating their schools for cleanliness. He began a long-range plan to set up a differentiated pay structure to reward risk taking and to set a new norm for a learning organization. He developed a comprehensive planning and improvement process to complement the OBE initiative. This was enhanced by the assistant superintendent for instruction, who had been hired to help with instructional assessment, as well as with other responsibilities.

Don reflected on the process of changing interaction patterns with teachers and principals:

For example, teachers at one school called me out there and wanted me to tell them about signing waivers for differentiated pay. We had quite a scene because they have never been able to make these decisions before. Now that it's "nitty gritty," they are unsure whether they want to be doing these things. I find myself playing the linker— here's what they are doing in so-and-so school, call them.

I just get other people involved in making decisions. For example, I just asked the principals to make a lot of decisions; in our district we have principals and teachers making decisions about thousands of dollars.

I had one principal most upset about a decision made. I asked her, "Why didn't you say something? You were at the meeting for two hours."

These two strategies—educating the people and supporting and modeling collaborative interaction patterns with principals and teachers—underscore the fact that Don's actions were grounded in his visions. He could practice what he preached because he had thought out what had to be done in his agenda for action and then had provided consistent support for such an agenda. "The most important thing I have done is develop a planning process for schools and the district."

In summary, these strategies functioned to change the traditional, authoritarian norms of central office control and direction to norms of school and teacher autonomy and responsibility. Even the role of teacher association representatives (reps) was changing, as illustrated by the following incident: A teacher association spokesperson had been complaining in the community that morale was "real low" at Henderson Elementary School. Don's first response to the complaint was saying, "This issue has never come up during my visits to the school." Then Don arranged to meet with the principal and the teacher rep. In the process of the discussion, the teacher rep acknowledged that she had been reporting what only one other person in the school had said.

Don elaborated to the researcher on the future of the traditional norms of teacher association reps as ax grinders and advocates: "Pretty soon this group won't be needed any more. When teacher reps talk about poor student discipline, I ask about the school's improvement plans." Don was setting the norm that teachers, as well as administrators, are responsible both for what goes on in the schools and for making plausible recommendations as to what to do about problems.

School and teacher autonomy indirectly provide a new management tool for savvy superintendents. Traditionally, teacher reps have rattled their sabers about superintendents and tried to hold them responsible for all schools—an impossible predicament for the superintendent. Under the school empowerment model, superintendents, providing resources, staff development, support, and autonomy for schools to take care of their own problems, amass the goodwill credits that allow them to pass the buck to the school.

ANALYSIS AND CONCLUSIONS

Don's extensive earlier administrative experience enabled him to make the managerial moves that set the tone for long-term school improvement in the school district. Based upon a careful assessment of the Richmond County Public School District and the community, Don made some deliberate personnel moves, hiring an assistant superintendent for instruction and inducing the resignation of two teachers, two teacher assistants, and two classified employees. He provided fiscal management by working with the board to establish a long-term facilities policy and by politicking with local community groups to gain approval of a $575,000 budget increase.

Don Drake could then begin exploiting other contextual factors, such as board commitment, economic growth, and the OBE grant, to provide the much needed leadership. The board kept its promise not to micromanage while providing consistent support for Don's exertion of internal pressure within schools through such strategies as teacher-student curricular design groups. He noted, "We are one solid group now: What gets down on paper gets tested."

The board's support appeared connected to external business pressure for school improvement as part of the initiative for economic growth. As the schools made substantial progress toward instructional improvement, board members might have perceived less need to micromanage, if they had ever been so inclined.

One incident vividly illustrates the positive nature of board support. In April, when spirits were low because of budgetary problems and teachers and principals were exhausted from team meetings on curriculum and shared decision making, board members held a surprise wine and cheese party for all RCPS personnel at the local Coast Guard station. All the board members dressed up with wigs and costumes and sang 60s music, thereby modeling risk taking. Awards were presented for outstanding school-based planning teams. Don commented about the fundamental motives of his board: "They are serving on the board because they care about kids."

Continuing professional reading and writing supported Don's first vision that schools needed both external and internal pressure for change. The OBE grant provided some commitment to change and community focus for external pressure through task forces on identifying student outcomes. Again, Dr. Drake's extensive administrative experience had provided him the skills to educate the public and provide clear, simple communication.

Don implemented his second vision—the need to change school workplace culture—largely by supporting teachers and principals. He provided staff development in team building skills and modeled the collegial interactions requisite for a collaborative culture. These skills were needed for site-based management and shared decision making.

An analysis of how Don spent his time helps illuminate his administrative practice. Budget matters consumed 26% of Don's time for the entire year. He demonstrated his commitment to educate the public about needed changes by devoting 51% of his time to this purpose, including 22% of his time for meetings within the district, 16% for change facilitation, and 13% for meetings with community groups. Communication with board members occupied 12% of Don's time. Evaluation of staff, which consumed 3% of his time, reflected a relatively low priority across the entire year for managerial practice. Most of this was done during the first few months of his tenure when he took some decisive personnel actions. [NOTE: These time categories were derived from the study data. Percentages represent averages across nine interviews.]

In conclusion, Don appeared to illustrate a good match among context, person, and change strategies. The board support for school improvement, some deft personnel moves, the economic growth potential, the community press for students to gain new skills required for information age workplaces, and the OBE grant were all *contextual* factors on which Don could capitalize. Don's considerable administrative experience and his twin visions of the needs for pressure for change and collegial school work culture were a good *personal* fit both with the district context and with his *strategies* to educate the public and set collaborative interaction patterns with principals and teachers.

This is consistent with the findings of Johnson and Verre (1993), who asserted that school reform is most likely to occur when there is a good match among the district context, the strategies, and the person of the superintendent. In essence, the critical question is, Do superintendents' actions confirm their public pronouncements about school reform?

DISCUSSION AND THEORY BUILDING

Four extant theories can be used to extend and ground findings from this case study. First, Don's earlier administrative experience was crucial to a successful first year. Such a finding is consistent with the findings of Carter, Glass, and Hord (1993), who studied career paths of exemplary superintendents and concluded: "The exemplary superintendents were far more likely to spend a few years in central office positions before acquiring appointments as superintendents" (p. 61). Don's administrative experience also enabled him to make decisive managerial moves early during his first year, such as the appointment of a new junior high principal just after assuming his role as superintendent. That move clearly set a norm of professional accountability throughout the district.

Second, Don's use of power by providing knowledge and helping people make decisions and his tactics of staff development for team building and devolution of decision making to building level approximates the facilitative power described by Dunlap and Goldman (1991). Don used power artfully, not as dominance over someone but as exercised through another: " . . . where learning and problem solving are mutual and are negotiated on the basis of collegial, reciprocal norms" (p. 8). Power as facilitation, according to these authorities, (1) decentralizes and enlarges the decision-making process by encouraging involvement by more actors, (2) encourages solutions as a function of actors and not as a function of a bureaucratic system, and (3) reduces the degree to which administrators are perceived as comprising the "visible centers of schools" (p. 22). Don's exercise of power in the Richmond County Public School District was consistent with these principles.

Third, starting with his doctoral program, Don's reading and writing related to the intellectual and moral development of administrators (Pitner, 1987). His study of the history and philosophy of education illuminated ideological discrepancies between the status quo and how things should be, providing a foundation for facing the problems of RCPS. In addition, Don's vision was grounded in his strategy for developing his professional identity by using his reading and writing as a base for administrative actions, such as shared decision making and building collaborative relationships. The stronger his own professional identity, the more inclined he became to devolve decision making in the school district to others who could benefit from this opportunity. Drake, by empowering himself intellectually, could then empower others more directly involved in teaching and learning.

Last, Don's administrative actions provide an interesting variation of the initiating structure and consideration theory of Halpin (1966). Don's "structure" was unilateral during the first several months, especially as applied to personnel matters. In the latter part of his first year, he shifted to a set of three mental images for revitalizing school work culture, including structure, curriculum, and student work. Don's "consideration" included not only traditional qualities of empathy and human relations skills but also a clear sense that administrators need encouragement to embrace a new mind-set. This mind-set led to empowering teachers, sharing formulation of student outcomes with parents and community leaders, and clear, simple communication with parents. As observed in administrative actions of beginning principals (e.g., Achilles, Keedy, & High, 1994), managerial structure setting often precedes wide-scale use of consideration—instead of structure setting and consideration being simultaneous processes.

QUESTIONS FOR REFLECTION AND DISCUSSION

1. What are some ways Don provided strong leadership while sharing decision-making power?

2. How can superintendents balance management and leadership responsibilities?

3. What can be done to accommodate the fact that administrators and teachers are usually at different levels of readiness for site-based management?

4. How can superintendents empower administrators and teachers to make decisions without abrogating their responsibility to be accountable to the board of education?

5. How do you think Don's knowledge base and keeping current with professional literature impacted the Richmond Schools?

REFERENCES

Achilles, C. M., Keedy, J. L., & High, R. N. (1994). The political world of the principal: How principals get things done. In L. W. Hughes (Ed.), *The principal as leader* (pp. 34–68). Columbus, OH: Merrill.

Carter, D. S. G., Glass, T. E., & Hord, S. M. (1993). *Selecting, preparing, and developing the school district superintendent*. Washington, DC: Falmer Press.

Covey, S. R. (1989). *The seven habits of highly effective people: Restoring the character ethic.* New York: Simon & Schuster.

Dunlap, D. M., & Goldman, P. (1991, May). Rethinking power in schools. *Educational Administration Quarterly, 27,* 5–29.

Goodlad, J. I. (1984). *A place called school: Prospects for the future.* New York: McGraw-Hill.

Halpin, A. W. (1966). *Theory and research in administration.* New York: Macmillan.

Johnson, S. M., & Verre, J. (1993, April). *New superintendents and school reform.* Paper presented at the annual meeting of the American Educational Research Association, Atlanta, GA.

Lieberman, A. (1988). *Building a professional culture in schools.* New York: Teachers College Press.

Murphy, J. T. (1989, June). The paradox of decentralizing schools: Lessons from business, government, and the Catholic Church. *Phi Delta Kappan,* 70, 808–812.

Pitner, N. J. (1987). School administrator preparation: The state of the art. In D. E. Griffiths, R. S. Stout, & P. B. Forsyth (Eds.), *Leaders for America's schools: Final report and papers of the National Commission on Excellence in Educational Administration* (pp. 41–67). Berkeley: McCutchan.

Schlechty, P. C. (1990). *Schools for the twenty-first century: Leadership imperatives for educational reform.* San Francisco: Jossey-Bass.

Senge, P. M. (1990). *The fifth discipline: The art and practice of the learning organization.* New York: Doubleday.

11

LAURA
Providing Focus by Managing Attention and Meaning

Larry L. Dlugosh, The University of Nebraska, Lincoln

ABSTRACT.   Laura moved from a nearby school district to assume the superintendency of an inner-city elementary school district where decrepit school buildings were in stark contrast with large elegant hotels, major conference centers, and tall office buildings. This small school district, where most of the 2,500 children were poor and more than half were minority, was balkanized by interlacing access and egress ramps for interstate highways. A bond issue to replace two of the schools and remodel the two others was defeated several months before Laura was employed. Laura focused her attention on curriculum and instruction and the improvement of communications while refocusing the desire for improved facilities on the needs of students. Management of attention and management of meaning were required when complex personnel and political issues threatened to distract Laura from the goal of providing solid educational opportunities for all students.

D r. Laura Elder, a 49-year-old white female, had served for 20 years as an elementary teacher, elementary principal, and assistant superintendent prior to becoming superintendent of the Ringsee School District. Typical of other first-time women superintendents, she had extensive experience in curriculum and staff development. She had worked with at-risk students and with students in special education, Headstart, and preschool programs.

When first meeting Laura, one could not help but be impressed with her high energy level and her pleasing demeanor. She presented herself as a professional, yet approachable, leader. Laura was described to the press by the school board president as having "demonstrated the leadership style and qualities that will benefit our entire community, especially the children, who are our first priority." Laura told the local newspaper that she had been interested in the Ringsee district because its focus was truly on the children and that her focus was also "people oriented."

In addition to the demands of her career, Laura shared responsibility with her brother for the care of a dependent sister. She was devoted to her sister's well being, providing both encouragement and moral support. She shared her home with her sister and helped her with transportation to and from work. She also provided many opportunities for her sister to travel with her to conferences and conventions. Laura had previously been married but was not married at the time she assumed the superintendency at Ringsee.

THE SCHOOL DISTRICT

Ringsee, a kindergarten through eighth grade district, is one of several school districts located in a large and rapidly growing city in the southwestern United States. The district, unlike the rest of the city, exhibited only a small upward trend in its population growth. The majority of the district's residents were of lower socioeconomic status, as reflected in the 74% of the students who took advantage of the free and reduced price lunch program. Many of the small homes served as residences for two or more families. The ethnicity of the 2,500 students included 51% Hispanics, 41% Anglos, and 8% African-Americans. The district maintained four separate elementary school buildings. Four months prior to Laura's entry, the district rejected a $26 million school bond issue that would have replaced two of the buildings and remodeled the remaining two.

The business district contrasted sharply with the residential areas. Within the district were many fine hotels, conference centers, and office buildings. There was excellent access to major freeways, close proximity to several colleges and universities, and a major high technology company. The district had been dissected by the construction of an extensive system of access and exit ramps to an interstate highway system. A large percentage of the land mass in the center of the district had been sacrificed to the highway project. The long-term implication was that the district might lose much of its population as a result of the displacement of people caused by the highway construction. When Laura became superintendent, the anticipated situation had not materialized; in fact, population numbers were increasing slightly.

LEADERSHIP

Bennis (1989) concluded that successful leaders need to be aware of four critical leadership competencies: (1) the management of attention; (2) the management of meaning; (3) the management of trust; and (4) the management of self. These competencies appear to be so closely aligned that a practitioner must have the capacity to utilize all of them to build and sustain a credible leadership position.

The first two competencies, management of meaning and management of attention, were the initial focus for Laura as she began her superintendency. She knew it was important to create a vision or set of intentions for the district, thereby managing meaning. She sought to constantly communicate that set of intentions to all constituencies in the school district, reflecting her management of attention. Laura believed that although the students did not choose the conditions under which they lived and learned, they deserved an opportunity to learn in the very best educational environment the district could provide. In her eyes, the meaning of *school* centered on enhancement of the learning environments for children. Laura focused her own attention as well as that of the board of education, faculty, and community on that set of intentions.

According to Bennis, the third competency, management of trust, grows from the leader's capacity to be reliable and constant—to have a record of support for issues of quality and not falter when the going gets tough. In other words, the leader proves to be reliable by not shrinking in the face of controversy when critical issues are debated. Finally, the fourth competency, management of self, focuses on the ability of leaders to manage their physical and emotional well being so they will be able to perform in a variety of career-related situations.

THE SELECTION PROCESS

The school board announced its search for a new superintendent in March after the former superintendent announced his plans to retire. Laura had been familiar with the district for a long time because she lived in the same city and served as an administrator in a neighboring school district. She believed that the Ringsee district had great potential and that her goals were compatible with those expressed by the board of education. She was encouraged to apply for the position by her own superintendent and three other area superintendents whom she considered as her advisors and mentors.

The application instructions, developed cooperatively by school and community interests, requested detailed information about communication and leadership style, educational facility and instructional philosophies, experiences serving the needs of special students, and decisiveness. The board underscored the need for a decisive leader because of the concerns surrounding the continuing need to pass the bond issue and because it wanted the superintendent to establish the future direction for the district. In her application, Laura addressed each of the questions on the list and emphasized the importance of communication with staff, board, and community.

The board requested the assistance of the state school board association to act as a conduit for applications and initial screening of candidates. The association received and screened 47 applications, narrowing the list of candidates to seven semifinalists. The board conducted initial interviews with the semifinalists and selected three finalists, two male candidates with previous superintendent experience and Laura.

Following the identification of the seven semifinalists, a special interest group in the community invited each to interview with them. The group was composed of homeowners who were opposed to the bond issue because they believed successful passage of the bond would adversely affect their ability to win a lawsuit filed against a local high technology company. They alleged that the company had polluted soil and ground water, causing the value of homes in the area to be reduced. If a bond issue were passed and people had access to new or updated school facilities, the group feared home values might increase, lessening their chance of winning the lawsuit. Every semifinalist declined the invitation.

During her final interview with the board, Laura focused on the questions the district had highlighted in the application and answered all questions as decisively as possible. Her good feeling about the interview was reflected when she said: "I thought I fit well with the needs of the district, with what they were looking for. I have good communications and people skills, and the board was looking for someone with these skills." In May, the board voted to offer her a contract with the beginning date set for July 1. The board president, when informing the media of the board's decision, said, "Dr. Elder has demonstrated the leadership style and qualities that will benefit our entire community, especially the children, who are our first priority."

ENTRY: GOALS AND PLANS

Prior to being offered the contract as superintendent of the Ringsee School District, Laura had planned a well-deserved vacation. However, once the decision was made, she knew she was on a short timeline to complete her responsibilities at her former district and become familiar with her new district. In her new position at Ringsee, a lengthy "to do" list was already waiting. A principal needed to be hired for one of the buildings and people were waiting to hear what she would do about the facility problems and the failed bond issue.

With the approval of each district, she actually worked at both jobs during the month of June, enabling her to enjoy a brief vacation prior to becoming a full-time superintendent. Laura realized it would take some mental energy to leave her former district and become assimilated in the new job. When speaking about her transition from her former position to the superintendency, Laura noted: "It was difficult, more difficult than I realized, to leave my [old] district for the new position. I was well liked, respected, had good friends there." She added: "Mostly, I was concerned about whether I could do the job. Was I making the right move? I did not have very much administrative experience, so I wondered if I was ready."

As she began organizing her entry into the district, Laura had an opportunity to review information from the former administration of Ringsee District.

The past superintendent left a number of files, memos to the board and staff, things like that. I reviewed all of them. I had a chance to talk with the outgoing superintendent at length to gain his perspective and assessment of the district. This was helpful; I'm glad to have had this opportunity.

Laura framed and initiated an informal entry plan early in June. It included several components that focused on the district, the board, the community, staffing, and student achievement. In an attempt to become acquainted with the district and its people, she met with parent and community groups, business leaders, and neighborhood associations. Laura formulated a plan for communications within the school structure and the community. She began a process of sending information to the board every Friday to highlight what had happened during the week and to focus their attention on the next week's activities.

Laura's visibility at one meeting was important for her and her constituencies, but it also proved to be an eye opener. A serious environmental concern involved a major employer and community action groups in the Ringsee School District. The state's department of environmental quality held meetings in her area. She decided to attend and try to gather information about the environmental concerns and the impact the issue held for her school district. She said, "I learned a lot about the [environmental] problem and, most importantly, which special interest groups were active in the community; this was very helpful!"

Dr. Elder moved quickly to fill the vacant principalship. She met with community and parent leaders from the school needing a new principal to gain their input about the qualities they wanted in a building leader. She interviewed candidates and recommended a new principal to the board. Laura also realigned some administrative duties and was successful in hiring staff assistants for all principals so they could devote more of their time to instruction. She interviewed teachers and administrators to fill vacancies. She also streamlined some staff supervision procedures. Finally, Dr. Elder focused on student achievement by examining the curriculum of the schools and instructional methodologies employed by teachers.

As part of her plan to strengthen communications with the board of education, Laura immediately responded to their concerns about financial matters, set up a board/administrator retreat, and outlined a plan to address how the board and administration should deal with questions and complaints from the staff.

Laura Elder's goals were to be visible and decisive, to gather pertinent information and make sound decisions that would benefit students. She moved quickly to establish her identity as a decision maker. Summing up her entry, Laura stated: "I was very visible and I made decisions. If a decision was required, I made it! People—board members, teachers, and the public—told me they appreciated this!"

THE BOARD, ADMINISTRATORS, AND TEACHERS' ORGANIZATIONS

A five-member board, four women and one man, served as the governing body of the Ringsee School District. Laura stated:

The board was a very interesting group. They were very open about the district, the problems we faced, and about each other. Sometimes, they tended to second guess each other on some issues—lots of politics involved. I was careful to listen closely and not take sides with them as individuals.

At the outset of her superintendency, Laura faced several unique situations. The first was that a man and his wife both served on the board. They worked well together and were proactive for children in the district. Secondly, the terms of three board members would expire only four months after the hiring of the new superintendent. One of Laura's immediate concerns was that she might have a turnover of three-fifths of the board that hired her. She feared that newly elected board members might have a different philosophy.

One of the incumbents, a member of a special interest group opposed to the bond issue, chose not to run again. A second incumbent, the wife of one of the board members, decided to run for the board of the high school district that served Ringsee students after they completed their elementary education; she was successful in her bid. The third incumbent, the board president, was heavily challenged by bond issue opponents but was reelected. Two new board members took their seats in January and continued to support the new direction of the district and its new superintendent.

The administrative staff consisted of the superintendent, a business manager, a curriculum director, a director of special services, and four building principals. The curriculum director and special services director were focused on children, as were the principals. The business manager was quiet and conservative and initially was not open or supportive. He had been a close ally of the former superintendent and had gained a reputation for being extremely conservative with school funds, especially funds that were allocated for teaching materials and supplies. Laura was concerned that the business manager did not offer suggestions or advice, even when asked. At times she suspected him of withholding information that could have been helpful to her. Her initial feelings suggested that she needed to work with this individual to gain his trust and bring him into the new administrative framework.

The district's teachers were members of the Ringsee Federation of Teachers (RFT), an affiliate of the American Federation of Teachers. The local organization was active and had a good relationship with the board. The working relationship with the superintendent was cordial. Part of the reason for this may have been based on Laura's recommendation to appoint the former RFT president as the new elementary principal. The fact that she listened to the leadership of the teachers' organization and demonstrated faith in their recommended candidate opened pathways for good communications and trust between Laura and the organization.

EARLY ISSUES AND CHALLENGES

Personnel issues occupied much of Laura's time early in her tenure. The first challenge to Laura's leadership concerned the hiring of the new principal and occurred before she was officially on contract. Because Laura would be working closely with the new principal, she wanted to be active throughout the hiring process. The superintendent whom she would succeed was still on duty but was cordial about her involvement.

The former principal, who had been hired from outside the district, had not been well accepted by the staff and had lasted only two years in the position. Laura did not want a repeat of this situation. The two finalists included one person from outside the district and one who was president of the Ringsee Federation of Teachers. Laura liked both candidates but recommended the insider because of the teachers' confidence in him. She believed teacher support would be a key to his success.

Immediately, one of the board members rallied a special interest group against the recommendation and was successful in delaying the appointment during the regular board meeting. One week later, the board called an executive session and requested that Laura and the principal candidate be present. In the public part of the meeting, several parents—members of the special interest group and friends of the combative board member—spoke against the candidate. However, the room was filled with parents and teachers who supported him. The board listened and voted four to one in favor of Laura's recommendation. Reflecting on this decision, Laura said:

It was uncomfortable, but I felt good about my decision and the decision of the board. Throughout the first year of his appointment, the principal has demonstrated to the board and staff that he was an excellent choice.

The next challenge presented itself when information was forwarded to the superintendent about the inadequate performance of a teacher. Laura investigated the accusations but, although they were troubling, could find nothing that could justify a recommendation for termination. When she confronted the teacher with the complaints and rumors, the teacher decided to resign. Laura was comfortable with the teacher's decision, feeling it was best for the teacher and the district. These two critical incidents occurred early in the tenure of the new superintendent, and both were resolved in ways that were positive for the district.

Superintendents depend on their assistants and associates to carry out much of the work of the district. In that light, it is important for the superintendent to have confidence in the administrative staff and to trust their decisions. As mentioned previously, the central office at Ringsee included the superintendent and three directors—a business manager, a special services director, and a curriculum director. Laura had full confidence in and the immediate support of two of the central office staff but struggled with the third. Two of the directors were recent hires, but the third had been with the district for a long time and was closely aligned with the former superintendent.

Laura, by her own admission, lacked a full understanding of budget and financial matters. Hence, she needed confidence in and the support of the business manager. For the first few months she was not able to gain his support. It was difficult to access information about past operations from him or to "get a straight answer" to a budget question. As the year progressed, Laura described the relationship with the business manager as "cordial." However, it did not develop into the strong relationship that she believed was necessary for people who work together on important issues.

Several other critical issues were identified early and required attention throughout the first year. An antitax group made itself known to the superintendent during her first two months. This special interest group favored neither the construction of new buildings nor the remodeling of old structures if the millage had to be raised. The superintendent viewed this opposition as part of a larger problem she identified within the first month of her work.

The district was undergoing dramatic changes in terms of the population it served. The growing population increasingly included ethnic minorities with few financial resources. Teachers were not prepared for students from low socioeconomic backgrounds; their expectations and instructional methods were aimed at students who were more motivated by their home environment and had greater economic means. The general public was less willing to extend their resources to provide new schools for poor and minority populations. Laura wanted to devote a great deal of her time to assisting teachers in making adjustments that would accommodate the needs of their students. She also wanted to send a message to the community that all children need the opportunity to learn in a proper learning environment, regardless of their circumstances and backgrounds.

Control of rumors has been a perennial issue for both new and veteran superintendents everywhere. Laura discovered an active rumor mill in her district, though it was not located at any particular site nor did rumors emanate from only one source. However, almost anytime change was proposed, especially if costs were involved, rumors would begin, and the superintendent spent an inordinate amount of time trying to counteract them.

One example of this situation concerned the needs assessment that Laura proposed for the district. Teachers began a rumor that the needs assessment process was going to cost the district between $100,000 and $200,000 and that the money was likely to come out of their pockets in the form of minimal salary increases. The rumor spread quickly and caused teachers to offer less than lukewarm support for the needs assessment. By the time Laura heard of the rumor, it had spread far and wide, and she needed to counteract the rumor with appropriate information. The furor subsided only when the board approved $14,000 for the needs assessment, rather than the rumored amount.

The provision of educational opportunities for all children served as Laura's focus, her platform for the superintendency. It was obvious when speaking with her that she was very dedicated to this purpose for the schools. She made it clear that she meant business, and this attitude sent a positive message across the district. Laura was determined that her first year in the superintendency would be a success. It was, thanks to a great deal of support from the board and administrative staff.

STRUCTURES FOR CHANGE

One of the structures for change was established because of the bond issue that failed during the spring prior to Laura's arrival. After the failure, some residual tension remained in the district. An antitax group thought the bond proposal had been too costly, and bond issue proponents were frustrated at the defeat because of failure to satisfy program and instructional needs.

While the needs assessment, described earlier, was in progress, Laura recommended that the board hire an architect to determine what it would cost the district to comply with the requirements of the Americans with Disabilities Act. Regardless of the results of the general needs assessment, Laura knew that an architect would be needed to design means for increasing accessibility to the current facilities. The needs assessment and architectural review made it clear that the cost of improving the facilities had been overestimated. This allowed the district to reduce its request for funds without compromising the quality of the program or the proposed facilities.

The needs assessment information and architectural assessment, coupled with Laura's constant attention to the mission of the district and the reason schools exist, helped serve as structures for change. Laura was able to focus on what was needed to provide solid educational opportunities for all children. She concentrated on talking about the needs of children and the ability of the district to meet those needs at every opportunity. Bennis (1989) referred to these leadership competencies as management of attention through vision and management of meaning through communication.

EVALUATION PROCESS

The board used a standard process for the formal evaluation of the superintendent. It occurred once a year and involved written and verbal feedback during an executive session at the December board meeting. Laura's evaluation was excellent, as indicated by the board offering her a substantial pay increase for the second year of her tenure. They were particularly pleased with her capacity to communicate with them and with the relationships she had built among the staff and in the community. She had clearly communicated her goals and focused the attention of the district on its primary task, the education of children.

From time to time, during the first semester, informal feedback was also provided by individual board members, as well as teachers and administrators. Although it was reassuring to have positive feedback, it was sporadic and not sufficiently specific to enable Laura to draw any conclusions. The formal evaluation process at midyear served as an opportunity for the board and superintendent to touch base with district goals and the direction the district was headed. It confirmed for Laura that her attention to the mission of the district and communication about the mission had been well received.

THE YEAR IN PERSPECTIVE

During her first year as superintendent, Laura was successful in her ability to focus the attention of the school board, teachers, and community on three important issues: (1) the curricular and instructional needs of the students; (2) the manner in which communications were handled throughout the district; and (3) the school district's need for improved facilities to implement quality curriculum.

It was apparent that Laura was goal oriented and that her goals were directed toward assisting children to achieve success in school. She never departed from that theme, although there were ample opportunities to do so. Also demanding her attention were a spirited school board election, the pending lawsuit of homeowners against a major business in the community, the district needs assessment, and proposed legislation at the state level that would have been detrimental to the Ringsee School District. Added to the larger issues were the regular personnel issues, board and staff concerns, and the day-to-day operations of the district. It is important to note that the overriding set of intentions for the Ringsee School District, clearly established and articulated by the superintendent, focused her attention and her energies and those of the staff on the purpose and meaning of school.

The needs assessment and architectural review that Laura recommended served the district well, helping to resolve questions of the bond issue. Findings indicated that it would cost between $6 million and $8 million less than anticipated to remodel and build the schools needed by the district. The amount of the bond issue defeated in the spring prior to Laura's arrival was 28% higher than actually necessary to accomplish the facility goals of the district. This made it possible for the board to substantially reduce the amount of money it needed to ask for in the next bond election.

Laura was a confident and an energetic leader. Throughout the first year she relied on her mentors, four superintendents in the immediate area, for advice and encouragement. She was not afraid of work; her work week averaged between 60 and 80 hours, depending on the issues. Saturday mornings were used as a quiet time at the office, time to clear the desk, have some conversations with the directors, and respond to correspondence.

When asked if she was having fun as a superintendent, she replied, "I am. I really like my job." Although there were frustrations and some second guessing about decisions she had made or things she had said, she rated her first-year experience as "7 or 8 on a 10-point scale."

As the platform for her superintendency, Laura focused on providing educational opportunities for all children. It was obvious when speaking with her that she was serious about the purpose of schooling. She made it clear that she meant business, and this attitude sent a positive message across the district. Her first year of service was successful and was made so not only by her own talents and strategies but also by a great deal of support from the board and administrative staff. Laura successfully managed attention and meaning for her internal and external audiences. As a result, she developed the trust of the community, the staff, and the board.

QUESTIONS FOR REFLECTION AND DISCUSSION

1. How would you, as a newly hired superintendent of schools, proceed to identify and communicate a set of intentions for a school district?

2. How do you think Laura's focus on "attention" impacted the faculty and staff of the Ringsee School District?

3. Why is it necessary to provide continual reminders about school district goals to all constituencies?

4. How does effective management of attention and meaning lead to effective management of trust?

5. How did the other superintendents about whom you have read manage attention and meaning in their districts?

6. Whether districts are large or small, the superintendency requires a tremendous amount of personal energy to maintain relationships, build coalitions, and communicate effectively with varied audiences. How would you manage yourself to ensure you could meet the physical and emotional demands of the job?

REFERENCE

Bennis, W. (1989). *Why leaders can't lead: The unconscious conspiracy continues.* San Francisco: Jossey-Bass.

12

THERESA AND MARILYN
An Outsider and an Insider

Mary Woods Scherr, The University of San Diego

ABSTRACT.   Two female first-time superintendents, one an outsider and one an insider, each in an urban district, offer contrasts. During her first 5 months, the outsider superintendent worked 12 to 14 hours a day, 6 days a week, spending nearly 85% of her time building community support. In contrast, the insider superintendent knew she had strong support throughout the community; the board had named her as superintendent with community urging and without a search. Both of these women faced similar problems: shrinking resources and greater numbers of students with special needs who required expensive services. In addition, bitter wrangling and threats of concerted action by the unions marked the first year for each of these superintendents. Their day-to-day lives as superintendents illustrate not only the complexities, challenges, and time pressures of the superintendency but also their personal commitment to public schools.

THERESA'S STORY: BUILDING COMMUNITY SUPPORT

Although well qualified for a superintendency, Dr. Theresa Brownell spent 18 months in search of a position. According to Dr. Brownell, she was "always competing against all males and against sitting superintendents." When a professional friend of long standing recommended that she apply for the superintendency of Alpha District, "a perfect fit," she did so. Her "relationships with teachers, kids, and community members" had always been a "strong suit." The comprehensive search process that included community involvement enabled her to demonstrate one of her significant strengths, and she became the successful candidate, entering her first superintendency as an outsider. Previously, she had been an assistant superintendent in a much larger district in another region of the country.

Alpha Unified School District, with over 20,000 students, is a high achieving, Midwest district located in a city known for its strong support for public education. The district has the potential to move toward the year 2000 with improved programs for all children and, therefore, is "an exciting place to be." The elaborate long-range plan for the district very closely matched Dr. Brownell's own vision, with its focus on "success for all students, on equity issues, and on urban issues." In addition, one of the consultants to the board for the superintendent search assured her that the job was "doable" considering the size of the district and the public's support of education.

Although Dr. Brownell entered "an extremely high achieving district," minority students were increasingly "not achieving and were dropping out of school." A "migration out of the city" and into other districts "much more homogenous and with a much lower tax rate" had begun. She felt that if the district started losing its middle, it was "really going to be in trouble."

Two members of the board that hired her on a split vote were up for reelection during her first year, and the minority population was angry because no minority candidate was among the finalists. In addition, the teachers' union was powerful and accustomed to significant raises.

Theresa Brownell began her tenure aware that the number of students requiring special services was increasing. "Even the broadest range of our services just doesn't touch some students—and that's going to increase." The numbers of homeless children, migrant students, and the population receiving Aid to Families with Dependent Children (AFDC) were all increasing. Financial constraints would undoubtedly necessitate more modest salary increases than teachers expected based on previous experience. These critical elements that she inherited foreshadowed the critical events Theresa would face during her first year in the superintendency.

The challenges for Dr. Brownell in her first year as superintendent had multiple sources: priorities established by the school board; spoken and unspoken expectations from multiple, often conflicting, special interest groups; and the pressure from a powerful union, complicated by changes in financial support for public education. The board wanted to improve the image of the schools with the media. To address this priority, Theresa initiated major strategies to be involved with schools, the community, and the media—all of which were interrelated.

Dr. Brownell visited a school the first day on the job. She believed that it was "an important message to the staff and the community that the new superintendent was out in a school." During her first five months, at the rate of 10 per month, she visited every school and each work site. Theresa held coffees at school sites "for teachers to drop by." Visibility in the schools and community were integrally related to how she expected to build community support and improve the image of schools. As a matter of practice, she included students whenever the media took her picture. Within the first six months, she made substantial progress. The media were positive; the superintendent and the schools had a high profile.

She recognized that school board members have their own constituencies that can promote or erode public support. Thus, at the beginning of her tenure, she met with each board member for two hours to learn his or her "overall agenda, personal agenda, and expectations for the new superintendent." She tabulated the concerns and gave each board member a copy of her summary for verification.

Dr. Brownell initiated regular meetings with the editorial staffs of the newspapers and television stations once a month and spent a high percentage of her time "trying to reach out to the very diverse community—trying to be approachable and listen and respond" to each segment. She estimated that 85% to 90% of her time was spent on community relations to build support for public schools. To become knowledgeable about the community, Brownell conscientiously followed a plan guided by the Luvern Cunningham Constituency Wheel (Cunningham, 1992). The plan is designed for staying in touch with all parts of the community and making sure that no groups are omitted.

An analysis of her daily schedule for a 2-week period showed that her official day, Monday through Thursday, began at 7 A.M. and continued until 10 P.M. Fridays usually ended by 6:30 P.M. In addition, she had speaking engagements almost every evening, as well as on either Saturday or Sunday. The weekdays included visits to schools, meetings with business groups such as the Chamber of Commerce and Rotary Club, planning sessions with staff, briefings regarding board of education agenda items, meetings with editorial staffs, and public addresses. On one of the days that I shadowed the superintendent, the school board held an executive session at 5 P.M. It was immediately followed by the regular bimonthly meeting that lasted until 10:30 P.M.

After two months on the job, Theresa felt she had "a sense of community issues and what's working and what's not." She believed she had "heard from every different franchise group." As a result of her intense immersion in the community, she concluded:

I see the superintendency right now . . . [with] a great deal of hope for those who want to change and change in terms of truly having parents be partners in the system rather than baking cookies and raising funds; change in terms of the minority groups expecting me to retool staff to enable them to have relationships of respect and mutual trust in decision making on behalf of children rather than just a one-way street; . . . expectations from a mayor and county executive that I will somehow really expand the partnership in terms of delivering health, social, and educational services in a very collaborative model; . . . expectations from the fiscally conservative community that I will be true to my reputation of being a good fiscal manager and yet assure success for every student.

To involve the community in more than "baking cookies" and "raising funds," she introduced a citizen budget process. She suggested to the board that the citizens have an opportunity to comment on what is important to them even before she made her budget recommendations. Did the citizens wish to continue both a very high level of service and a high property tax? Theresa created a packet of materials illustrating three scenarios for the future, ranging from the highest percentage of increase in the budget to provide the same level of service to no property tax increase and reductions in services. She listed a menu of deductions that would need to take place if anything other than the same service went through, and she asked for citizen testimony. Extremely long meetings were held, with call-in television and radio on three different nights.

Brownell, a 47-year-old, began her superintendency at a time when educators throughout the state felt an urgent need for a "new type of formula for financing public education through state resources—a better balance than property tax alone."

For 9 of the first 12 months on the job, the union and the board were in negotiations that resulted in what a local newspaper described as bitter wrangling in a nasty tenor, marked by sick-outs, slowdowns, student protests (by those who feared a sick-out would prevent them from getting college applications completed), and picket lines at school board meetings. One board meeting became "a huge shouting, screaming, walkout" after the union won a court ruling and the board announced its intention to file an appeal. A threatened strike, the first in 20 years, was avoided in an eleventh-hour negotiating session. Both sides claimed victory. Both sides also acknowledged the ill will created by the long, drawn-out negotiations and recognized the need to heal relationships between the board and the union.

During the slowdown, Dr. Brownell kept a very low profile. Other district administrators directly responsible for public relations and labor negotiations were the spokespersons. The superintendent refused to be goaded into teacher bashing or responding to gibes. She doubled her time in schools and explained to the media that her role was to keep the situation as stable as possible. When her critics demanded to know where she was when a sick-out closed several schools, a district spokesperson answered: "She's been in her office since 4 A.M. deciding which schools should close and which should remain open."

The district had developed day-to-day contingency plans to survive a strike. For a few days nearly half of the schools were closed. To assure that all efforts were coordinated, updates were prepared almost hourly. The board's reaction to the detailed contingency plans was complimentary.

Throughout these tension-filled months, Theresa experienced a great deal of autonomy as a superintendent. School board members were sensitive to the differences between board-member and superintendent roles. On one occasion, a member called to apologize for micromanaging. The district had engaged in comprehensive long-range planning prior to Dr. Brownell's arrival in the district. To implement the plan she felt she had to *motivate staff to be responsive to students and parents . . . moving staff to be positive, to do problem solving and to be accountable.*

She also planned to move the district toward an outcome-based system.

The focus needs to be on learning outcomes and not programs . . . the district continues to add programs, wonderful programs.

She explained that she wanted the programs evaluated on the basis of learner outcomes and believed it necessary to provide each school with the necessary data to begin making structural decisions.

Looking toward the beginning of the next school year, she said that she hoped schools would have plans

that are learner outcome focused; that by race, by gender, and by socioeconomic level they are very clear about where they are going with certain groups of youngsters who have not typically been successful in the school system. By year's end, they can point to growth in achievement and participation and positive attitude about learning and where they have brought students from point A to B who were not typically successful. We are trying to institutionalize the focus on students and student success.

The central staff became involved in reorganizing to become more school site-based. The focus of administrator meetings became "leadership and team building—becoming agents of change in a positive, total quality type of way—emphasis on customer service and communication." A new phone line was installed—a "one stop kind of call that parents and community members can make when they have concerns and issues they cannot get addressed elsewhere." The goodwill established by regular meetings with the editorial board and Theresa's visibility in schools and in the community resulted, in spite of the tensions, in more favorable press than had been customary in previous years.

STRATEGIES AND SUPPORT

Theresa had an excellent secretarial staff that developed a computer tracking system. The system provided a "tickler" for every assignment due to the superintendent, the board, or the community. The superintendent answered phone calls from her car when en route to schools. She worked on a plan to reorganize the district office to include a position of deputy superintendent. She switched meeting schedules to provide a block of time once a week for paper work so she was not overloaded on the weekends. She also planned to save one weekend a month when she could be out of town and not attend a meeting or give a speech.

Theresa felt the future hope for urban superintendents was to "build political alliances that [would be] required to get the resources to get the people moving together on behalf of a children's agenda." She also emphasized the importance of "the leader who continues to establish trust relationships and tells the story and keeps the vision uppermost in everybody's mind as we go through this time of change."

Almost monthly, Brownell referred to notes taken at a workshop "with ten very successful superintendents" to make sure she was "keeping up." Two or three times a month she talked to colleagues. Although she did not think of communication by telephone as one of her strong points, she recognized the need for networking. She also visited the sites of colleagues. Networking was both a strategy for success and a source of support. However, her chief source of support came from her husband. "We've always been a team," she explained. They had taken turns pursuing doctoral degrees. Even though they were geographically separated by several states (before her husband was able to relocate), Theresa still found in him her major source of support.

She also received strong support from the women in the community who held significant leadership positions in both politics and higher education. Her arrival in town as the first woman superintendent in the district was marked by a welcoming celebration. Dr. Brownell also felt fortunate to have a board that was committed to education and to children. She considered the board members truly unique. Some of her other colleagues experienced so much conflict with their boards that they were "scrambling to try to figure out how they were going to be [able to continue] speaking to their board" at the next meeting. In addition, the mayor and county executive were both committed to children. She described the city as

an incredibly rich community in terms of educational background, resources, and willingness to make the city what it needs to be for the future.

Dr. Brownell made a definite overture to the faith community and spent a lot of time in different churches every Sunday. As a result, the faith community was extremely supportive. She also received support from the broader community where she spent most of her time.

FRUSTRATIONS AND REWARDS

The recurring theme during Dr. Brownell's first few months was lack of time. She needed more time to "physically survive," to work with the board members, to be with teachers, and to build support for change at the district office. She needed time to workout and time to take vacation days. During the first nine months, she worked most weekends and did not have a single full week of vacation time.

Theresa also explained that unwillingness to change on the part of the central office staff was a big frustration. Many of the administrators had been in the district for a long time, and because the district had enjoyed a wonderful reputation, they were not motivated to change.

She felt she needed to devote more time to the board, to stay in touch on a one-to-one basis. Because the long-range plan for the district so closely matched Dr. Brownell's own professional vision, she did not find her priorities in conflict with those of the board. However, communication with members did take time.

Dr. Brownell wanted to give more time to teachers. The previous superintendent had an adversarial relationship with teachers, and they were unsure of someone who wanted to collaborate. "They don't trust me yet," she concluded after a few months in office. The district was at an impasse with the union over participatory management. "They are labor, and they want no involvement in management decisions and don't want to be accountable for them."

Other difficulties included land acquisition that involved dealing with both the city and county government and which required extensive negotiations that raised racial, social, and economic issues. The decision regarding where to locate a new school and pressure from a minority group to fire an administrator were examples of other time-consuming problems.

While shadowing her for two days during site visits, I experienced her heavy schedule, but I also gained several significant clues to the rewards she experienced. For example, since the beginning of her superintendency she kept a scrapbook of news articles featuring students. She sent a laminated copy along with a letter of praise to each student featured. A mother of one of the high school girls wrote a thank you note to say what an inspirational model Dr. Brownell was for her daughter. Also that day, while visiting a middle school, one of the students looked up as we entered the classroom and said to another, "I know who *she* is. *She's* the superintendent." Another example occurred the next day while driving between appointments. We stopped at a Taco Bell for lunch, and just as Dr. Brownell was saying that "this is as good as it's going to get," two high school girls walked up to us in line and beamed at the superintendent, saying: "We go to Lincoln High, and we met you last week." The superintendent enthusiastically engaged them in a conversation about activities at the school.

By visiting the schools, Theresa Brownell demonstrated a strong commitment to the improvement of instruction and to serving as a role model for young women. The importance of relationships with students, staff, parents, and the broader community was central to her philosophy. It was so central to her conception of the superintendent's role that she was unwilling to reduce her time in the schools and community in spite of her concern that paper work and meetings at the district office could overwhelm her. Fully aware of how much time community building took and of its difficulties, Theresa spoke of

trying to reach out to the very diverse community and trying to be approachable and listen and respond to all of them simultaneously, which is difficult at times.

The community's response to public education was one of the most rewarding aspects of being the superintendent of the Alpha District:

. . . the willingness of people who were ready for change and now have an agenda to move forward and a vision . . . trusting that that vision is student-centered and truly committed to 100% success for every child . . . being able to take that message to a community that is so willing to help and be involved.

MARILYN'S STORY: CHALLENGES FOR AN INSIDER

When the superintendent in a large Southwestern district became a finalist for another position, the school board began receiving "widespread public support . . .

from all around the city" for a particular central office administrator to be named as the next superintendent. Eventually, therefore, Deputy Superintendent Marilyn Collins, at age 59, became the superintendent of the Delta Unified School District. This urban district enrolled over 125,000 students of which 60% were minority students and over 40% were below the poverty line. Dr. Collins, a minority woman, had been in the district for over 25 years, moving up from teacher to principal to central office administrator before becoming superintendent. The board's decision to offer her the superintendency without a search was unanimous.

Although Dr. Collins was hired because the board was happy with the direction in which the district was going and she had been a part of the progress, she felt it necessary to articulate her vision: "People will question—wonder if we're going in the same way or whether something is new." After a short time in the superintendency, she believed that staff members were reassured that her vision would not send the district in a new direction.

Requests for speech making increased dramatically over those of the prior superintendent. "I don't know whether it's because I'm new, because I'm good, or because I'm cheap," she laughingly commented. She thought the political environment, namely statewide school financing problems, contributed to the requests, and tried to get as many of the requests on her calendar as possible. She spoke to local organizations three or four times a week.

Like the Alpha district, the Delta district was experiencing changing demographics, budgetary constraints, expectations for more public involvement, union problems, and media demands. The Delta district was growing, and "the new students cost more to educate because of language differences, because of special education needs, and because of reading difficulties or learning issues—problems related to poverty."

The shortage of money for city and county agencies, for nonprofit organizations, and for the public schools was forcing collaboration across boundaries once considered sacred.

It's the feeling on the part of each of us that our work touches one another, and as resources become restricted, it's important to know what the other is doing . . . and push toward greater collaboration and efficiency.

Integrating services for children from a variety of agencies had already begun in Delta district, and extensive plans to expand those collaborative efforts were well underway.

Traditionally, citizen involvement has meant serving on advisory committees. However, today "people want to be involved from the development of something and not just have things handed to them." For instance, a large group of business people working with the district to establish a new high school, "helped to shape the curriculum," and to "shape and provide training in total quality." Another group of citizens worked with the district to develop a health careers magnet school. Involvement at these levels "takes a lot of time because they want to sit with you and work through the development."

The union protested a decision of the board, considering it a unilateral action in violation of the contract. They expressed their displeasure by issuing a resolution of intent to engage in concerted action if the administration did not take strong steps toward collaboration. Efforts to promote more collaborative management-union relationships were initiated by the central office staff.

Meetings related to the media also take a superintendent's time. The media have "strong feelings about their rights and responsibilities." These feelings sometimes conflict with administrators' belief that as public officials they are "charged with running schools, maintaining safety and order, and looking out for children and their learning environment." These disagreements necessitated new guidelines for working together.

The time Theresa and Marilyn required to learn the needs of the district and to gain support from the community varied dramatically. The difference between being an outsider and being an insider was clearly a major factor. After four months on the job, Dr. Brownell reported that she spent nearly 85% of her time in building community support. When I asked if she felt that was due to being an outsider, she answered with a resounding "Yes."

Dr. Collins was aware that what might be an advantage for an insider superintendent could also be a disadvantage. She stated:

For the person who is on the inside and knows where the skeletons are, I think we tend to be impatient to get on with a number of change efforts and so you may push on the organization faster than it is ready to be pushed. On the other hand, it may be that you are able to seize the opportunity and the momentum and to get some things done. . . . The class size reduction proposal is an example. . . . I could cut through to the bottom and suggest places where people could make the cuts . . . shift resources . . . that no one from the outside could probably do as quickly. . . . This took decisions to shift . . . some $9 million . . . at a time when we have critical financial problems. . . . In that context it was quite a change . . . not without pain, not without concern, not without all of the uproar that would go along with something like that. But if you were from the outside, I think it would be very, very difficult for you to pull off.

In the following statement, Dr. Collins explicitly described the advantages she saw of being an insider:

One of the things I had going for me was the knowledge that lots of people supported me, and I enjoyed their respect for my integrity. . . . that's at the core of your leadership . . . even the things that you don't know how to do will be forgiven until you learn how to do them. But if you have to go in and establish your character, your integrity, those basics, then every little thing can stand out as a major flaw. The support I had was an important plus going into this. Everybody is going to make some mistakes; some problems are just brand new mutations. [You] just need to use your knowledge, your relationships, and the expertise of others.

Marilyn also discussed disadvantages for an insider:

Certain communities have been waiting over a period of time for certain changes. . . . Someone from the inside is expected to be able to know that . . . and be able to move. . . . Someone from the outside is given more of a honeymoon and can stand on the learning curve, so to speak, a little longer time.

Dr. Collins also believed that if a new superintendent did things differently from the expectations, particularly the expectations of staff, he or she would be in trouble:

If you take a risk and do some things that are maybe a little alien to their culture . . . you are not forgiven as quickly. . . . You should have known; you should have known that wasn't something we liked.

Throughout this discussion, Dr. Collins presented disadvantages as well as advantages of being an insider. In conclusion she said: "The real advantage is one of credibility. If you have it and are an insider, I think it is a tremendous boost because you don't have to develop that."

STRATEGIES AND SUPPORT

Early in her tenure, Dr. Collins met with the board of the administrators' association. She stressed the importance of all the leadership groups. She believed that

understanding, buying in, so to speak, and the more you can develop that understanding and answer their questions and give them a chance to make comments and suggestions, the more commitment you're developing along the way.

She also met with the teachers' association board of directors during her first two months, a meeting that she termed *significant.*

Within the first two months, Marilyn held a mini-retreat with school board members, asking them to reflect on her performance. She also shared her perceptions of the board's performance and discussed communications between board and staff members. She planned to hold these "close conversations" with the board throughout the year and to maintain "shorter time frames for talking to one another . . . and have a chance to correct things more quickly."

To model with her central staff the processes she hoped they would follow, she emphasized open communication. She considered it absolutely essential that the cabinet be supportive of her efforts. She admitted that she found herself "with one foot in old behavior," just like everybody else, while moving into new ways of behaving:

We have to constantly talk about it. As a cabinet we are encouraging each other to be open in that regard. . . . We take time in each cabinet meeting to go around and do what we call reflections. In reflections people can . . . take a minute or so . . . talk about what has happened during the week . . . what is coming up . . . some of the learning . . . how you think things are going. Team building is developing out of those discussions.

A portion of each cabinet meeting functioned as a study group:

We are doing a common reading, Reinventing Government [Osborne and Gaebler, 1992] . . . We take a couple of chapters and different cabinet members lead

*[the discussion] . . . a different approach by each cabinet member . . . the budget
people leading some . . . the data assistant . . . the attorney. . . . so it is not the usual
instructional consultant. . . . When we reach the last chapter, we want to reflect back
. . . and come to grips with the whole book.*

These discussions encouraged interdisciplinary thinking and the ability "to see [the
situation] in a proactive way."

Cabinet meetings were held in a different school nearly every week. The principals from that school cluster were invited to join the cabinet. In addition, three principals from different levels rotated membership on the cabinet each month, and the
middle managers from the central office were also included on a regular basis. In
these ways, the superintendent tried to keep a maximum number of people involved
with cabinet discussions without overwhelming the meeting with too many participants. Because education is "a people intensive business—nurturing and developing
your staff," Marilyn spent a lot of time trying to get resources for staff development
and thinking how best to use them.

Dr. Collins was acutely aware that the role of the superintendent required her to
be "in touch" with the "external public as well as the internal public."

*Today's world requires that you not only inform but also be informed; so the idea of
involving others, and knowing how, and how many, and what kind of representation to
involve is key. . . . You have to listen in so many different areas in order to come up
with that collective response . . . not in any way offensive to any particular group . . . a
delicate balance. . . . That's important.*

Working with the board also required a heavy time commitment. Board members
are political people who must be responsive to their constituencies. That awareness
meant she needed to talk with them to assure them that a collective vision represented their interests as well as her interests as superintendent—a task she described
as "leadership at its best."

When Marilyn Collins talked of the need for resources, she also talked of the
need for time and solitude. When asked what she discovered about the role of the
superintendent that she had not anticipated, she responded: "I had not estimated the
overwhelming impact on your time. Although I was very, very busy as a deputy
superintendent, I still had underestimated the impact it would have on time."

The role also included more dimensions than she had expected. For example, a
conflict over affirmative action forced the district to shut down a construction site
until the controversy could be resolved; and two cases of meningitis at a secondary
school catapulted her into health care discussions and medical policies. Even though
she had been acting superintendent periodically on numerous occasions, she found
that being the district spokesperson "kicks it [the responsibility and pressure] up to a
different level." Her tenure, like Theresa's, was also complicated by the fact that the
state was considering major changes that would impact the financing of education.

The demands and influence of the media also called for particular skills. As
superintendent of the largest district in the county, she knew the focus was always on
her district, and she increasingly realized that she was "constantly on-stage."

Dr. Collins described herself as "spiritually centered" with "deep roots in the church as a strong anchor."

For African Americans, the church has played such a central role dating all the way back to the days of slavery. . . . That has been a core family value that parents have pushed. . . . Since most of us came from a poverty background . . . and did not have access to a lot of other options, the church became an all encompassing kind of experience . . . continues as an important strand.

To reduce stress, on the way to work she tried to focus on what she described as "a few words of anchoring or prayer for a balanced outlook for the day" rather than think of her work as problem-oriented. She described herself as someone who likes and is comfortable with people but is also "very comfortable spending time alone in reflection and reading." From conversations with Dr. Collins, it appeared that she had good friends, relationships that she valued, and a lot of support from family and the community.

FRUSTRATIONS AND REWARDS

The only frustrations for Dr. Collins appeared to be lack of time and the continuous realization that things do not change as fast as she would like. As to what was most satisfying about being a superintendent, she was not sure whether her views applied to just the superintendency or whether they represented the way she felt about life:

I think you have to love what you are doing, and it has to be personally rewarding . . . you don't get paid enough nor could you get paid enough for what you do. . . . The rewarding thing for me in the urban school district is that . . . I see the connection between what I do, the kinds of things I am pushing, and the neediest students in our society. [It's] rewarding when I can see some of those things moving in that direction.

CONCLUSIONS

The differences between being an outsider and an insider during a first year as superintendent was clearly captured in the words of the superintendents themselves. In spite of the difference in size between the two urban districts, the major challenges they faced during their first 12 months were remarkably similar: changing demographics, an increase in the number of students requiring special services, severe financial constraints, and greater expectations of public involvement. The major personal challenge was how to find the time to meet the demands of the position.

Long days were typical for both superintendents, but, at several points during the study, Marilyn, the insider superintendent, reported significantly lower levels of stress. When asked about the job after just two months in office, Marilyn replied, "It's starting to fit." In response to the same inquiry, Theresa replied, "Stretched pretty thin."

Theresa Brownell, the outsider, spent 85% of her time in the community to gain public support for education and to hear what the various groups were saying so she could respond to their needs. Marilyn Collins was able to build support for her vision with her board, her cabinet, and her managers early in her tenure. Although she gave frequent speeches, attended civic meetings, and made regular television appearance, she began her tenure with strong public support and firm support from professional friends both within and outside the district.

As an outsider, Theresa once remarked that she did not know how long anyone could keep up with the daily schedule. On one occasion early in her tenure, a woman in a department store recognized the new superintendent from newspaper pictures and introduced herself as a former superintendent in another state. Dr. Brownell was surprised to hear herself blurt out, "How long did you last?"

Dr. Collins had a staff she knew well and to whom she was able to delegate with confidence, another example of a difference accruing from insider status. While waiting for an interview with Dr. Collins during a site visit, I heard a secretary tactfully explain, "Dr. Collins relies on the assistant superintendents to resolve that type of problem. They are the ones who know the individual school situations most clearly. I suggest you talk with Dr. Whitney. Her number is . . . or, I can transfer you now."

In contrast, Dr. Brownell found it necessary to institute a hot line as a "one-stop call" for parents who could not get answers to their problems. During her first few months she met with parents several times to try and determine why their children's needs were not being met. When asked specifically why district staff members could not meet with these parents, Theresa explained that she was not sure they could convince parents that the district was committed to quality services for *all* students, and she did not want families moving out of the area.

Should the gender of these two superintendents be considered in a discussion of their professional roles? Sandra Harding (1986) maintains that gender is a "fundamental category" (p. 57). Women superintendents are usually treated differently because of pervasive sexism in society, and they may fulfill the role differently from most men because of socialization and/or different career experiences.

In her scrapbook, Theresa Brownell saved a note from a principal apologizing for the "appalling introduction" the superintendent had received from a staff member and thanking her for the "gracious manner" in which the superintendent had clearly indicated its inappropriateness and sexism.

I asked Dr. Brownell if she perceived gender differences between men and women superintendents. "Absolutely," she replied. "I have a list." The list included inappropriate and illegal questions surreptitiously asked during recruitment as well as recurring inappropriate questions asked during interviews. The newspaper articles proved that both her wardrobe and hair style generated criticism, two topics far less likely to be under scrutiny for men.

Marilyn Collins, the Delta superintendent, did not volunteer any anecdotes regarding gender. One explanation may be that she was promoted within a district where 50% of the principals were women. Moreover, even before Marilyn's promotion, women comprised 50% of the superintendent's cabinet. This ratio of female administrators is far larger than in most of the nation's school districts.

During one interview, Dr. Brownell explicitly explained her preference for collaboration and non-adversarial relationships. She had no concern for who gets the credit. Neither of these women used expressions typical of administrators, which, according to Kempner (1989), are terms borrowed from the world of sports, the military, or business, such as *making things happen*, *taking charge*, and *a can-do attitude*. According to Kempner, in coaching and in the military, "the leader has singular responsibility for moving the team, platoon, or organization forward. Orders are taken from higher authority without question" (p. 109). In contrast, schools are emphasizing collaboration and community school partnerships. Kempner believes that business terminology is also inappropriate because

> public education is not profit oriented . . . [and] the creative education of children is not necessarily an efficient process. . . . This adoration of business by educators is a "corporatist" mentality based upon a capitalistic orientation that separates the owners of the means of production from the laborers (p. 109).

Because of their career backgrounds, both Marilyn and Theresa took far more active roles in curriculum development than their male predecessors. As reported by Glass (1992), female superintendents typically have taught longer than male superintendents.

It is important to note that although Dr. Brownell was aware of gender differences in leading, the superintendents she admired were not limited to women. She specifically referred to a male colleague whose district she visited during her first year to learn the specifics of his organizational plan.

Both women began their tenure extremely well qualified for their positions. Both had extensive knowledge. However, Dr. Collins had strong relationships within the district and knew which members of her staff would be loyal and which members had what kind of expertise. In contrast, Dr. Brownell had to gain the confidence and trust of the board, her senior staff (especially the cabinet), and the community. Because she had moved to a new area, she had no support system in place either within or outside the world of education. She did, however, receive an enthusiastic welcome from the community. Women in positions of leadership, political as well as academic, greeted her in a celebratory spirit. The community continued to be a source of strong support.

Over a decade ago, Klein (1983) noted the distinction between research *on* women and research *for* women. This chapter explicitly seeks to benefit both prospective and current female superintendents by exploring multiple aspects of the superintendency as experienced by two women, each in a different setting. Recent research (Rosener, 1990) has indicated that women tend to exhibit a different way of leading: more collaborating, more listening, and minimizing the hierarchy in organizations. These differences, however, can easily be masked unless researchers are alert to the types of questions that need to be addressed. "The submergence of women in an all-encompassing male or genderless category distorts their unique experiences" (Bensimon, 1989, p. 144).

According to Gilligan (1982) and Lyons (1983), women tend to follow a "care orientation" when making moral decisions. They place greater emphasis on relationships than do men. They are also more likely to consider the particular context and whether a decision will maintain a relationship, hurt a relationship, or relieve a burden. Men tend to follow a "rights orientation," placing greater emphasis on fairness, rights, and principles. The "rights orientation," also referred to as the "justice orientation," is the basis of our legal system. With the current emphasis on caring, expressed most notably by Nell Noddings (1992) in her book *The Challenge to Care in Schools*, superintendents need a care orientation for decision making, as well as a justice orientation. Both orientations are needed in a superintendent's repertoire so that the one most appropriate for the situation can be followed. Unfortunately, only the justice perspective has been studied and observed by most administrators.

A similar perspective was expressed by Tom Sergiovanni, in an interview with Ron Brandt (1992), when he said:

> Management literature traditionally was written by men for men, and its values—individualism, competition—define success in a masculine way. . . . Women tend not to define success and achievement that way. They are more concerned with community and sharing (p. 47).

The interviews with Marilyn and Theresa revealed that these two women stressed the importance of listening and collaborating. Their language did not stress "command and control," and they most definitely did have the courage to care. However, these data are only suggestive. Not all authors consider gender "a fundamental category." Further research is necessary to document the unique ways in which women may fulfill the role of superintendent.

Chapman began this volume by describing the need for well trained superintendents (Murphy, 1991) and reporting the short tenure of urban superintendents (Daley, 1990; Scherer, 1995). Tallerico, Burstyn, and Poole's (1993) work warns of the many reasons women exit the superintendency. One of the women studied in this chapter did not know of a single woman superintendent who had signed a second contract. On the contrary, every woman superintendent she knew did not desire another term. The findings in this chapter suggest questions that must be addressed by both researchers and practitioners to better prepare and support women superintendents.

Both of the superintendents in this study stated that they would quit when it stopped being fun. Considering their schedules and pressures, I'm reminded of a cartoon from the *New Yorker* showing one ant at the top of the hill and another ant trudging up the hill with a huge load on his back, calling out, "I'll quit when it stops being fun."

QUESTIONS FOR REFLECTION AND DISCUSSION

1. How can women superintendents be supported in their new positions?

2. How can superintendents be better prepared for urban problems related to having more students to educate that cost more to educate (students with problems related to poverty); budgetary constraints requiring collaboration across agencies; union-management and a public more demanding of engagement?

3. More specifically, how can superintendents gain the skills necessary to build collaborations across agencies?

4. How can they involve multiple community groups, often in conflict with each other, in school planning?

5. How can the burden of the superintendency be lessened? Is the role less and less feasible now that male as well as female superintendents usually have working spouses?

REFERENCES

Bensimon, E. M. (1989, Spring, published in 1991). A feminist reinterpretation of presidents' definitions of leadership. *Peabody Journal of Education, 66*, 143–156.

Brandt, R. (1992, February). On rethinking leadership: A conversation with Tom Sergiovanni. *Educational Leadership, 45*, 41–45.

Cunningham, L. (1992). *Monitoring, mapping, and interpreting the sources and content of change.* Gahanna, OH: Leadership Development Associates.

Daley, S. (1990, December 26). School chiefs dropping out, plagued by urban problems. *The New York Times*, p. 1.

Gilligan, C. (1982). *In a different voice.* Cambridge, MA: Harvard University Press.

Glass, T. E. (1992). *The 1992 study of the American school superintendency: America's education leaders in a time of reform.* Arlington, VA: American Association of School Administrators.

Harding, S. (1986). *The science question in feminism.* Ithaca, NY: Cornell University Press.

Kempner, K. (1989, Spring, published in 1991). Getting into the castle of educational administration. *Peabody Journal of Education, 66*, 104–123.

Klein, R. D. (1983). *How to do what we want to do: Thoughts about feminist methodology.* In G. Bowles & R.D. Klein (Eds.), *Theories of women's studies* (pp.88–104). London: Routledge & Kegan Paul.

Lyons, N. P. (1983, May). Two perspectives: On self, relationships, and morality. *Harvard Educational Review, 53*, 125–145.

Murphy, J. T. (1991, March). Superintendents as saviors: From the terminator to Pogo. *Phi Delta Kappan, 72*, 507–513.

Noddings, N. (1992). *The challenge to care in schools.* NY: Teachers College Press.

Osborne, D. E., & Gaebler, T. (1992). *Reinventing government: How the entrepreneurial spirit is transforming the public sector.* Reading, MA: Addison-Wesley.

Rosener, J. B. (1990, November–December). Ways women lead. *Harvard Business Review, 68*, 119–125.

Scherer, R. (1995, June 19). Big city school superintendents are posting high dropout rate. *The Christian Science Monitor*, pp. 1, 18.

Tallerico, M., Burstyn, J., & Poole, W. (1993). *Gender and politics at work: Why women exit the superintendency.* Fairfax, VA: The National Policy Board for Educational Administration.

13

PHILBERT
Battling Bond Barriers

William M. Gordon, Center for Program Design, Saluda, North Carolina

ABSTRACT.   Though Philbert was only 42 years old, he had 18 years of experience as a school administrator when he became superintendent of a 1,400-student rural district. Philbert's predecessor had operated in a relatively laissez faire manner, leaving building principals to operate in their own spheres. Though principals would be receiving more direction, Philbert wanted them to assume more prominent leadership roles. He helped principals to develop as instructional leaders by working with them individually, encouraging them to gain new skills, and directing them to set goals and objectives for their schools. Although concerned about educational leadership, the most time-consuming challenge facing Philbert was securing the passage of a bond issue that had failed three times before he was employed.

Philbert Green is a white male in his 40s. He is bald and left-handed, so we hit it off immediately. His first superintendency was in Wee Hawkin Local School District, a 112-square-mile rural district 40 miles south of a major metropolis.

The system is a William Bennett paradise. It is composed of mostly white farmers; less than 1% are Black and none are Hispanic. There is one Asian-American family. Approximately 19% of the students qualify for the free-lunch program; these students come from a large trailer park—a virtual mobile ghetto located on the "main road." The school board, until the last election, was all white male; it now includes one white female. Apparently the board members all go to church and attend all football games. Board meetings end early during planting and harvesting seasons.

Although a large Amish population lives in the area, only ten Amish families have chosen to enroll children in the district. The farms in the community are small to mid-sized, so few inhabitants derive their sole support from agriculture. Because the district has little industry, it is not wealthy. Wee Hawkin's per pupil expenditure is approximately $1,000 below the state average and $250 below the county average. The modest resources available limited the district's program, salaries, and facilities.

Wee Hawkin Local Schools employed 85 certified staff, of whom 64 were class-room teachers. The teaching staff was a veteran group with 69% having 10 or more years experience in the system. However, only 26% of teachers held graduate degrees. In addition to the certified staff, the system employed 46 classified staff, including 13 bus drivers and 8 food service workers.

Four school buildings served the students of Wee Hawkin Local. The superintendent's office was in a building that also housed the bus maintenance garage. The 35-year-old high school was the district's "new school." Of the other three buildings, the junior high structure was 88 years old, one elementary school was 72 years old, and the other 116 years old. Though some additions to these three buildings had been made over the years, the most recent addition had occurred 30 years earlier.

The student population of Wee Hawkin had remained at approximately 1,400 for some years and was expected to continue at this level through the end of the century. Average daily attendance was 94.9% of the average daily membership. Achievement of high school juniors and seniors who took the ACT equaled the state average and slightly exceeded the national average. The dropout rate of 8% was impressively modest considering the significant presence of Amish in the area. (Amish families generally encourage their children to quit school as soon as compulsory attendance laws permit.)

THE NEW SUPERINTENDENT

Philbert Green was 42 years old when he was selected to be the superintendent of Wee Hawkin Local School District. Prior to his appointment as superintendent, he had spent 3 years as a high school language arts teacher, 1 year as an elementary principal and special education coordinator, 4 years as an assistant junior high principal, and 13 years as a high school principal. During some of those 13 years, he also served as an assistant transportation coordinator and a district athletic director. Of his years as high school principal, 6 were in a 1,200-student school in a mid-sized city.

Because of Philbert's experiences as an administrator, he decided he would like to have the opportunity to head a school system. Having made this decision, Phil wrote to the state superintendents' association, informing them that he was in the market for a superintendency and requesting their assistance. His only condition was that the position had to be in the state.

When assessing his personal strengths, Green cited curriculum and public relations, having experienced success in both areas during his tenure as high school principal. Strengths he did not cite were his very friendly nature and ability to place people at ease almost immediately. Phil Green could best be described as laid back, a good listener, and comfortable with those in his presence. A board member indicated that he was selected for the position mainly because of his public relations skills and the fact that there had been three recent failures of bond issues.

After a visit by Wee Hawkin board members to his district during the interview process, they agreed unanimously to offer him the position. Green reported that he had not been able to determine where his support on the board came from. During the selection process, he had observed an indifference in how the board members dealt with each other, leading him to infer that the members did not know one another well.

The Wee Hawkin district (K-12) had barely 200 students more than the high school Philbert was currently administering. However, he was drawn to the position because he saw an opportunity for personal development, a school system that appeared to be fiscally well managed, and a rural location similar to one he had enjoyed in his early years as an educator.

When the time came for Green to decide whether to accept the position, he faced two issues. First, he was concerned about his own children's educational opportunities. His present position was in a strong mid-sized school system that enjoyed good public support and a variety of educational opportunities for its students. He knew the new system would have a more limited set of program offerings and would be void of the cultural diversity of the larger system he would be leaving. Housing for his family was his second concern, because the contract required the superintendent to reside in the community. In fact, once Green accepted the position, the absence of adequate housing and his commitment to comply with the board's mandate forced him to live in a small apartment.

INITIAL CHALLENGES

The greatest challenge that Philbert faced was financial. He knew he had to maintain the fiscal integrity of the system while addressing significant deficiencies in facilities and programs. The tax base was low because of the prevalence of agricultural land and the absence of industry.

Green focused on getting acquainted with the people, listening to their concerns, and determining what they saw as educational needs. He also faced the reality that the past three bond issues for facilities upgrade and replacement had failed by substantial margins.

As a first step in reviewing the system and charting a direction, he established a 20-member steering committee. The committee was composed of school personnel and citizens from the community and chaired by two of the members. This group became a strategic planning committee. First, they gathered information about all aspects of the district's operation, programs, and curricular offerings. Various members of the committee chaired focus groups to involve community members in planning for the district's future.

In the curriculum area, students had not done well on the state proficiency examinations in mathematics and science; deficiencies were evident in both instructional materials and equipment. Only a few computers were available in the district. Philbert also found that the teaching staff was in need of in-service workshops.

DISTRICT CLIMATE

Although it is not fair to say that the district had no direction, it is accurate to note that the former superintendent had given building administrators only modest leadership. As a result, each principal independently determined his own direction. There was a void in planning and an absence of objectives beyond the immediate needs of the schools and classrooms.

Recognizing the signs of long-term administrative neglect, Phil worked with each principal reviewing the school's performance and looking to the future. Each principal was directed to work with his staff and to prepare some goals and objectives for the school. Likewise, the administrative team devised district-wide goals, providing direction hitherto unknown in the district.

Throughout the beginning stages of the new administration, the school board remained supportive. However, Philbert learned little about each member other than his or her level of involvement in the district and some personal information generated through informal contacts and board meetings.

A dispute developed within the high school booster organization at a critical point in the bond issue campaign. The illusive bond issue would enable the district to build a new high school. However, a contingent of the boosters felt that building plans did not adequately address the athletic facility needs of the school. Thus, they began a campaign to have the plans changed to include more elaborate facilities. Tempers flared and boosters squared off against one another when the group could not reach consensus. This did not bode well for bond issue efforts.

There was relative labor peace in the district. The teacher organization was the state affiliate of the National Education Association. A local classroom teacher association existed, but it was a loosely organized group and fairly passive. A new professional agreement had been negotiated just prior to Phil's employment, but there were some specific areas that needed to be finalized. When he met with association officials, he indicated that, as superintendent, he would not work outside the agreement, pledging himself to work closely with the association's leadership.

The central issue left from negotiations was clarification of the teachers' conference time; the negotiated agreement called for each teacher to have 200 minutes per week. The need for clarification arose when some principals interpreted the 200 minutes to be within the teaching day rather than within the student day. The matter was finally resolved to everyone's satisfaction. This was Phil's first encounter with the association and his first opportunity to reach an accord with his teachers over a contested issue.

In Philbert's state, county superintendents have certain controls over local superintendents. For example, though a local school board selects the local superintendent, the county superintendent must also give approval before the individual is given a contract. Likewise the county superintendent must give approval to a local school board's budget and to any plan to place a bond issue on the ballot.

The county superintendent for Wee Hawkin was particularly active in local school matters, exercising his oversight roles with vigor and in positive ways. Early in Phil Green's tenure as local superintendent, the county superintendent provided helpful technical assistance and contacts with the Wee Hawkin school board and personnel.

However, the county superintendent's most valuable contribution was a day-long retreat led by personnel from the state affiliate of the National School Board Association (NSBA). During the retreat, the Wee Hawkin board was made aware of the proper role of a school board member. They developed a series of consensus-driven "We Agree" statements. This involvement by the state association helped the board and superintendent work together on some value-driven issues that the board had not resolved when the new superintendent was employed.

GETTING THE JOB DONE

The paramount task given the new superintendent was to get the thrice-failed bond issue passed. Funds were needed to build a new high school and remodel the existing one into a middle school for sixth through eighth grades. The movement of sixth graders into a middle school would eliminate crowded conditions in the two elementary schools and would allow the district to close its 88-year-old junior high school.

The bond issue became an all-consuming task for Phil Green, requiring him to shift his energies away from some areas he considered of equal importance. When the issue was put before the public in November, it failed by 11 votes. In March, the bond issue failed again, but this time there was a tie vote. In May, on Phil's third try, the issue passed with a margin of 148 votes. Unlike Hank, whose story is told in chapter 4, Philbert persisted until the district gained the public support it needed.

Though the bond issues focused on critical needs Philbert had to address, other important areas needed his attention. He was keenly aware of research on effective schools and believed that rural students as well as city children would benefit from the application of this body of research. For instance, consistent with the findings of Edmonds (1979), he wanted his principals to become strong instructional leaders. Green recognized that instructional leadership requires principals to spend time with teachers in their classrooms, so he appointed an additional principal, eliminating the need for one principal to commute between two elementary buildings.

With this position in place, Phil made it clear that he expected the principals to assume more prominent leadership roles. He was trying to implement the research of Andrews and Soder (1987), which found that principals who are strong instructional leaders are instructional resources for their teachers, observing in classrooms, providing feedback on instructional strategies, and helping teachers use test results to improve student achievement. Seeking to help principals become strong instructional leaders, Philbert provided training in effective schools and in instructional supervision.

Green's focus on the teachers was within the context of their classroom instruction. Curriculum articulation, clear goals, and expectations commonly shared are characteristics of effective schools (Austin & Reynolds, 1990). Hence, Philbert required courses of study for all grade levels and courses, making it clear that teachers were to follow the curriculum as prescribed. He spent a great deal of effort on his principals, working with them individually within their buildings. He had each principal, in conjunction with his staff, develop mission statements. In schools that have been found to be effective, "there is a clearly articulated mission for the school through which the staff shares an understanding of and a commitment to instructional goals, priorities, assessment procedures, and accountability" (Bullard & Taylor, 1993, p. 16). Green insisted that principals become aggressive supervisors who are conscious of outcomes.

Though technology was not abundant within the system, the staff was not using what was available. Green started developing programs of in-service for teachers and administrators with the expectation that technology would become an integral part of classroom instruction.

DOING IT RIGHT

When Phil arrived, he found that job descriptions were nonexistent for many positions; and those that existed were outdated, without a common structure, and not viewed as important documents. Hence, all job descriptions were revised and made current, and Phil implemented a system to ensure they would be reviewed periodically.

Green found the board's policy manual consisted of a collection of resolutions passed to address immediate issues. It was by no means a coherent document that could be used to properly govern the system. After contacting the state school board association, he engaged a consultant to work with the board to completely revise and update the district's policy manual.

Through the years, some board members had developed a tendency to bypass the superintendent and go directly to teachers or administrators when they wanted information or something done. Philbert addressed this vexing issue with a manual of operation, developed through his office with assistance from the board. He wanted administration and staff to operate consistently with clear expectations and lines of authority. A consequence of his early efforts was that the board became clearer in its responsibilities for policy, reducing its tendency to micromanage.

Philbert's most profound realizations, when he first became superintendent, were feeling overwhelmed by the quantity of work to be done and recognizing how alone he was in making most of his decisions. Even though the job looked immense, he remained in control, taking time to stop and reflect when difficult issues arose or conflicts developed.

AS THE YEAR EVOLVED

Though the bond issue was a never-ending project until it passed, Philbert Green did not allow even the two failures to distract him from his responsibility to lead the school system. He quickly discovered that he needed to better manage his time because of the extraordinary commitment the bond issue required of him. To this end he purchased a *Franklin Day Planner*. It helped him to prioritize his time and to organize his own preparation for the tasks he had to complete.

Green's two additional priorities were working with his principals and with the community. The bond issue required 50 to 60 meetings over the course of the year, and Phil faithfully attended each one. He remained until the last question was asked and answered, which enhanced his stature and built trust in the community.

Phil also turned to some outside consultants for assistance. His school board attorney, a part-time employee he inherited with the job, worked for a firm located in a city 40 miles away. Although this posed some communications problems, a productive working relationship evolved. For guidance, Green relied on the state school boards association and the state association of school administrators. Though he felt a need for someone who could assist him with grant applications, he was unable to find such an individual.

Philbert found that the school district treasurer, the high school principal, and his secretary were the people in whom he could confide. Trusting them, he sought their advice and counsel in certain situations. Through his work with the bond issue, Green developed a good working relationship with the board. Increasingly, they demonstrated reliance on his judgments and supported his decisions. He thought his prime resources for decision making were his previous experience as an administrator and the ability to look logically at situations, approaching them in a calculating fashion.

Through Phil's first year, he remained comfortable with himself, often relying on his good sense of humor when the going got rough. His humor, calm approach, and affability gave him the ability to lighten a situation and to gain trust as he dealt with people. He believed that to be successful he had to build relationships so that people would feel at ease with him and his decisions.

MEMORABLE EVENTS

As he reflected on memorable events in his first year as superintendent, Philbert related two that stood out. One had an element of humor and the other anguish.

The first incident involved a student with a developmental handicap. The young man usually took a bus to the high school where he transferred to a second bus that took him to his school of instruction. On this particular day in February, he arrived at the high school but missed his connecting bus. Fearing consequences for failing to arrive at his proper destination on time, he took one of the buses from the compound and tried to drive it to his school. Lacking driving skills, he and the bus ended up in a ditch along the road leaving the high school. The bus was recovered, the student was unhurt, and the incident proved to be little more than a good story.

The second incident was of a more serious nature. A teacher who was also a coach had an affair with a high school student. When confronted with the accusation and some evidence, he acknowledged the situation. A letter of reprimand was given to the teacher. He subsequently resigned before the matter could be acted upon by the school board.

The superintendent reported that the teacher, who was tenured, would have been dismissed if the matter had been placed in the board's hands. He indicated that he had been extremely careful to afford the teacher every due process consideration but was relieved that the matter had been resolved through the resignation.

REFLECTION AND VISION

Philbert Green felt this initial year as a superintendent had been a successful one. He had survived constructing his first board agenda, saying: "Thank God for a great secretary!" He had learned to work productively with the board of education. He had built an effective administrative team.

With the conclusion of the school year, Phil attributed a large portion of his success to his 18 years of experience as a building administrator and his prior central office responsibilities. He opined that he did not see how anyone could assume the duties of a superintendent without first having had extensive experience in other aspects of public school administration, especially as a high school principal.

Hanging tough and passing the bond issue on the third try had built credibility with the board and his staff. He had persuaded the board and staff to introduce current technology into the school's programs and in the operation of the school system. The high school library became more than a book repository; it became a center for learning with computers and support materials.

The comfort with the status quo had been breached, and in the process, Philbert had developed trust within the organization and the community. He had made it a point to learn the name of every employee in the system during his first weeks, and he had taken care to call people by name when dealing with them. This, he felt, had assisted him in building relationships and trust among all of his staff and constituencies.

Philbert Green's vision for the future was greater ownership of the schools by the staff and community. He hoped they would develop more willingness to take risks, to try new things, and to build community pride in the schools.

QUESTIONS FOR REFLECTION AND DISCUSSION

1. Jackie West (Chapter 3) and Phil Green were both rural superintendents who felt the isolation of their leadership roles. Imagine conversations between the two of them during their first year as superintendent. What would they discover they had in common? What could they have learned from each other?

2. How could Phil's laid back manner and people skills have helped him as he set out to change the behaviors of principals?

3. What are some factors that might explain the differences between the way Hank (Chapter 4) and Philbert responded to bond issue defeats?

REFERENCES

Andrews, R. L., & Soder, R. (1987, March). Principal leadership and student achievement. *Educational Leadership, 44,* 9–11.

Austin, G., & Reynolds, D. (1990). Managing for improved school effectiveness: An international survey. *School Organization, 10,* 167–178.

Ballard, P., & Taylor, B. O. (1993). *Making school reform happen.* Boston: Allyn & Bacon.

Edmonds, R. (1979, October). Effective schools for the urban poor. *Educational Leadership, 37,* 15–24.

14

MISTAKES BEGINNING SUPERINTENDENTS MAKE

William M. Gordon, Center for Program Design, Saluda, North Carolina

ABSTRACT. Mistakes are inevitable when doing a job for the first time. However, the goldfish bowl in which superintendents live and the broad impact of a superintendent on administrators, teachers, and students produce a situation in which mistakes are highly public and consequences can be far reaching. Board members and administrators, who may be understanding when teachers or students make mistakes, are far less likely to forgive the one chosen as their chief executive officer.

There is a fine line between the successful and unsuccessful beginning superintendent. As the Beginning Superintendent Study (BSS) unfolded, these successes and failures were confounded with evidence that the behaviors of some superintendents leading to success were the very same behaviors as those of others who experienced failure. Thus, the elusive human behaviors and circumstances of successful new superintendents, though placed in better focus through this study, are yet to be definitively isolated and measured in specific terms. However, even with the foregoing observation, the BSS isolated some issues that appeared to be critical for the beginning superintendent.

There is an old joke that has been applied through the years to head coaches that can also describe a new superintendent: "He left as he arrived—fired with enthusiasm." The most observable characteristics of the new superintendents were enthusiasm and planning for the new position. Many of their dreams were built as individuals toiled in the profession in lesser roles, preparing for this very special leadership undertaking. As a result of these dreams, the new superintendent often brought to the position visions and plans, formulated in other districts, that had little basis for fact in the new situation. Therefore, when constraints began to interface with preconceived ideals, enthusiasm would often give way to procedure and visions to realities. Once this process of institutionalization began to establish itself, the forces of the status quo became the norm, and new superintendents as change agents, visionaries, and leaders found themselves defined by the system rather than defining the system they had envisioned upon arrival.

UNSHARED VISION

The new superintendents seem to have recognized the importance of *vision*, that characteristic of successful leaders that Bennis and Nanus (1985) described as the capacity to create and communicate "a mental image of a possible and desirable future state of the organization" (p. 89). However, the mistake several of them made was failing to recognize the critical nature of having the school district reflect "the hopes and dreams, the needs and interests, and the values and beliefs of teachers, parents, and students as well" (Sergiovanni, 1990, p. 20). Sergiovanni declares the need for a leadership dimension called "purposing," which combines a leader's vision with forging a *shared covenant:*

> The key to successful schooling is building a covenant, comprising purposes and beliefs, that bonds people together around common themes and that provides them with a sense of what is important, a signal of what is of value. A covenant is a binding and solemn agreement by principals, teachers, parents, and students to honor certain values, goals, and beliefs; to make certain commitments to each other. . . . It is the compact that provides the school with a sense of direction on the one hand and an opportunity to find meaning in school life on the other (p. 20).

The areas of change and boardsmanship presented new superintendents with their stiffest challenges. Some of them not only overlooked the need for purposing but also demonstrated lack of sensitivity to the human side of an experienced staff that was more comfortable with the status quo than in seeking new horizons. Many of the new superintendents failed to realize that individuals who had occupied positions for a period of time or who had committed themselves to a district through the years were, in most instances, comfortable with things as they were and saw no reason to change. Also, many had seen superintendents come and go, so the new superintendents had to first win over the troops before they could proceed with any substantive changes. Finally, some staff were hesitant to commit to change because it could affect job security or could foster criticism, especially if a new superintendent did not last.

TOO MUCH TOO SOON

A significant mistake occurred when the new superintendent wanted to change it all "yesterday." This person quickly inventoried all of those problems he or she felt must be addressed immediately. Generally, the superintendent was able to find a small cadre of like-minded individuals, in the schools or the community, who encouraged the envisioned changes. In many instances, those providing the encouragement had their own agendas that were not always congruent with those of the new superintendent. Hence, when difficulties arose, new superintendents found that they waged battle alone or struggled to move forward without the necessary commitment from the bulk of the organization.

A new superintendent, who was terminated at the end of his first year, was bold enough to reflect upon some of his misadventures. He pointed out that his primary mistake was "overplanning and trying to accomplish [his] plans in too short a time period." When he took over the district he perceived a district in deep trouble, and he saw his role as getting it out of trouble as quickly as possible. Thus, he became Harold Hill, the legendary band leader in "The Music Man," high-stepping down Main Street in River City, Iowa. The problem was that none of the 76 trombones were behind him, so he waived his baton and stepped smartly out front, becoming a one-man parade as everyone else sat on the curb watching. He opined that if he had taken time to find out what the staff and board perceived as problems, and if he had learned the local culture, it would have been a much happier experience for all.

PROMISES, PROMISES

A partner of the "too much too soon" pattern is the mistake of making hasty promises or commitments while seeking the position or shortly after securing it. In retrospect, the BSS superintendents who had difficulty in this area made what they considered innocent or uncomplicated commitments on which they were unable to deliver. When this occurred, credibility was undermined and, after several such instances, people began to doubt the individual's ability to deliver on anything. In most cases, the source of this problem could be traced to making promises without adequate information, without a complete knowledge of the history of the problem, or approaching with more enthusiasm and will to please than ability to deliver. A more insidious source of this mistake was committing to people who had old axes to grind. Once new superintendents learned the art of deferring commitment until a course of action was well planned, they found the problem of unmet promises rapidly disappeared.

OFFENDING SCHOOL BOARD MEMBERS

Relations with the school board were probably the most tenuous area that new superintendents in the BSS had to face. School board members, by definition, are not trained educators. As such, they have notions on how schools should operate based upon a variety of influences, few of which are gathered from accepted practice, educational literature, or research. Difficulties generally arose when the board felt left out of the formulation process for new initiatives. They took offense when it became apparent that the new superintendent had worked with or informed only a portion of the board, excluding or minimally informing the remainder.

There were instances where the new superintendent recommended personnel action that involved staff who had special, indeed long-standing, relationships with one or more board members. So when a board member said to one new superintendent, "I put Smedley in his position as principal," he was also saying that before you criticize Smedley or tinker with Smedley's duties or position you had best get my blessing. In this instance, the new superintendent failed to pick up on the board member's special relationship with the employee. In one disastrous situation, the superintendent recommended termination of an incompetent teacher without realizing that the teacher had chaired the board president's election campaign. When the superintendent rather than the teacher left the district, he commented, "Someone on my staff should have told me [about the election campaign]."

There were instances where the new superintendent had been effusively optimistic about a project and, consequently, raised board members' expectations to unrealistic levels. In one case, the new superintendent had not been entirely candid with the board concerning the financial health of the district. This mistake resulted in some public pronouncements by board members that later had to be rescinded, embarrassingly.

A significant mistake occurred when one new superintendent failed to pick up the nuances of what board votes meant. When her board voted eight-to-one or seven-to-two on certain issues, the votes followed a pattern. What escaped the new superintendent was that, in many instances, a losing vote was cast by the board's only minority member who represented the views of a significant portion of the total school community.

On another occasion, a new superintendent who failed to recognize the significance of the negative vote by her minority member found herself with a serious problem. It occurred following an eight-to-one board decision to place a tax issue on the ballot. After several weeks of campaigning, the new superintendent awoke to read in the morning newspaper that her "united board support" had evanesced because her single minority member had come out publicly against the proposed sales tax increase. The board, in its deliberations concerning the tax, had not taken their minority colleague seriously and had refused to commit funds to the restoration of personnel and facilities, two areas that most directly affected the minority board member's constituency.

NOT DOING HOMEWORK BEFORE BOARD MEETINGS

Some new superintendents encountered difficulties with boards because of insufficient communications with individual members between meetings. These superintendents failed "to bring along" the individual board members and to educate them to the programs being undertaken or the needs that were being addressed. One new superintendent stated: "I was so busy running the district that I just didn't feel it was necessary to always be talking to board members about day-to-day issues. I quickly found out this was a mistake."

Another new superintendent learned the hard way that the board meeting was not the time to intervene with new ideas or become overly involved in the board's deliberations. He observed, in retrospect, that the board meeting was an opportunity to give leadership and to respond when members directed their comments to him, but it was not a time to be surprised or to surprise board members. It certainly was not a time to use intemperate language.

This superintendent related that, at times, he found himself protecting egos, responding to pet projects that never seemed to go away, and reacting to total misconceptions and sometimes intentional inaccuracies. He learned, after some initial attempts to intervene, that his best strategy was to be relatively quiet, especially when the board was in open session. He found that the time to exercise his leadership was when the board was not in session.

After a series of initial mistakes and being taken by surprise in open meetings, he made it his practice to always contact each board member individually prior to every agenda setting meeting and board meeting. He also met with his board president on the day of the meeting, but before the open session, to answer any questions. This enabled the president to be well informed and, during the public meeting, to remain on center stage and project the image of control and leadership. "Board presidents like it this way."

In another district, such an intense rivalry developed between the board president and the new superintendent that little was ever accomplished with both posturing for control. The loser was the new superintendent who, though retaining his job, lost a significant amount of his ability to lead the board and school community.

POWER POLITICS

Where does the power in a system lie? Who is the controlling voice? What traps need to be checked before embarking on a course of action? These are important questions for a new superintendent.

When one new superintendent failed to take her time and learn where the various pockets of power were in the district, she experienced difficulties where none should have been encountered. The most revealing feature of the power base within her school district was that it was found in pockets and not confined to a single group. She quickly realized that the special interest groups were single-issue oriented and that she could retain their support so long as their areas were supported or left unchanged. Therefore, when the football team and band became problems, she realized she needed to have the support of the booster groups and the board member who had a special commitment to the sports related groups.

This superintendent also sought out the pockets of citizens and staff who had special allegiances. Later she was careful to say that groups with their own special power bases should not be exempt from oversight and supervision. However, she believed it was important for her to be aware of these groups in order to win them over to her positions rather than unnecessarily create groups hostile to the tasks that needed to be completed.

The notion of power base should be viewed as becoming alert to the politics of the district. At the superintendent's level, education is a political undertaking, and it is important to know the rocks and shoals in the political waters. Several new superintendents pointed out the necessity of learning about local politics quickly. In most districts, the boards of education are collections of individuals with separate constituencies. Many board members also have their own personal contacts within the schools and central office. These personal contacts usually extend over many years to times when the board member had children in the district's schools or when they were students there. As a result, board members are not hesitant to gather information privately and outside normal communications channels.

Another aspect of knowing the power bases in the district became apparent when one new superintendent underestimated resistance to cultural change. She was an adept leader in that she could persuade, cajole, and convince others to follow her lead. As superintendent she realized that the neighboring city's urban problems did not stop at her suburban boundary. Thus, she undertook change that addressed the needs of the at-risk population that was scattered throughout her district, but was not its centerpiece. As she proceeded to infuse multicultural components into the curriculum and to include at-risk children and their parents in her coalition, board members who represented the white, conservative, middle- and working-class residents viewed the changes as detrimental to the students in their constituencies.

Deborah Meier (1995), a principal who is famous for the phenomenal improvement in student achievement at her inner-city school in East Harlem, recognized this issue when she pointed out, "Democratic schools are impossible to implement without an aware and supportive public" (p. 82). The opposition from influential community leaders in the BSS superintendent's district was critical, and the breach with her board eventually lead to her resignation as superintendent.

FICKLE LOYALTIES

Loyalties are strange behaviors that the new superintendent must identify. The issue of loyalty had several implications for the new superintendents in the BSS. In one instance the new superintendent attached herself too quickly to a particular group within the organization. This quick identity tended to create an in-group of loyalists who assumed real or imagined power at the expense of the remainder of the organization who saw themselves as the out-group with a need to attach somewhere else. That somewhere else turned out to be groups and individuals who had narrow views of the district and who, for the most part, felt that things were fine as they were and that new programs or changes in procedure were unnecessary. This out-group became, in effect, a stealth force within the organization that intentionally, or at times unintentionally, obstructed or delayed programs.

A second aspect of loyalties focused on the new superintendent's predecessor. Former superintendents invariably leave friends and supporters. This is true whether the former superintendent was released or had retired or died. These old loyalties are the normal consequence of any organization, and it was important that new superintendents recognize and respect them. In several of the BSS districts, the former superintendent remained as an employee of the district, complicating the development of new loyalties.

The mistake made by one new superintendent was to criticize the past. The staff quickly identified a pattern of criticism on his part, and resentments developed that undermined new initiatives and the orderly transition that the new superintendent sought. This was especially critical with the immediate central office staff and the building principals with whom the new superintendent was in daily contact.

Some new superintendents failed to recognize the need or value of developing loyalties toward them from within the organization. This is not to say that new superintendents had to be all things to all people; however, there was a need for a support system in the district. The superintendents discovered they needed to move slowly and to assess just where and how connections should be made, lest they form alliances that would alienate them from key stakeholders.

FAILURE TO IDENTIFY PROBLEMS

One new superintendent came into the system intent on allowing things to progress as they had in the past. Trouble surfaced at once. Another new superintendent who followed this course found, to her dismay, that the board expected just the opposite— that is, they wanted her to build teams and to lead the system in a new direction. When she was perceived as reluctant to take an active leadership role, the vacuum was filled with elements of the former administration.

This perception of a lack of leadership so dogged her administration that she failed to achieve the desired level of control and position of authority she sought. This new superintendent was attempting a balance because, as she related, she had been warned about "arriving with promises that can't be fulfilled or with unrealistic plans to make extensive changes immediately." The result was that she failed to provide a level of leadership that demonstrated competence to identify problems and to move toward their solution.

BLUNT TALK

Several new superintendents got into difficulty when they "told it like it was." It must be kept in mind that a new superintendent is just that—a person new to the job. Those who hire the new superintendent do so for a number of reasons. Sometimes there was a perceived need for change; sometimes the former superintendent moved on, retired, or died; and sometimes the former superintendent was simply fired. But, for whatever reason the former superintendent departed, there was always left behind a number of faculty, staff, parents, board members, and community who felt the district was a good one, that the children were bright and capable, and that the former superintendent had done a good job. Therefore, when the new superintendent came on strong with criticisms, there was the immediate reaction of "What does he know? He just got here."

One superintendent reported that he told the truth, at least as he saw it, about low academic achievement, and repeated his observations both privately and publicly throughout the school district and community. He quickly found that many people did not agree with his rather harsh appraisal, viewing it as unkind. In fact, he was quickly informed by some prominent citizens and board members that he was misinformed and that if he knew the community better he would be more temperate in his remarks. In retrospect he reported, "If I had gone privately to some of the key community leaders and board members voicing my concerns and observations and asking for their counsel and assistance, I could have gained their support." Instead he suffered serious criticism and personal attacks.

ALONE AT THE TOP

Some new superintendents were surprised, and some uncomfortable, with the level of isolation their new position entailed. All had come from positions where they were not the final word on issues. Though many perceived their former posts as important leadership roles, they had not fully understood the magnitude of the decision making required of the superintendent. Suddenly they were responsible for all the school children in the district, a school board, faculties, administrators, programs of instruction, budgets, expenditures, bond issues, personnel, academics, athletics, musical and dramatic performances, parent and citizen groups, drug education, special education, facilities, and all the other facets of a school district. These responsibilities were daily and most required immediate attention and action. Some superintendents discovered that there was no one available with whom to brainstorm about ideas or pending decisions. Even when staff were available, superintendents new to their districts did not know who could be trusted, especially when the staff included administrators who had competed unsuccessfully for the superintendency.

Initially, for most, the new reality of their isolation was overwhelming; but as superintendents settled into their position, they recognized that time management was a necessary art. With practice, the ability to focus on one issue, to the exclusion of others, became easier.

Once they learned how to allocate their time and to identify and separate issues that could be delegated, some new superintendents became more focused and secure. One new superintendent reported that the single most important thing he had learned was effective time management. This enabled him not only to enjoy the position but also to have time with his family and friends.

Another new superintendent, believing she could do the job herself, had neither an assistant nor full time secretary. Her lack of adequate support, plus the isolation of the position, caused her to make the following observation:

I often get the visual image of myself as the man on Ed Sullivan spinning the plates. You know that by the time I get the last plate spinning, I have to rush back to the first plate to keep it spinning, and I am always fearful I am going to break one.

Superintendents who remained overwhelmed by the endless demands and time pressures of the role became troubled and ultimately left the superintendency. Not surprisingly, the plate spinner resigned at the close of her second year.

HAZARDOUS HOUSE CLEANING

Personnel administration, in its myriad forms, is a crucial area for the new superintendent. Credibility demands that personnel decisions be perceived as evenhanded and without bias. When personnel matters were postponed or a reprimand for poor performance was delayed or seen as deferential, the leadership role of the new superintendent was undermined.

Likewise, when one new superintendent was perceived to have been brought in to clean up the system, virtual instant mistrust developed on the part of the staff. Warren Bennis and Burt Nanus (1985) highlighted the importance of trust in their classic book, *Leaders*, when they said:

> Trust is the emotional glue that binds followers and leaders together. The accumulation of trust is a measure of the legitimacy of leadership. It cannot be mandated or purchased; it must be earned. Trust is the basic ingredient of all organizations, the lubrication that maintains the organization (p. 153).

When the new superintendent failed to dispel the mistrust and went forward with changes that affected teacher planning periods and use of professional leave, suspicions were simply corroborated. Because this new superintendent had failed initially to establish trust and communication links with his staff, instead focusing on gaining control over what he perceived as a laissez faire administrative structure, he had no power base of his own.

The result was that, when problems arose that could and should have been addressed through simple communications within the district, there was neither trust nor personal relationships available to the new superintendent to resolve what were actually minor issues. Eventually the lack of quality communications and trust led the new superintendent to retire early; he "simply found that being a superintendent was not as fulfilling as being an assistant superintendent." He also found, to his dismay, that the problems were simply never ending and that he had no outlet or sources of collaboration within his own district.

OVERLOOKING THE OBVIOUS

Several of the new superintendents included in the BSS undertook the passage of tax referendums. Their efforts met with varying degrees of success. In one instance, the new superintendent's primary focus was to generate positive votes among the community's many retirees. With his attention focused on the retirement community and the rest of the electorate beyond the schools, he made the mistake of assuming school employees would automatically support the issue because it directly affected their livelihoods. As a result, no one generated enthusiasm among the district's teachers and support staff, in effect, not franchising the district's sales force. Though the referendum might not have passed even with the support of district personnel, the results were significant. The vote was 65% against the referendum in a state where passage required an abnormal majority vote of 60%.

THE HIGH COST OF SAVING MONEY

One new superintendent was a certified strategic planner and had worked as an outside consultant leading school districts through the strategic planning process. He decided to save some money and lead his new district through the process. He quickly discovered two salient facts: The process itself was too time consuming for a superintendent who was also learning his job, and the strategic plan was seen as his plan rather than the community's or the board's plan. Even though the strategic plan had substantial merit and in the end was appropriate for the district, it was neither warmly accepted nor properly implemented.

Because 55.5% of the first-year superintendents in the BSS reported that they were selected to be change agents (see Table 2-8), many of them faced the need to decide whether to use inside or outside consultants. Schmuck and Runkel (1988), long recognized as experts in organizational development in schools, provide helpful insights on this dilemma. Their assessment of advantages and disadvantages of inside consultation and outside consultation are summarized in Figure 14-1. Building trust and collecting accurate, unbiased information may also be issues for beginning superintendents who decide to be their own consultants.

CONCLUSIONS

Although all superintendents made mistakes as they began their administrations, their mistakes were primarily the product of their own enthusiasm and myopic focus on the job. Dealing with a school board appeared to be the source of many mistakes. One embarrassed his board members by correcting their misinformation in public meetings. Others failed to realize the importance of keeping board members informed of issues big and small.

Associated closely with board relations was the broader area of communications. The need for better communications with the board, district personnel, and public created numerous problems. Most new superintendents seemed to quickly master the communications demands placed upon them. Several indicated it was difficult for them to adjust to the constant telephone interruptions and the severe demands on their time, as well as the need to monitor newsletters and other printed information distributed by the district office.

Nearly all new superintendents in this study arrived feeling they could and should be responsible for making changes in their new districts. Even though they were the persons who recognized the need for change or who had received a directive for change, several made mistakes when instituting the change. Some had difficulty

INSIDE CONSULTANT	
Advantages	Disadvantages
1. More easily available	1. Work demands of regular duties interfere with projects
2. Knows useful information about the setting	2. May not be seen as expert because they are locals
3. Can get to the task faster	3. Knowledge of district may be biased
4. Can avoid political mistakes an outsider might make	4. Fact of "common fate" may dissuade from taking risks
5. Shares a "common fate" with the clients and can inspire immediate trust	

OUTSIDE CONSULTANT	
Advantages	Disadvantages
1. Can more easily take on large projects beyond the ready capacity of the district	1. Time and effort needed to find the right consultant
2. Has expert power	2. Requires more time for getting to know district, regardless of how open people may be
3. Can collect information for an unbiased diagnosis	3. Requires cash outlay
4. To extent trusted—some people usually trust an outside expert immediately—staff members will confide things they would be fearful of telling an insider	4. Though some will trust immediately, others may take longer to trust an outsider, or worry about possibility of embarking upon risky journeys
5. Freer to take risks of change	

FIGURE 14-1

Comparison of Advantages and Disadvantages of Employing Inside or Outside Consultants to Facilitate Change

Note: From *The Handbook of Organization Development in Schools* (3rd ed., p. 458) by R. A. Schmuck and P. J. Runkel, 1988, Prospect Heights, IL: Waveland Press.

defining effective approaches to initiating change, several failed to identify potential resistors to change, and a few attempted to initiate changes without adequately involving staff and the school community.

Most of the mistakes made by the new superintendents were not by themselves devastating to the individual's administration. In many instances, simply revisiting the area where problems had occurred and mending some fences, retreating from a position, or adjusting behavior resolved the issue. Only a few mistakes were serious enough to threaten long-term success or shorten the individual's tenure. It could be observed, by and large, that mistakes of new superintendents were similar to those of any new school administrator, but at the superintendent's level the impact was magnified by public scrutiny and district-wide consequences.

QUESTIONS FOR REFLECTION AND DISCUSSION

1. How can enthusiasm be both a friend and a foe to beginning superintendents?

2. How might the concept of *purposing* have helped the superintendent who met resistance to her vision of better serving multicultural populations and at-risk students?

3. As you reflect on the case studies, what strategies did some superintendents use to overcome the temptation to attempt too much too soon?

4. Which of the mistakes of beginning superintendents do you think individuals hired from outside the district are most likely to make? What steps can outsiders take to avoid or overcome them?

5. What kinds of strategies for working with a school board are necessary in order to avoid the mistakes of beginning superintendents reported in this chapter?

REFERENCES

Bennis, W., & Nanus, B. (1985). *Leaders: The strategies for taking charge.* New York: Harper & Row.

Meier, D. (1995). *The power of their ideas.* Boston: Beacon Press.

Schmuck, R. A., & Runkel, P. J. (1988). *The handbook of organization development in schools* (3rd ed.). Prospect Heights, IL: Waveland Press.

Sergiovanni, T. J. (1990). *Value-added leadership: How to get extraordinary performance in schools.* San Diego: Harcourt Brace Jovanovich.

15

HARSH REALITIES
Politics, Corruption, and Immorality

Carolyn Hughes Chapman, The University of Nevada, Reno
Samuel G. Chapman, The University of Oklahoma

ABSTRACT. Life is political, but the superintendent's life is an extreme example. A superintendent is a professional who functions in the crucible of public expectation, opinion, and support. On the one hand are professional knowledge, exemplary practice, ethics, and moral leadership. On the other hand are competition for finite resources and dealing with special interests, traditions, and unethical or immoral behaviors.

When immoral or unethical behavior is uncovered in a district, new superintendents face dilemmas with long-term consequences for their credibility. Prior mismanagement of school funds was difficult to resolve, but even more challenging were situations in which school personnel were charged with assault, sexual harassment, or abuse. Superintendents needed to protect students while balancing concern for protecting the rights of individuals with keeping boards informed and recommending appropriate action.

Because school districts are political entities that operate within state and federal laws, long-standing court cases and changing state school finance legislation painted the external political picture for more than a third of the superintendents in the Beginning Superintendent Study (BSS). Desegregation cases and legal challenges to equity in state funding patterns brought immediate pressures on new superintendents.

POLITICS OF DESEGREGATION AND SCHOOL FUNDING

For one new superintendent a critical early challenge was preparing a set of educational initiatives with the intent of convincing the federal judge to modify the contentious court-ordered busing plan that had been in place in the district for two decades. Hence, the judge's approval of the superintendent's proposal gained her enormous political support before she had been in the district even two months. As superintendent, she continued to promote educational initiatives to enable students to rise above the effects of poverty and prior segregation.

Threats to the fiscal stability of districts created political challenges for other new superintendents. Even some districts that had appeared to be "in good shape, financially" were caught unprepared when resources declined suddenly due to plummeting state tax revenue, military downsizing, or newly legislated limitations on districts' taxing capability. This resulted in unanticipated needs to reduce costs and limit employee salary increments. Such actions are never popular moves and were especially difficult for new superintendents seeking to develop their support in the district. Delays in state funding decisions while legislatures wrangled about school finance created additional pressures on other new superintendents.

Kathleen, whose story is told in Chapter 6, appeared to have developed important political insights as the wife of a former state senator. As the new superintendent, she inherited a sales tax referendum requiring her to quickly learn the complex elements of preparing tax propositions, petitioning the state legislature, and appearing before the bond commission to gain its approval. She developed a specific agenda of expenditures that a successful referendum would make possible, including salaries, instructional materials, maintenance, compliance with the Americans with Disabilities Act, in-school suspension, counselors, and debt service.

Kathleen's work was complicated by the fact that many business and political leaders opposed the referendum because they had not been consulted before it was proposed. Nonetheless, she built support for the referendum by working with parents, school employees, and the larger community. She went to see every elected official in the district and arranged to address every public board and civic organization. Her intense energy and commitment drew enough political support that voters approved the sales tax referendum.

Kathleen could concentrate her political efforts for increased funding within her district, but Jackie's small rural district, described in Chapter 3, was threatened with the loss of a third of its budget by state legislative action. Although she prepared for the worst by involving district personnel and community members in discussing potential cuts, she also used her political skills to ward off the disaster. Realizing that "local school people and communities exert a major influence over state policies" (Spring, 1988, p. 75), Jackie organized a community meeting featuring the local state representative and state senator. She also wrote to the governor and state commissioner of education, explaining the devastating impact of proposed budget cuts. Jackie's persistence in meetings, letters, and telephone calls helped to set the stage for an eleventh-hour legislative decision that cut only 4% from the district's budget.

CITY POLITICS—OPPORTUNITY OR THREAT?

Mayors of large cities have taken increasingly direct roles in school politics during the 1990s. Urban schools, plagued by low student achievement, high dropout rates, and violence, have become a target for action by mayors such as Richard M. Daley in Chicago and Rudolph Giuliani in New York City. Mayor Giuliani expressed frustration at his lack of control over the city's public school system. However, New York City's seven-member school board included two appointed directly by the mayor, and the budget process gave the mayor control over school finances.

Giuliani's desire for even greater control was evident when he declared that "the next chancellor [superintendent] should be selected jointly by the board of education and [himself]" (Scherer, 1995, p. 18). Former New York Mayor Ed Koch criticized Giuliani's intervention in school governance saying, "Rudy has shot himself in the foot politically and damaged the education of the children in this town. . . . Why would [potential chancellors] want to come here knowing the mayor is going to try to break them and run the system?" (Scherer, 1995, p. 18).

Perhaps Mayor Daley realized Giuliani's dream when, in the summer of 1995, he was empowered to abolish Chicago's board of education and appoint a superboard to replace it. Daley used his new powers to dramatically change the nature of school district management:

> Not only were the top management positions exempted from educational-certification requirements, the criteria for the positions virtually eliminated those "ed admin" types. In addition, because both the managers and the smaller, five-member board were both directly appointed by the mayor, neither group was protected from direct partisan, political influence (Hess, 1995, p. 28).

One of the BSS superintendents was employed in a city where the mayor used a different form of political influence. In Renfield, where political motivations and discord among school board members had long impeded educational progress, the mayor promoted the election of a reform school board. The public elected four new members to the seven-member board with the promise that they would concentrate on education rather than politics.

This board of education selected Susan as the new superintendent, as described in Chapter 9. She was drawn to the city because of the reform board, believing that the situation was optimal for promoting positive change. When Susan was hired, a local political commentator who had supported her selection observed:

She might have a hard time . . . if she doesn't play politics the way they're played here. . . . We have a mayor who's sort of in control of the school board, and if she doesn't play ball, she'll be run out of here.

Within months, the board yielded to the mayor's urging and rescinded its decision to place a desperately needed tax levy on the ballot. For the most part, though, the board was supportive of its new superintendent.

The need for additional fiscal resources became increasingly evident. Limited funds and the reluctance of the board to place a tax levy on the ballot led to many months of negotiations with employee unions and angry threats of a teacher strike, described in the city paper as "inappropriately destructive and needlessly inflammatory." After vitriolic attacks on the superintendent that spewed venom that "had no justification and were detrimental to collective bargaining," a pact was ultimately reached with the teachers' union.

During the next election, the mayor supported additional reform candidates for the school board, though an incumbent protested, "If the mayor wants to remove politics from the system, the first thing he should do is keep his hands out of school board elections." The mayor's political machine was successful; now every member of the board had been elected with the mayor's support. After delaying for nearly two years, the board finally placed a tax levy on the ballot in May. In spite of vigorous campaigning, the referendum failed by a three-to-two margin. Elimination of all sports and massive layoffs loomed; the district was in deep financial trouble. A typical headline read: Schools Told to Cut All Sports; Rejection of Levy Blamed in Call for 1,070 Layoffs. Even in the face of such gloomy prospects, the mayor opposed asking the public again to approve the tax levy on the November ballot.

According to the city newspaper, the superintendent "begged and pleaded with board members; they ignored the mayor's advice and followed hers. The levy did slightly better than the one in May, but, as the mayor had predicted, it failed." Within days the mayor began criticizing the pace of the district's reform and suggesting consideration of private school vouchers. Shortly after the levy failed, the mayor and the board had a private meeting from which the superintendent was excluded.

In February of her third year, Susan announced her resignation, saying that politics caused her to leave the district. A former board member who had been defeated by one of the mayor's candidates commented:

I'm a little disappointed in her, but she was coming to realize that the mayor was her boss. With his control of the board and the corporate establishment, he could have made life miserable for her. She stood up to him, to her credit, and that put her in a difficult position.

One of the newly elected board members added this perspective:

I don't believe she had ever been in an environment that is so political, where you have to work with the mayor, the business community, and the politicians on every major initiative.

Although the support of powerful politicians can help a superintendent, their support also entails risks. The Renfield mayor had promoted the election of a reform school board that, he promised, would focus on education rather than politics. However, the mayor's political reality led him to impact the decisions of board members he helped to elect. His unwillingness to support needed tax referendums placed not only educational reform but also district solvency in jeopardy.

INTERNAL POLITICS OF BOARDS OF EDUCATION

Though external political intervention can create highly visible pressures on superintendents and school districts, internal political activities of school board members can create less visible, but nonetheless compromising, situations. For instance, some superintendents were asked by individual board members to employ friends or relatives, circumventing standard personnel procedures. Such requests can be threatening to new superintendents because boards of education have the power to hire and fire them. Eugene, whose story is told in Chapter 8, was asked to employ a board member's friend. Rather than bowing to this political pressure, Eugene firmly told him that all candidates for employment must be processed through the district's hiring procedures administered by the personnel office and that all appointments would be made on the basis of merit.

Even after employees are on the school district's payroll, political alliances with school board members can leave them feeling invulnerable to supervisory expectations. These feelings seemed to intensify when the alliances were based on race. Employees who believed they had been employed because of intervention of particular board members were fiercely loyal to those board members, expecting continued protection, regardless of the quality of their work.

By no means unique to school board members, such political alliances are explained by Flinchbaugh (1993):

> One of the unwritten but very active understandings among politically active individuals is that if a person does something for someone, the receiving person assumes a political debt that the giver can recall in the future. . . . Politically active people are constantly maneuvering, dealing, manipulating, persuading, and so on, in ways that make it unclear as to what is political intent and action and what is unethical or illegal action. . . . The greater their political power, the greater is the likelihood that crafty politicians will be successful in such activities for a while even though their actions are illegal (p. 418).

In addition to using their political position to benefit their friends and solidify their power base, some board members tried to use their role to secure favored treatment for their own offspring. When Keith learned that board members were asking teachers to give their children parts in the school play or leading roles on sports teams, he intervened courageously. As reported in Chapter 8, Keith was well aware that his job security was at risk, but he took the morally high ground, asking that board members desist from such requests.

Doing the right thing, even when it means disagreeing with a member of the board responsible for one's employment, is a mark of a superintendent's moral strength. As Sergiovanni (1990) pointed out:

> Moral questions about leadership are unavoidable. . . . Leadership combines management know-how with values and ethics. Leadership practice, as a result, is always concerned with both what is effective and what is good (pp. 28–29).

UNETHICAL, ILLEGAL BEHAVIORS

Nearly all of the BSS superintendents were confronted with unethical or illegal behaviors in their districts. Although most instances involved school employees working in their official capacities, one case found a school board member accused of sexual harassment in his professional role outside the school. Police investigation appeared to substantiate the charges, but found insufficient evidence to file criminal charges. Nonetheless, the allegations continued to make headlines, and the board member ultimately resigned, citing family and church obligations.

Although, in this case, no action was required of the superintendent or other board members, a plethora of other instances arose in the BSS that found school employees engaged in unethical or illegal behaviors. In one financially strapped school district, an audit found that an employee, assigned as a sixth-grade teacher by the district personnel office, had not taught a class for the entire school year. Instead she served as an assistant principal while her class was taught by a substitute teacher, inappropriately inflating costs for the district.

The amounts of money involved in problem behaviors by school employees varied with the size of the school districts. The payroll employee in Eugene's district wrote checks to herself for a few hundred dollars. In another district, investigation of what at first appeared to be an error in computation revealed that $650,000 had been misappropriated and used for projects other than the ones for which they were authorized. A manager of computing services in Renfield admitted ordering more than $4 million in goods and services without board approval. In each instance, the superintendents needed to inform the board of the situation and develop procedures to safeguard against similar incidents in the future.

Although inappropriate fiscal behaviors were troublesome to new superintendents and created negative public perceptions of the schools, even more troublesome were the instances in which school employees were guilty of physical assaults. Though some of the incidents occurred before the new superintendents arrived in their districts, they continued to create problems until they were resolved.

One such incident involved an assault on a Black teacher by a white principal who "grabbed her by the arm and dragged her out of her classroom at the school." The principal was removed from his post and assigned to administrative duties in the district office. He was later convicted of assault and unlawful restraint and ordered to do community service. Dissatisfied with these legal consequences, the teacher loudly voiced complaints in meeting after meeting of the school board. After many months of protest and litigation, the board offered the teacher a $67,000 settlement, which she accepted.

In another case, a slam-dunked basketball struck a physical education teacher in the head. The teacher whirled around and threw his keys at the student. They hit the student in the head requiring several stitches. Clearly, the administrative reprimand the teacher received was justified. Though the parent originally filed a police report, she dropped the criminal complaint and filed civilly.

A 40-year-old male teacher who had been teaching in the district for 8 years was charged with throwing a first grader against a bookcase, stepping on his stomach, and kicking him. A week later he was alleged to have kicked another pupil in the stomach while the pupil was sitting on steps during recess. The same teacher had been reprimanded for slapping a student in another school the previous school year. District policy had prohibited corporal punishment for more than 5 years, so he was suspended with pay. Following a prolonged investigation, the superintendent recommended termination, and the school board acted on that recommendation citing "willful and persistent violations of board policy."

SEXUAL ABUSE AND HARASSMENT BY SCHOOL EMPLOYEES

In addition to other unethical and illegal behaviors, sexual abuse and sexual harassment by school employees were brought to the attention of a third of the new superintendents. Although the complaints were prompted by current events, it was clear that similar behaviors had occurred under previous superintendents. This pattern was indicative of a growing body of evidence that reveals

> repeated failures by school employees to properly report sexual offenses and by school leaders to act on the reports. Teachers in all states are required by law to report any suspicion of child abuse. . . . Many times superintendents and principals investigate reports themselves with the primary aim of keeping a lid on scandal (Graves, 1994, p. 12).

Often the new superintendent learned the history only when new charges emerged. For instance, only after a middle school teacher and coach was accused of sexual involvement with an eighth-grade girl did Jackie find out that, earlier, a teacher had been terminated because of sexual indiscretion toward a student. She reported:

They let him go last year, and they released him, but they paid him off. In other words, they bought him out. Well, this same kind of thing is happening now, exactly the same kind of thing. They also knew about this guy for awhile. . . . [Parents] had brought this to the attention of the board in the past, but the administration didn't do anything about it.

Jackie learned of the charges against the middle school teacher when parents called the school counselor, asking to meet with her on the Friday before Christmas break. Jackie placed the teacher on administrative leave, pending investigation. Over the Christmas holidays, the district attorney's office investigated and decided to file felony charges. At that time, it appeared that the teacher had touched girls inappropriately, but later it was determined that he had also had sexual relations with one of the eighth-grade girls. The board supported Jackie's recommendation for termination, and the prosecutor followed through on the criminal charges.

Investigation of this middle school teacher brought to light other instances of inappropriate teacher behavior in the district. Jackie described them, saying:

He [a high school social studies teacher] looks the pretty girls up and down with his eyes, and practically undresses them with his eyes. I've heard that at least five times. . . . He picks on the vulnerable kids, and some of the things he does physically, you wouldn't believe. He'll take their finger and squeeze it real hard and smash it on the top, and he makes the kids do push-ups in front of him and looks down the girls' blouses. . . . With the boys, one of the punishments was what they call a mustache burn: they'll hold a can across the upper lip very, very hard until it burns; or the eyebrow burn where they pull it across the eyebrow. It'll pull the eyebrows apart and burn.

Jackie was stunned to discover that teachers were totally unaware of what is legal and what is illegal. Consequently, she scheduled a child abuse seminar. Some of the greatest offenders did not come "because they knew it all." However, the new information about child abuse laws and Title IX spread rapidly around the small rural district, especially when other teachers in the district had children in the offenders' classes. Jackie thought they had decided to change their behaviors, but she knew continued vigilance would be necessary.

Other instances of sexual abuse by school employees included a case where a male teacher accused of sexual involvement with female students attempted suicide and was subsequently treated in a mental hospital. Although most of the cases of sexual abuse encountered by new superintendents involved female students, a male staff member in Eugene's district was charged with inappropriate behavior with young men. He was placed on administrative leave with pay pending investigation. The district did not take more decisive action because the teacher resigned, and the police investigation led civil authorities to take over the case, removing it from the district's jurisdiction.

The male coach accused of inappropriate sexual behavior toward female students in Keith's district was reprimanded and removed from his coaching responsibilities but allowed to continue teaching. Shakeshaft and Cohan's (1995) study of sexual abuse by school personnel found that 11.3% of accused sexual abusers received reprimands.

In Philbert's district, when a tenured teacher and coach was confronted with evidence that he was having an affair with a high school student, the teacher resigned before the school board could act on his resignation. Shakeshaft and Cohan found that this was the most common outcome when teachers were accused of sexually abusing students—38.7% resigned, left the district, or retired. Of these, superintendents reported that 16% went on to teach in other schools.

Interestingly, all the cases of sexual abuse by school employees discovered by the new superintendents involved teachers who were also coaches. This pattern is consistent with the findings of a survey of North Carolina superintendents that revealed "over 20% of the superintendents listing a reason for dismissing a coach reported that the coach was dismissed because of a morality charge" (Wishnietsky, 1991, p. 164).

In every case where the BSS superintendents heard allegations of sexual impropriety, they worked to protect students while respecting due process rights of employees. Their work was complicated by the fact that few districts had outlined procedures for reporting and investigating allegations of sexual abuse by staff members. This situation was also true in the 225 districts studied by Shakeshaft and Cohan.

At one time, superintendents may have felt that their duty was done when they were successful in preventing a scandal or getting sexual abusers out of the district. However, federal courts have found school districts civilly liable for sexual abuse and sexual harassment by their employees. In a landmark case, the teacher resigned on condition that all charges against him be dropped, and the school closed its investigation. However, the Supreme Court ruled, in the 1992 case of *Franklin v. Gwinnett County [Georgia] Public Schools*, that Title IX permits students to sue for damages. In the first Title IX case to go through a jury trial, a federal jury, in October 1994, awarded a female student $400,000. She charged that the director of her vocational school offered to reduce her class schedule on the condition that she have sex with him every week until she graduated. After reporting the incident to the police, she recorded on tape a similar offer the director made to her on the subsequent day (Yaffe, 1995).

Given the legal and fiscal consequences for failure to act responsibly when school employees are accused of sexual abuse or sexual harassment, superintendents are recognizing the critical necessity of having clear procedures in place to deal with such allegations. Although the due process rights of employees must be respected, it is important for superintendents to realize that in administrative hearings, including those involving school boards, the standard of proof required is "preponderance of evidence rather than the higher criminal standard of guilt beyond a reasonable doubt" (NASSP, 1992). Importantly, school districts are not required to defer dismissal until the completion of the employee's criminal proceedings arising out of the same sexual misconduct (*Rosenberg v. Board of Education*, 1985).

AVOIDING LAND MINES

The harsh realities of the superintendency, including politics, ethics, and immorality, are land mines waiting to explode under unwary feet. Although soldiers in lands where guerilla warfare has long been in progress will inevitably stumble on a few of these land mines, the odds of their survival are enhanced by thorough preparation. Review of school policies related to ethical and moral issues is a crucial early step for all new superintendents. Revising policies and procedures and providing training for administrators and teachers may be necessary in some districts as a means of preventing abuses.

Superintendents need to be armed with knowledge of the law and court decisions and be willing to make courageous stands in face of strong opposition. As Sergiovanni (1992) points out, "To a large extent, moral commitments explain the decisions people make and the behavior they exhibit" (p. 19). Though the situations appeared to threaten the survival of new superintendents, political, ethical, and moral issues provided opportunities for them to model the kind of behaviors they hope will characterize their employees and students.

QUESTIONS FOR REFLECTION AND DISCUSSION

1. What do you see as the assets and the liabilities of having a city's political leaders take a strong interest in the schools?

2. A number of the mistakes of beginning superintendents described in chapter 14 involved board politics. How can a new superintendent distinguish strategies for building board support from actions that would compromise moral leadership?

3. What factors need to be considered when deciding whether to protect a district from scandal or to confront unethical or immoral behavior?

4. What steps do you think a superintendent should take to prevent or prepare for those situations in which unethical or immoral behavior occurs?

REFERENCES

Flinchbaugh, R. W. (1993). *The 21st century board of education: Planning, leading, transforming.* Lancaster, PA: Technomic.

Franklin v. Gwinnett County Public Schools. 112 S.Ct. 1028, (1992).

Graves, B. (1994, October). When the abuser is an educator. *The School Administrator, 51,* 8–20.

Hess, G. A., Jr. (1995, November 29). Chicago's new perspective on district management. *Education Week,* p. 28.

National Association of Secondary School Principals. (1992, September). *A legal memorandum: Sexual misconduct by school employees.* Author.

Rosenberg v. Board of Education of School District No. 1, Denver Public Schools, 710 P.2d 1095 (Colo. 1985).

Scherer, R. (1995, June 19). Big city school superintendents are posting high dropout rate. *The Christian Science Monitor,* pp. 1, 18.

Sergiovanni, T. J. (1990). *Value-added leadership: How to get extraordinary performance in schools.* San Diego: Harcourt Brace Jovanovich.

Sergiovanni, T. J. (1992). *Moral leadership.* San Francisco: Jossey-Bass.

Shakeshaft, C., & Cohan, A. (1995, March). Sexual abuse of students by school personnel. *Phi Delta Kappan, 76,* pp. 513–520.

Spring, J. (1988). *Conflict of interests: The politics of American education.* New York: Longman.

Wishnietsky, D. H. (1991, January/February). Reported and unreported teacher-student sexual harassment. *Journal of Educational Research, 84,* 164–169.

Yaffe, E. (1995, November). Expensive, illegal, and wrong: Sexual harassment in our schools. Kappan Special Report. *Phi Delta Kappan, 77,* pp. K1–K15.

16

THROUGH THE LENS OF LEADERSHIP THEORY

Mary Woods Scherr, The University of San Diego

ABSTRACT. The term leadership arouses passion and excitement, suggests status and power, promises improvements, and provokes academic arguments regarding its definition and the appropriate perspectives. The leadership views expressed by first-time superintendents and an analysis of their case studies demonstrate that both traditional and nontraditional approaches to leadership theory were evident. Understanding leadership as it relates to the status and power of the superintendency holds considerable promise for improving public schools.

Educational researchers with a mission of unraveling the threads of connection that link good teachers with excited, engaged, committed students have reported extensively on discipline-specific pedagogy (Grant, 1988). Of course, numerous aspects of good teaching cross departmental lines. Likewise, crucial aspects of good leadership are central to a variety of contexts: political, academic, business, and religious institutions. However, a discussion of leadership that focuses exclusively on generic characteristics may not be as useful for practitioners as a discussion that also includes context-specific aspects, in this case, aspects of leadership specific to the superintendency.

Heilbrunn (1994) called for the study of leadership within context. The Beginning Superintendent Study (BSS) provides an opportunity and a responsibility to look at leadership within the context of public schools.

INSPIRATION AND VISION: "LIFT YOURSELF ABOVE THE MOON"

Most of the BSS superintendents talked about the importance of inspiration or the importance of a vision to inspire staff. They stressed the need to continually articulate the district's vision, and considered the superintendent the number one spokesperson. One superintendent explained:

I think the inspiration, hoping to inspire the staff, is going to be the first thing . . . inspiring the people within the district—the central office, the teachers in particular— to believe in themselves. . . . getting them on board . . . being proud to work for the [district] because they've been bashed incessantly in the press.

In her opening of school speech at a breakfast for several thousand teachers, she explained what the staff could expect from her:

First and foremost, you can expect me to focus my energies on making things better for children, not for adults; but at the same time, you can expect me to show a great deal of love and respect for teachers.

She described her philosophy as "top-down support for bottom-up reform" and assured her staff they could count on her to act on that philosophy. She also passionately urged teachers to trust her and to believe in the potential of children and not "dwell on the environments from whence children come . . . [but instead on the schools] to which they come."

Another superintendent emphasized high expectations for students and linked school improvement to the need for quality service to parents:

[It is] extremely important for the leader to articulate the vision . . . wherever she goes—whether to the editorial board or the business community. I think the second thing with regard to leadership for our district right now is the whole issue of customer service . . . and quality service to parents. . . . [We expect] 100% success for every

child and [the staff's commitment] to do whatever they need to do to enable children to be successful. . . . and they will respond to the needs of their colleagues and the demands of the broader community with regard to the services and the process of delivery.

The following words express another superintendent's personal vision:

. . . to be able to inspire by my own modeling and deep belief and strategize others to be able to rise to that level of empowerment to defeat the odds. . . . because the odds are so great that if you only dwell on the odds you would never see yourself achieving . . . so you almost have to lift yourself above the moon, and see yourself moving toward it.

COMMUNITY SUPPORT: "DOWNING ROAST BEEF AND MASHED POTATOES"

Building community support was an essential part of every superintendent's role. Even a superintendent who was promoted from within the district felt the need to speak often to community groups. She gave far more addresses throughout the district than her predecessor and attended the meetings of key civic organizations. As another superintendent explained:

You've got to win the community over—and I just about kill myself and I know my colleagues do [also]—working six and seven days a week—doing two or three community things every weekend. . . . It's very important for me to be out and about. I go to Rotary with 500 men every Wednesday and try and get down roast beef and mashed potatoes and be at the Optimist Club on Friday and be at the football games.

This same superintendent carefully consulted the Cunningham Constituency Wheel (Cunningham, 1992) as she accepted speaking engagements to be sure she did not miss any important segment of the community (see Chapter 12).

STRUCTURES FOR CHANGE: THE BEST TIME . . . IS EARLY

First-year superintendents developed a wide variety of structures for change. One superintendent felt so strongly about the need to get to know the community and foster collaborative action that he built in an "entry plan" as part of his contract. He followed guidelines developed by Jentz et al. (1982) that state the need for "structured collaborative inquiry" and "activity mapping." He also accepted their recommendation regarding timing: The best time for a leader to establish new structures for change is early in a new position (see Chapter 3).

While developing a process for budget development, this superintendent realized there were "no definitive district goals, and that the budget process could be used for setting goals that would be implemented through the School Improvement Team (SIT) and District Improvement Team (DIT) structures." He worked with the DIT and the school board to develop a mission and five belief statements intended to guide decisions. To guide the mission and belief development process, the superintendent provided the board with a credo explaining much about his leadership philosophy and style.

Other first-year superintendents instituted a wide variety of structures for change. These changes included large-scale reorganization of the district, new processes for involving the public in budget development, and the establishment of a hot line for "one-stop" phone calls to resolve problems that had not been addressed satisfactorily at the school level. Nearly all of these changes represented the desire of new superintendents to be more responsive to the community, provide a higher quality of education, and promote school-community partnerships.

TIME AND STRESS: "EVERYBODY'S VYING FOR MY TIME"

The lack of time was a recurring, consistent theme. A few managed to "save" time to workout or be with their families; others worked evenings and most weekends and had trouble figuring out how to survive. Nearly all expressed the desire for more time to work with their boards, the central staff, the teachers, and the community. New superintendents often felt that everyone was vying for their time. The importance of time management, which is so central for educational leaders, especially superintendents, has led Heifetz (1994) to note the necessity for leaders to manage themselves as well as their external and internal environments. The need for management prompted him to see the elaborate distinctions between leadership and management as not particularly useful.

Most of the superintendents needed strong support from their district staff in order to survive. As a consequence, nearly all discovered the need to nurture the organization.

NURTURING THE ORGANIZATION: "THINGS STARTED TURNING AROUND"

"Oh, here we go again," thought one superintendent when she learned that her central office staff members were feeling isolated and neglected. In a previous job, she had gradually realized the organization needed some care—that people "wanted access"—a way "to cut through all these layers and have access to the top staff member." Recognizing that she was "not going to get anything done" unless she had staff support, she began

spending more time working on the organization itself. . . . then things started turning around to the point that, when I left, many of these people who had been adversaries and underminers were actually in tears, afraid that the next leader coming in was going to go back to the more traditional organization.

Although she experienced resistance from her central office staff early in her tenure, one superintendent intentionally gave high priority to being in the schools and in the community and developing clear communication with the school board. It is highly likely that this central office staff felt isolated and did not know where they fit into the new superintendent's plan. However, toward the end of the first year, she initiated a series of retreats and reorganizational plans that gained the support of the district staff.

The superintendent who had been promoted from deputy superintendent, and, hence, had a working relationship with central staff, also felt some urgency to reassure district staff. She had to carefully articulate her views so the staff would hear from her that the district was not turning in a new direction.

SYMBOLS: "NO DAIS WITH ALL THOSE PEOPLE . . . "

One woman superintendent entered a district ready for change, ready for a superintendent that symbolized something different. She explained, "I was very different not only in that I was a woman but also in that I had spent most of my career in curriculum and instruction as opposed to the business side." In planning the opening of school meeting, she decided not to have a traditional program: "No one will introduce me; there will not be a dais with all those people sitting on it."

On the first official day on the job, another superintendent visited a school because she felt it was extremely important that she be out in a school. As a matter of practice, she also included children with her whenever the media wanted a photo or when she was on television. During the recruitment process she found it helpful to tell stories illustrating that she could be "decisive" and "tough" with unions, characteristics boards often want in a superintendent and ones that they feel might be lacking in women. She also included such stories in nearly every speech she gave.

Some superintendents convinced the school board that the first 15 to 20 minutes of the board meeting should focus on education:

I try and highlight the children . . . and remind the board what we are about. We are televised now, so kids are up front in every telecast. I think it is critical for the superintendent's identity to be with kids and successful students.

RELATIONSHIPS: CARING FOR CHILDREN; CARING FOR STAFF

One superintendent was described as a caring leader with employees, parents, community, and students, both on the personal level and on the district level. She considered her greatest challenge to be "keeping children as the focus since there are so many extraneous aspects to the superintendency." She reminded the staff of their responsibility to educate all students and instituted in-school suspension, so, as one teacher reported, "kids weren't in the streets anymore." She worked to shape the culture of the district (Deal & Peterson, 1990). As a potter, she shaped their belief that all students should be in school. She also acted as a healer. In addition, she took the time to address each group of employees at their site to remind them "of [their] rich history in the district."

LEARNING ON THE JOB: "SPINNING PLATES"

All the superintendents worked incredibly hard. Those who were newcomers in a state had to master the intricacies and nuances of state financing. Nearly all had to prepare budgets under severe financial constraints. Some had to overcome cynicism expressed by staff, as well as community members, who were against the tax because the district "didn't spend money wisely."

To overcome opposition to a district tax, one superintendent listened and acknowledged the feelings of the community. She then prepared a capital improvement proposal that dedicated all funds for a 10-year period, causing the employees to regain faith in the system. Enough of them joined the ranks of voters to pass the tax. Within a very short time period, she had to learn the intricacies of bond financing while also mastering other details of a new job. Her emphasis on relationships was balanced by her hard work in mastering technical issues.

She described the multiple, complex tasks of the superintendent using the metaphor of "spinning plates," recalling a circus stunt man, seen in her youth, who managed to keep plates spinning on several poles at the same time. She stated that "by the time I get the last plate spinning, I've got to rush back to the first plate to keep it spinning, and I'm always fearful I'm going to break one."

BOARD MANDATE: "CLEAN UP THE SYSTEM"

One superintendent was hired by a board with the mandate to "clean up the system" and gain control of a district whose past leadership had been laissez faire. He worked to improve communication with the schools and the community, and to create an image of a superintendent who was "in charge."

As might be expected, his efforts met with mixed results. His termination of an ineffective support staff member was supported by the teachers. His efforts to emphasize time-on-task, to replace a demeaning coach, and to induce an ineffective principal to leave, thus making room for a more instructional principal, were greeted with community and district support. He allowed teachers to contribute their sick leave to a colleague with a heart condition, an action symbolic of a superintendent who cared.

On the other hand, he took away teachers' "freedom" during their planning periods and limited their use of professional leave. In spite of these unpopular decisions, the negotiations toward the end of his first year progressed smoothly, even though the teachers were granted few of their requests.

Because the superintendent lived in a nearby community, he felt he had insider status, a view only partially correct. He attempted to pass a $3.5 million bond issue without involving teachers or administrators in the planning process. A 65% negative vote signified either a sense of naiveté or a strong unrealistic belief in his personal leadership and communication skills. He followed the traditional change strategy of adding staff; he did not exhibit specific strategies for collaborating with the district staff or the community.

TRADITIONAL LEADERSHIP THEORY

The preceding examples of central themes emerged from interview data on the superintendents' first year. Many of their views of the superintendency, which guided the formation of their first-year priorities, clearly reflect strong influence from the traditional frameworks of educational leadership and from the business literature.

An article by Slater (1995) describes four different traditional perspectives of leadership: (1) structural-functionalist; (2) political-conflict; (3) constructivist; and (4) critical humanist. Slater begins by stating that the questions most frequently asked about leadership are "What is it? Why is it important? and What are its conditions?" (p. 449). How these questions are answered "depends in no small degree on our assumptions about the nature of social organization" (p. 449). He proceeds to address each question from the four different perspectives. For the purpose of this chapter, we consider the definition of *leadership* from each perspective.

According to the structural-functionalist perspective, leadership is a set of "measurable behaviors and skills." Slater highlights the work of Hoyle, English, and Steffy (1985), who describe leadership competencies in *Skills for Successful School Leaders*. They include designing, implementing, and evaluating school climate; building public support for schools; developing curriculum; instructional management; staff evaluation; staff development; allocating human, material, and financial resources; and conducting educational research, evaluation, and planning.

Slater adds to the list using the work of Andrews and Sonder (1987), who explain that the effective instructional leader is a resource provider, an instructional resource, a communicator, and a visible presence (p. 9). Slater notes that they "articulate a vision of instructional goals, set and follow clear standards for instruction and teacher behavior, and are out and about" (p. 145). Other researchers cited by Slater (1995) identified many of the same behaviors.

The case studies clearly indicate that the superintendents, indeed, included those behaviors in their first-year activities. Their words illustrate the superintendents' central concern with vision, the importance of building community, developing staff, managing resources, and being "out and about."

From the political-conflict perspective, politics and conflicts most noticeably revolve around relations between the superintendent and the school board. Understandably, the new superintendents were anxious to establish that they were responsible for administration and the board for policy. Many of the superintendents reported conducting workshops with the board for this purpose. Lack of time to spend with individual board members was cited as a frustration. In some cases, the board members participated in so many committees that it was difficult for the superintendent to keep up with the committee work.

A constructivist perspective calls attention to the meaning behind actions. Their words indicated the superintendents' sensitivity to the symbolism of their actions. They, therefore, included instructional reports with teacher and student participation at school board meetings, welcomed teachers to a breakfast meeting without any introduction or use of a dais, included children in their photographs, and visited a school on the first official day on the job.

From a critical humanist perspective, nearly all superintendents in the study fostered change by developing new structures, usually in collaboration with staff and often in collaboration with community members. They were committed to social change, seeking to transcend "the limits of existing social arrangements" (Slater, 1995, p. 453, citing Burrell and Morgan, 1979, p. 32).

One of the superintendents clearly identified her own form of leadership: "[The] best term from the textbooks is transformational [leader] because somehow I need to be able to have a vision . . . to know the people, the player, the things, and all that, and the particular skills." She was identifying her views with transformational leadership as described by Burns (1978) in his classic work, *Leadership*.

Another superintendent also applied the principles of transformational and moral leadership as described by Burns (1978). In a city where educators had long been subjected to widespread criticism, she helped educators believe in themselves and in their power to make a difference. She believed that educators and the public shared aspirations and values for their children, and she crafted strategies to help people realize their common aspirations and build consensus as the means for meeting commonly recognized needs of students.

The traditional frameworks explain why leadership means different things to different people. Therefore, definitions are "almost as numerous as the researchers engaged in its study" (Hoy & Miskel, 1996, p. 373). Rost (1991) deplores this lack of agreement and is not comforted by explanations for the ambiguity surrounding the term *leadership*. He has defined leadership as "an influence relationship among leaders and collaborators who intend real changes that reflect their mutual purposes."

Heifetz (1994) is not alone when he questions the desirability of a definition for *leadership:*

> It seems to me that scholars might usefully consider that leadership is less an "is" than a "should be," and that our arguments might center not around who has most accurately described objective reality (or perhaps prevailing cultural assumptions) but around what image we can usefully offer to people who in part shape their self-images by our conceptions (p. 286).

Unfortunately, this explanation appears in the endnotes rather than the main text of Heifetz's *Leadership Without Easy Answers*, so many readers may not notice it.

The case studies emerging from the BSS offer at least glimpses of what on-the-job leadership should be, and perhaps can be. Superintendents demonstrated a strong commitment to improving schools for students who often are not well served by school systems and an equally strong commitment to meeting the challenges of a rapidly changing world.

NONTRADITIONAL LEADERSHIP THEORY

In a response to Slater's article, Maxcy (1995) calls for going "beyond leadership frameworks." He urges his readers to consider leadership in today's culture, seeking to understand "contemporary meanings of leadership by shifting our inquiry into the larger 'ways of life,'" and to be more interested in leadership for democracy (pp. 477, 478).

In another response to Slater's (1995) review of the leadership literature, Marshall (1995) questions the reliance on research that has excluded women and people of color. She searched for definitions "that are separated from hierarchical positions in bureaucracies and for frameworks for leadership in organizations where collaboration, nurturing, and inclusivity, relationship-building and caring, and social justice are asserted to be goals" (p. 486). She describes four viewpoints that challenge traditional frameworks by raising "critical questions left unasked and unanswered by the recent efforts to review leadership theory and research for education" (p. 486): (1) politics of knowledge; (2) feminist critique; (3) challenge to bureaucracy; and (4) critical theory.

An awareness of the politics of knowledge causes one to consider the relationship between knowledge and power. Whose knowledge is accepted? Whose is ignored? Marshall (1995) asks why leadership scholars "continue to search for a value-free definition of leadership" and whether "schools and their leadership are value-free" (p. 486).

Heifetz (1994) points out that

> we may like to use the word *leadership* as if we're value free, particularly in an age of science and mathematics, so that we can describe far-ranging phenomena and people with consistency . . . [but] we cannot talk about a crisis in leadership and then say leadership is value free (pp. 13–14).

In other words, "we cannot continue to have it both ways" (p. 13).

The feminist critique emphasizes the experiences and perspectives of women and minorities, data that until recently have been excluded from theory-building research. Alternative ways of leading have not previously been included in the mainline literature, because traditional leadership theory was

> developed by white males observing white males holding leadership positions in bureaucracies. The behaviors, perspectives, and values of women, minorities, and others who could not get through socialization and selection systems in bureaucracies . . . were, therefore, excluded from theory and research on leadership (Marshall, 1995, p. 487).

More recent research suggests that women do differ. They differ in the ways they speak, using more inclusive language and fewer terms suggesting "take charge and control" (Kempner, 1989). Women differ in their ways of knowing (Belenky, Clinchy, Goldberger, & Tarule, 1986), often seeking to understand rather than criticize. Women also are more likely to follow an ethic of care in moral decision making, emphasizing a desire to maintain relationships, consider the context, and alleviate burdens (Gilligan 1982; Lyons, 1983). In addition, women have been found to be different in their ways of leading (Rosener, 1990, 1991), frequently more collaborative and more concerned with resisting bureaucracy (Cooper, 1995).

Although the minority BSS superintendents did not express unique theories of leadership, they did note that people seemed to have different expectations for them. The Hispanic superintendent, whose parents had been migrant farm workers, was employed in a district with 35% Hispanic students. Headlines in the local newspaper celebrated this aspect of his background so vividly that he was concerned lest he not be seen as "the superintendent of all the students in the district."

Despite such concerns, minority superintendents consistently reported expectations that superintendents of color would provide for needs of minority youth and support long-repressed feelings of alienation by minority staff members. Happily, the Hispanic superintendent was able to intervene effectively when problems with youth gangs arose in the community for the first time, and he was able to collaborate with Hispanic civic groups to address the issues.

Among the minority first-time superintendents were also those who had grown up in housing projects of inner cities. Not surprisingly, each of the minority superintendents expressed strong commitment to meeting the needs of children living in poverty. Their efforts to improve schools reflected their understanding of the importance of a strong instructional focus for effective teaching of poor and minority youth (Andrews & Sonder, 1987).

Women and minorities experience both internal and external pressures to support bureaucratic structures, and they do so "to survive and advance in the hierarchy"; yet they also "resist bureaucratic procedures" (Cooper, 1995, p. 244). Bureaucratic organizations are too often considered the norm for schools and this model is seldom questioned. Marshall leads her readers to wonder whether or not we can embrace an educational model that fosters nurturance and collaboration instead of competition.

Critical theorists stress moral and democratic practices in schools, question the status quo, and seek to enlighten and empower. They ask What aspects of schooling perpetuate inequities? and What assumptions, policies, and practices enforce the status quo? Sergiovanni (1992) has called for a reconsideration, suggesting that we start thinking of schools as communities instead of organizations. He believes that, as professionalism is emphasized, the need for traditional leadership is lessened.

Marshall concludes her article by asserting that traditional views of leadership do not identify women and minorities who exhibit leadership and do not identify those leaders committed to reducing poverty, sexism, racism, and violence—problems that she sees perpetuated in the factory model, competitive schools. "Combining critical and feminist perspectives," she suggests, "would provide a framework for leaders who are carers, people who constantly work to maintain relationships, community, caring, and connection" (citing Gilligan, 1982; Noddings, 1992).

BRIGHT ORANGE: THE PROMISE OF COURAGEOUS CHANGE

Bright orange was the color of their leadership, the leadership exhibited by these first-year superintendents: intense, dramatic, and inspiring. The year was filled with frustrations as well as rewards and obstacles along with successes, but always active and full of suspense. The BSS captured the color of the daily lives of these first-year superintendents and their trials and triumphs. In her critique of traditional frameworks, Marshall (1995) stated: "If leadership is bright orange, leadership research is slate gray" (p. 486, citing McCall and Lombardo, 1978, p. 3). Actually, the research on educational leadership is gradually becoming more alive, more colorful, and in the case of superintendents, more truly representative of their professional lives. It is less gray than it was in the 70s, when McCall and Lombardo wrote their dramatic assessment.

More recent publications offer different perspectives and hold promise of courageous change as well as a promise of what leadership should be and, perhaps, can be. *Women Leading in Education*, edited by Dunlap and Schmuck (1995), is a rich collection of chapters related to the preparation and socialization of women, alternative ways of leading, and visions for the future. Regan and Brook's (1996) *Out of Women's Experience: Creating Relational Leadership* includes the personal stories of 11 women school administrators who gradually discovered their own authentic voice and together created an alternative model—relational leadership. They discuss the attributes of relational leading, including collaboration, caring, courage, intuition, and vision. These concepts were of concern to most of the BSS superintendents.

Mainline textbooks for educational administration are beginning to acknowledge different perspectives. Hoy and Miskel (1996) refer to "emergent nontraditional perspectives." Although, as the authors readily admit, most of the text emphasizes traditional perspectives, three nontraditional approaches are described, including postmodern and poststructural approaches, critical theory, and feminist theory. These are included because they "present a major intellectual challenge to the established knowledge about organizational behavior, and they force discussion of important, but often ignored, organizational problems" (Hoy and Miskel, 1996, p. 17). I suggest this is a strong rationale for a much more comprehensive discussion of these approaches.

Robert Starratt's (1996) *Transforming Educational Administration: Meaning, Community, and Excellence* offers a nontraditional perspective that can be briefly described as taking a "critical turn" (Foster, 1996, p. xii), but blends both the "critical and appreciative arts" (p. xiii). After explaining "the special nature of educational administration" and why we must move beyond "administrative pathologies," Starratt develops three main aspects of educational leadership: "(1) administering meaning; (2) administering community; and (3) administering excellence." These divisions link purpose, vision, action, and the strategies needed to overcome the status quo.

In Murphy's (1995) report on the St. Louis Working Conference on School Reform Implications for the Preparation of School Leaders, three dimensions of leadership were highlighted: "(1) nurturing the educational agenda; (2) promoting continuous growth and improvement; and (3) fostering purposive relationships and collaborative action." The themes that emerged from the data on first-year superintendents reflect a central concern for these three dimensions.

The BSS superintendents asked many of the questions associated with the less traditional frameworks. They were especially concerned with equity issues, serving students not usually successful in schools; seeking ways to promote collaboration and lessen traditional bureaucracy; seeking to establish caring relationships; and addressing the unasked questions regarding schooling. Both traditional and nontraditional ways of leading were often demonstrated by the men as well as the women. It is apparent that looking through different lenses holds promise for improving schools in ways more appropriate for a democracy—ways that better meet the needs of all students.

Progress has been made in representing women's experiences and perspectives in the leadership literature. Less progress has been made in including the voices of minorities. However, the gray is beginning to take on a more colorful hue. Recent research and publications hold promise of courageous change for the improvement of schools. To resist the slide back toward the gray of the status quo, it is important that scholars and practitioners affirm their commitment to multiple lenses, alternative approaches, and diverse perspectives.

The case studies heighten awareness of the enormous amount of time demanded of the superintendency. It is important to ask questions usually unasked, to consider how bureaucracy can be resisted, to seek alternatives to hierarchy, to develop collaboration across agencies, and to advocate for children before state legislative bodies. These tasks require not only time for the actions involved but also time for study and for reflection.

The role of the superintendency developed during an era when virtually all superintendents were men whose wives were not employed outside the home. More women are now becoming superintendents, and most men have working wives. In addition, there appears to be more desire for a lifestyle that values time for a personal life. Concurrently, problems associated with poverty, drugs, and violence have created far greater stresses on the schools and their superintendents.

This book began by recognizing the rapid turnover of superintendents as a deterrent to sustained efforts by school districts to improve schools. I am haunted by the comment of one superintendent: "I'm stretched very thinly—if it doesn't change, I won't do this for long." Perhaps the most important question is not What *is* leadership for a superintendent? but How can the superintendency be reconfigured so the role is more humanly possible?

QUESTIONS FOR REFLECTION AND DISCUSSION

1. What aspects of traditional leadership theory did you find most frequently expressed by the words and behaviors of the new superintendents?

2. What evidence did you see in the case studies that superintendents were applying nontraditional approaches to leadership?

3. How might a candidate for a superintendency assess the match between his or her leadership style and the expectations and needs of the district?

4. How should the presence or absence of such a match affect a candidate's decision to accept a superintendency? If a mismatch exists, how can or should that impact the initial year of the superintendent's tenure?

5. What do you see as the ideal mix of traditional and nontraditional approaches to leadership for superintendents in today's school districts?

REFERENCES

Andrews, R. L., & Sonder, R. (1987, March). Principal leadership and student achievement. *Educational Leadership, 44*, 9–11.

Belenky, M. F., Clinchy, B. M., Goldberger, N. R., & Tarule, J. M. (1986). *Women's ways of knowing: The development of self, voice, and mind.* New York: Basic Books.

Burns, J. M. (1978). *Leadership.* New York: Harper & Row.

Burrell, G., & Morgan, G. (1979). *Sociological paradigms and organizational analysis.* London: Heineman.

Cooper, J. E. (1995). Administrative women and their writing: Reproduction and resistance in bureaucracies. In D. M. Dunlap & P. A. Schmuck (Eds.), *Women leading in education*. New York: SUNY.

Cunningham, L. (1992). *Monitoring, mapping, and interpreting the sources and content of change.* Gahanna, OH: Leadership Development Associates.

Deal, T. E., & Peterson, K. D. (1990). *The principal's role in shaping school culture.* Washington, DC: U.S. Department of Education.

Dunlap, D. M., & Schmuck, P. A. (1995). *Women leading in education.* New York: SUNY.

Foster, M. (1996). Foreword, in Starratt, R. J. *Transforming Educational Administration.* New York: McGraw-Hill.

Gilligan, C. (1982). *In a different voice: Psychological theory and women's development.* Cambridge, MA: Harvard University Press.

Grant, G. E. (1988). *Teaching critical thinking.* New York: Praeger.

Heifetz, R. (1994). *Leadership without easy answers.* Cambridge, MA: Harvard University Press.

Heilbrunn, Jacob. (1994, Spring). Can leadership be studied? *The Wilson Quarterly, 18,* 65–72.

Hoy, W. K., & Miskel, C. G. (1996). *Educational administration: Theory, research, and practice.* New York: McGraw-Hill.

Hoyle, J., English, F., & Steffy, B. (1985). *Skills for successful school leaders.* Arlington: VA: American Association of School Administrators.

Jentz, B., Cheever, D. S., Jr., Fisher, S. B., Jones, M. H., Kelleher, P., & Wofford, J. W. (1982). *Entry: The hiring, start-up, and supervision of Administrators.* New York: McGraw-Hill.

Kempner, K. (1989, Spring, published in 1991). Getting into the castle of educational administration. *Peabody Journal of Education, 66,* 104–123.

Lyons, N. P. (1983, May). Two perspectives: On self, relationships, and morality. *Harvard Educational Review 53,* 125–145.

Marshall, C. (1995, August) Imagining leadership. *Educational Administration Quarterly, 31,* 484–492.

Maxcy, S. J. (1995, August). Beyond leadership frameworks. *Educational Administration Quarterly, 31,* 473–483.

McCall, M. W., & Lombardo, M. M. (Eds). (1978). *Leadership: Where else can we go?* Durham, NC: Duke University Press.

Murphy, J. (1995, September). Rethinking the foundations of leadership preparation: Insights from school improvements efforts. In *Design for Leadership,* Fairfax, VA: *National Policy Board for Educational Administration, 6,* 1–4, 6.

Noddings, N. (1992). The challenge to care in schools. New York: Teachers College Press.

Regan, H. B., & Brooks, G. H. (1996). *Out of women's experience: Creating relational leadership.* Thousand Oaks: CA.

Rosener, J. B. (1990, November-December). Ways women lead. *Harvard Business Review, 68,* 119–125.

Rosener, J. B. (1991, January-February). Ways men and women lead (response in debate). *Harvard Business Review, 69,* 155–160.

Rost, J. C. (1991). *Leadership for the twenty-first century.* New York: Praeger.

Sergiovanni, T. J. (1992, February). Why we should seek substitutes for leadership. *Educational Leadership, 49,* 41–45.

Slater, R. O. (1995, August). The sociology of leadership and educational administration. *Educational Administration Quarterly, 31,* 449–472.

Starratt, R. J. (1996). *Transforming educational administration: Meaning, community, and excellence.* New York: McGraw-Hill.

17

THE ROAD TO THE
SUPERINTENDENCY

Doris A. Henry, The University of Memphis
Charles M. Achilles, Eastern Michigan University

ABSTRACT.   Traditional educational administration programs have been criticized on many fronts for not adequately preparing individuals to become successful superintendents. In response, some innovative programs have emerged in recent years. These upbeat approaches emphasize executive skill development and include not only intensified academic studies but also supervised internships. Some programs also provide continuing education and supportive coaching for individuals who enter their first superintendency. Several of the BSS superintendents participated in such innovative programs. Six examples of programs to prepare superintendents illustrate approaches that follow the recommendations of the BSS superintendents and meet the Professional Standards for the Superintendency (AASA, 1993).

At a time when the nation is deeply concerned about the performance of its schools, and near-to-obsessed with the credentials and careers of those who teach in them, scant attention has been paid to the preparation and qualifications of those who lead them.

(Peterson & Finn, 1985, p. 42).

To the extent that preparation programs for superintendents are included in the general criticism of education, they are painted by the broad brush of that criticism. Though speaking of administrators in general, rather than superintendents in particular, Guthrie (1990) stated, "The preparation of professional education administrators is one of the weakest components of United States education" (p. 228). Expressing a similar viewpoint, the Subcommittee on the Preparation of School Administrators for the American Association of Colleges of Teacher Education declared, "Dramatic changes are needed in programs to prepare school administrators if they are to lead their schools and faculties rather than just manage them" (Shibles, 1988, p. 1).

As described in Chapter 2, the superintendency was created in the middle of the nineteenth century when schools were not the complex organizations that they are today. In 1969, Gregg observed that

> the administrator could learn his profession effectively on the job by trial-and-error processes. Little, if any, formal specialized preparation was needed, and none was provided. The minimal formal education which was designed for teachers was deemed sufficient for those who would be administrators (pp. 993–994).

A preparation program for the superintendency and preparation for the superintendency are not necessarily the same. This is because few prospective school administrators initially enter a preparation program with the immediate goal of becoming a school superintendent. Typically, the process of moving through the ranks to become a superintendent takes considerable time, and movement into one's first superintendency may occur well after completion of a formal preparation program. A common pattern is that a person earns a master's degree; works as a principal and, perhaps, as a central office administrator for some time; and then, at a later time, takes courses required for certification as a superintendent.

In 39 states, school superintendents are required to gain additional certification beyond that required of principals (NASDTEC, 1991). Certification as a superintendent, in most states, requires completion of additional university courses, and, in some cases, a sixth-year or educational specialist degree. Hoyle (1989) summed up what he saw as problems in current approaches to learning the superintendency:

> Preparation programs for school administrators are often fragmented, unfocused, and lacking a carefully sequenced curriculum. Moreover, they can easily extend over a period of years. The preparation process can be a hit-or-miss, piecemeal selection of education courses, institutes, and academies, rather than a planned, systematic program of professional studies (p. 376).

In spite of this dismal picture, the BSS superintendents favorably rated their own programs of graduate studies as preparation for the superintendency. Some 26.7% identified them as "excellent"; 60% rated them as "good"; and none of them rated their programs as "poor." The views of the BSS superintendents were surprisingly similar to those of superintendents and principals surveyed in a 1987 study by the National Center for Education Information. Hoyle (1989), who reported on this study, noted that "one in four superintendents and principals said that their university preparation was 'excellent'; some 50% said that it was 'pretty good'; only 1% of the superintendents and 2% of the principals described their preparation as 'poor.'"

THE NATURE OF THE SUPERINTENDENCY

A superintendency is not necessarily a superintendency is not necessarily a superintendency. According to Glass (1992), "Of about 15,000 school districts in America, about 80% have fewer than 3,000 pupils" (p. 7). Hence, it is not surprising that many leaders of larger school systems begin their careers in small districts. Large urban superintendencies have more complex problems that occur more frequently than those of the small-district superintendency of less than 3,000 pupils. And somewhere between the urban and the rural superintendencies are a large collection of school leadership positions in suburbia and in small cities.

Although the persons applying for the superintendency have had specific training provided by an institution of higher education, variations among districts may point to the need for more site-specific internships. This is currently not provided by most institutions preparing individuals for certification.

Because few people move directly into a superintendency immediately upon completion of an entry-level preparation program, one major stumbling block is continuing to consider preparation for the superintendency as "pre-service." It is probably better described as a continuing professional development process that begins with one's initial preparation program and includes a continuing crescendo of courses and experiences leading to the district-level leadership position.

Superintendents are faced with complicated demands that require continuous renewal of skills related to change, ambiguity, and diversity. Added to the urgency for quality superintendency preparation is the projected retirement of many superintendents across the nation. Based on the average age of superintendents presented in Chapter 2, as many as 50% could retire in the next decade. This projected retirement challenges faculties in departments of educational leadership to rethink and revise their programs to reflect the changing times.

PREPARATION PROGRAMS

The university has been the predominant place for preparing superintendents. "Preparation programs are essentially diverse collections of formal courses that, taken together, do not reveal consistent purposes or a systematic design" (NASSP, 1985, p. 2). One major criticism offered by Goodlad (1984) was that the certification and accreditation processes are too costly and cumbersome.

The National Commission for the Principalship (1990) stated that certification focused on skills and requirements that are different from what is needed in the field. In a comprehensive analysis of preparation programs in educational administration, Murphy (1992) noted that "university programs are often diametrically opposed to conditions that characterize the workplace milieu of schools" (p. 89).

Preparation programs are disconnected to practice. "[Institutions] that had emphasized a solid grounding in theory, the social sciences, [and] rational decision making . . . were discovered to be well off the mark as effective preparation for the chaotic life of a principal or superintendent" (Crowson & McPherson, 1987, p. 49). Many university-driven programs that prepare superintendents have not changed as society and education have changed. The traditional courses that were offered decades ago are still the staples of the program.

Pitner (1988) notes that "the denigration of professional training by practitioners is by no means confined to the field of school administration" (p. 378). Pitner identifies major studies from such fields as medicine, business administration, and law to bolster her claim. However, there are recent trends in leading schools of medicine and of business administration to replace much of their traditional lecture-rote-regurgitation curricula with problem-based learning (PBL); and that trend, by osmosis, is seeping into preparation for school leaders (Bridges & Hallinger, 1991).

BSS SUPERINTENDENTS REFLECT ON THEIR PREPARATION

As noted earlier, 86.7% of the BSS superintendents rated their graduate programs as "excellent" or "good." Although one superintendent was appointed the same year he completed his doctorate in educational administration, others finished their academic preparation years earlier. Some had earned their terminal degrees as long as 17, 18, 23, or 25 years before becoming superintendents. By no means did this time gap correlate with age: a 59-year-old new superintendent had completed her degree 3 years before and a 42-year-old had completed his 18 years earlier.

When the BSS superintendents were asked to list one major strength of their graduate programs, seven listed the "quality of educational administration courses," six cited "field contacts or practical work in districts," and four noted the "high quality of professors." Other strengths noted included the "high caliber of fellow students" and "availability of noneducation or cognate courses."

Although four of the BSS superintendents reported that their graduate study program had "no weaknesses," four others mentioned "poor quality of specific educational administration courses." Three of the BSS superintendents felt the major weakness in their programs was "lack of opportunity for full-time study," and three others criticized the "lack of quality internship."

Some of the BSS superintendents attended workshops, seminars, and academies in addition to their university-based preparation programs. Two of these, the AASA National Superintendents Academy and Superintendents Prepared, are described in detail later in this chapter.

Although their overall assessment of their graduate education programs was generally positive, the BSS superintendents were also asked to identify areas in which they would have benefitted from stronger preparation. Most frequently, the BSS superintendents felt a need for more preparation in fiscal matters, reflecting the fact that major fiscal problems emerged during their first year that were beyond the knowledge that they had gleaned when they interviewed for the jobs. They also felt weak in strategies for conducting bond issue campaigns, dealing with sudden loss of revenue or unanticipated costs, correcting financial practices of the previous administration, and managing massive capital outlay. Several superintendents reported that they could have better assessed the fiscal status of their districts if they had stronger preparation in school finance and school business management.

The BSS superintendents recommended that such courses should be more extensive and that the instructional delivery should include simulations and hands-on activities. One superintendent suggested that more management, marketing, and financial analysis training would be useful; another recommended more work on budget development; and still another believed that basic accounting is needed, including how to read spreadsheets and use computer-based accounting programs. Financial training is especially needed by superintendents whose first position is in rural districts where they are usually directly responsible for all financial affairs. Although specialized personnel may handle finances in larger districts, even there some superintendents discovered the importance of understanding fiscal management when they needed to correct mismanagement or suspected discrepant transactions.

Communications was another common area of need expressed by the BSS superintendents. One superintendent said that he thought he was communicating effectively to others but that his efforts often went awry.

Coupled with communications is skill in interpersonal relations. Several mentioned a desire for more skill in delegating wisely and developing staff. Though one superintendent said that she based many actions on intuition, superintendents need to make reasoned, objective judgments about people, a skill not readily gained from textbooks. Interpersonal relations concerns were not only with the personnel within the district but also with political entities.

The BSS superintendents wanted to develop their skills in group dynamics, consensus building, and working with legislators and other people in the political arena. Some of the superintendents had to go before government officials to solicit support. Here they discovered that school finance is as much a political process as a technical one. "Superintendents need to be extremely adept at the politics of it all."

Perhaps because 55.5% of the BSS superintendents were hired to be change agents, as reported in Chapter 2, a number of them reported a need for more training in change strategies and how to bring about improvements. They wanted to understand systemic reform and "new models of organizational life [such as the] total quality movement and learning organizations."

Other recommendations from these first-year superintendents included the need for knowledge and skill in the "street smarts" of organization and political life. Some recommendations were direct: more on technology, current research, law (open meetings and school board rights), collective bargaining, designing a board agenda, developing policy, changing demographics, and dealing with "right wing fundamentalists." These are survival skills of good management.

Some of the BSS superintendents explained the rationale for their recommendations. They felt that if they had been more perceptive during the interview process, they might have been able to sniff out problems and dysfunctional aspects of the district before accepting the position. Many were surprised about the condition of the district when they were confronted with a crisis. This was especially true of the fiscal matters.

The superintendents overwhelmingly said that the courses would be better if they were "hands on" and experience based. In-basket activities, simulations, problem-based learning, role playing, and case studies would be good ways to deliver instruction. Because some of their most helpful classes were taught by practitioners, the BSS superintendents felt that there should be some way in which practitioners are actively engaged with people preparing for the superintendency. A common complaint was too much theory and not enough experience. This is literally a return to the stance of Cubberley, that pioneer superintendent-professor of the early twentieth century described in Chapter 2, who focused on solving educational problems (Glass, 1992).

One suggestion was that people acquiring a superintendent's certificate should have internships in rural settings as well as the usual urban/suburban settings. Though these are the kind of districts where most universities place people for field experiences, relatively few first-year superintendencies are in urban districts or wealthy suburbs.

The BSS superintendents sought strategies for dealing with crisis issues. All superintendents in the study had some crisis, such as child abuse, upon which they had to act. Child abuse is a growing concern for administrators.

Another crisis area was handling stress. One superintendent said that he needed to know more about protecting his own health while being a superintendent. Another talked with a therapist as a way of handling stress, and still another saved time each day for exercise.

Mentors were helpful in some crises. Networking and socialization to the superintendency are not a formalized part of most preparation programs. However, as Glass pointed out in Chapter 2, mentors were particularly important for minority and women superintendents.

One first-year superintendent did not suggest courses; he suggested four processes and ideas. His first criterion was experience as a principal, and especially experience as a high school principal. In his terms, "There is no crap like high school crap: discipline, community demands, factions, faculty reluctance to change, athletics, parents, the law, teen pregnancy." Second, a person must "know thyself." This might be accomplished through assessment center work, Myers-Briggs Type Indicators (MBTI), discussion, education platforms, introspection, and reflection. The person must also come to grips with key questions such as, How comfortable am I with delegation? Finally, "the preparation program should push a person to become familiar with classic and current literature and research on teaching and learning and to get some idea of change processes and of the politics needed to get the job done."

Interestingly, only one of the BSS superintendents mentioned additional work in curriculum and instruction. Perhaps most of them had a strong curriculum and instruction background, but most likely their first year was primarily consumed with management challenges. This was true for one of the BSS superintendents, Dr. Martha Post.

THE CAREER PATH MAY WIND UNPREDICTABLY

Dr. Martha Post's story offers a perspective on preparation from the viewpoint of an unusual career path to the superintendency. Dr. Post was an insider. She was the only BSS superintendent to grow up in the same community where she began her teaching and administrative careers and raised a family. The only period of time she left the community was to attend college.

Martha started as a fourth-grade teacher, became a media specialist, and was eventually selected to be the district media coordinator for the elementary schools. Next, she was appointed as director of purchasing and finance. Later she moved into the role of assistant superintendent for business before becoming deputy superintendent of the 8,000-student district.

Before Martha even considered the superintendency, the superintendent, who was contemplating another position, declared he would not leave unless Martha agreed to replace him. She declined. Even in the face of her reluctance, the superintendent began to groom her for the position. He made his point—two years later she accepted the superintendency.

Dr. Post's path to the superintendency was different from the others in the study. She had considerable experience in one of the areas described by the others as being the most difficult—finance and fiscal affairs. In addition, as second-in-command, she had been instrumental in developing a strong focus on school improvement. In fact, the district had attracted national recognition as a leader in the school effectiveness movement. The board members wanted to continue with what they had in place, and Martha wanted to preserve what her efforts had helped to initiate.

At the outset, Martha thought that her experience and training in the district would make her transition relatively easy. Unanticipated events later tempered this perception. Even her finance background and intimate knowledge of the community did not fully prepare her to cope with military downsizing at a large base in the district, which resulted in loss of both students and revenue. Although challenged by this unexpected turn of events, Martha did not panic, crediting her calm composure to her experience on the business side of education.

Dr. Post experienced another strong stressor. She became a superintendent in the community where she grew up and had spent her entire career. As a first-time superintendent she asked, "If I am not successful as a superintendent, then where will I go?"

The BSS superintendents said that experiences as a building principal and a central office administrator were valuable aspects of their preparation. These experiences positioned them well for being selected as the instructional leaders of their districts. The importance of central office experience, as well as being a principal, was illuminated by the research of Glass (1993). Based on his study of career paths of superintendents, he reported, "Exemplary superintendents were far more likely to spend a few years in central office positions before acquiring appointments as super-intendents" (p. 61).

Regardless of their path to the superintendency, most first-year superintendents in this study identified areas in which they wished their preparation had been stronger: (1) financial issues; (2) communications and interpersonal skills; (3) political issues; (4) personal stress; and (5) crisis issues, such as child abuse.

INNOVATIVE PROGRAMS EMERGE

Although the call for changing educational administration preparation programs has been sent from many varied sources, little change has been made in most university-based programs for training superintendents. Seminars, academies, and workshops have been conducted by professional associations to assist superintendents in learning the ropes and gaining the expertise needed to be successful in the job. These on-the-job options supplement certification or licensure requirements set by the states.

A few innovative preparation programs tailored to the challenges facing today's superintendents have emerged. Most of these programs work with aspiring superintendents for more than a year, and some continue to provide support for individuals who enter their first superintendency. Some focus on a particular type of superintendency, such as those for urban superintendents.

Although some of these programs are associated with higher education, others are not. The programs summarized here include (1) the Cooperative Superintendency Program (CSP) at the University of Texas, Austin; (2) the Urban Superintendents Program (USP) at Harvard University; (3) Superintendents Prepared; (4) the Institute for Executive Leadership at Lewis and Clark College; (5) the Bell South Program for Exemplary Superintendents in Tennessee (BEST) at East Tennessee State University; and (6) the AASA National Superintendents Academy. The following sections include summaries of each program's purpose(s), goals, structure, and curriculum content.

Cooperative Superintendency Program

The Cooperative Superintendency Executive Leadership Program (CSP) at the University of Texas, Austin, has been in place for more than two decades. It received national recognition in 1987 when AASA designated it as an exemplary program for administrator preparation. Nolan Estes, former superintendent of the Dallas Independent School District, coordinates the program.

The CSP is completed over a 24-month period that integrates university-based course work and assessment, field research, and an internship (Loredo & Carter, 1993). In the year preceding each new CSP cycle, a talent search begins by inviting candidates to submit a portfolio that includes a comprehensive professional and personal curriculum vitae, complete graduate and undergraduate transcripts, recommendations by professional referees, admission to graduate status, evidence of administrative performance and developmental growth, and a written self-portrait. Those selected as finalists go to Austin to participate in a day-long appraisal seminar in mid-April. Successful candidates begin their 2-year program in June.

Additional diagnostic activities provide formative evaluation to guide individual program development for CSP fellows. The research-based spiral curriculum is organized around a conceptual framework for leadership, including general education, instructional leadership, general administrative leadership, human relations and interpersonal leadership, personal capabilities, and multicultural perspectives.

In addition to University of Texas faculty, practitioner-scholars, including outstanding superintendents, share their specific expertise and insights during seminars. Each fellow works with four mentors chosen from the fields of government, industry, university, and public education. Because at least one of the mentors is involved in initial diagnostic processes, fellows receive feedback and support from the beginning of their program.

Mentors play a key role in the professional development of fellows during their field experiences and dissertation development. This process is enhanced by participation in Peer-Assisted Leadership (PAL), described by Loredo and Carter (1993):

> The PAL program pairs students with practicing superintendents. Partners learn how to collect information about each other by shadowing and conducting reflective interviews; thus PAL activities afford fellows the opportunity to become more intelligent about their own leadership behaviors and those of a peer. PAL participants attend six training sessions and also engage in follow-up activities between training meetings (p. 130).

In addition to their work with the PAL program, CSP fellows participate as members of a vertical problem-solving team in the planning and implementation of school improvement projects. Discussions about school problems engage the collaborative efforts of the superintendent, a central office administrator, a principal, a teacher, a classified employee, and a school board member on the vertical team.

The Urban Superintendents Program

The purpose of the Urban Superintendents Program (USP) at Harvard University is to prepare people to become superintendents of urban school districts. The single-focused program was created in 1990 by the collaborative efforts of superintendents and the Harvard faculty. The director, Dr. Robert Peterkin, was formerly a superintendent in Milwaukee, Wisconsin, and in Cambridge, Massachusetts. Urban superintendents throughout the United States who serve on the Superintendent Advisory Panel provide direction for this program.

This is "a doctoral program intended to prepare superintendents who are capable of, and committed to, undertaking the analysis and action necessary to a campaign of authentic, systemic educational change" (Peterkin, 1994, p.2). The students complete a doctorate with specific preparation to be a superintendent. No more than ten students are admitted each year following an extensive selection process. Each student receives a $20,000 fellowship for the first year and a stipend of $30,000 for the 6-month internship during the second year.

The Harvard Urban Superintendents Program has three components. First, intensive, accelerated course work is provided during two summers and the intervening fall and spring semesters. The courses focus on law, teaching and learning, leadership in organizations, microeconomics, qualitative and quantitative methods, school finance, negotiations, adult development and school leadership, communication, and politics, including policy making and political action in education.

During the second year, the students are selectively placed with urban superintendents, full time, for a 6-month internship. "The intern-mentor relationship is such that the superintendent involves the student in all aspects of the superintendency—both routine and challenging—and regularly engages the student in dialogue about what the superintendent does and why" (Peterkin, 1994, p.2). Students return to Harvard University at least twice during the internship for intensive 3-day seminars. They are also connected through electronic mail to continue the support and networking that has been established during the first year.

The third component of the Harvard program is the dissertation. Students select and research a complex problem of urban educational leadership. "The problem is illuminated by a formal inquiry that brings theory as well as qualitative or quantitative methods to bear on professional practice" (Peterkin, 1994, p. 3).

A preliminary assessment indicates progress toward meeting the program's goals. Indicators include completion of the doctorate within four years, employment at the superintendent or cabinet level in urban school districts, and movement into new urban leadership positions.

Superintendents Prepared

The establishment of this innovative program, led by Floretta McKenzie, former superintendent of the District of Columbia Public Schools, was hailed as a significant effort to improve preparation of school district leaders:

> To increase the number of educational leaders prepared to meet the rising demands of urban school systems, five major foundations are supporting a multi-year, national effort to identify and expand the pool of candidates for large city superintendency (Foundations back efforts, 1992, p. 2).

Superintendents Prepared was designed and is operated by The Institute for Educational Leadership, The McKenzie Group, and the Joint Center for Political and Economic Studies. The program, based in Washington, D.C., offers "an experiential, nontraditional approach to leadership development" (Foundations back efforts, 1992). The sponsoring foundations are The DeWitt Wallace-Reader's Digest Fund, The Ford Foundation, The Pew Charitable Trusts, The Prudential Foundation, and The Rockefeller Foundation.

Goals are to provide a strong emphasis on the development of political and managerial skills, communications, community mobilization, state-of-the-art educational strategies, and the many complex social and financial issues particularly confronting urban school districts today. No more than 30 applicants are accepted each year. Participation is not limited to educators; persons in other fields, such as business, law, or the military, are also welcome to apply.

The program is structured around five key components. The first is an intensive, 2-week summer institute to assess leadership skills, attend expert briefings and seminars on critical educational issues, and develop an individual leadership development plan.

The second aspect is an individual leadership development plan that is intended to tailor the program according to the individual's leadership training experiences. The third component is the participant observing complex working environments. The fourth element is a summer institute on managerial and financial issues and on marketing and placement preparations. The fifth, and last, component is establishing a network of support among the leaders and other emerging superintendents.

One of the BSS superintendents participated in the Superintendents Prepared. She considered this program to be very helpful in preparing for her superintendency and looked forward to meeting periodically with her Superintendents Prepared colleagues as her first year progressed.

The Institute for Executive Leadership

This university-based program at Lewis and Clark College, in Portland, Oregon, helps participants to obtain a basic superintendent certificate in the state of Oregon.

The focus is on problem-based learning and clinical knowledge in educational administration. Approximately 20 students form a cohort for the five-quarter program. Some students have doctorates but lack certification for the superintendency.

Each of two weekend retreats each quarter begins with a challenge course. There are "monthly meetings of two evenings and a full day Saturday. The content and pedagogy . . . focus on clinical knowledge in educational administration" (Schmuck, 1992, p. 67).

Simulations, exercises, and case studies provide an opportunity for the students to practice, receive feedback, reflect, and practice again. Practicing superintendents discuss specific issues. From these contacts networks are formed.

Bell South Program for Exemplary Superintendents in Tennessee

The purpose of the Bell South Program for Exemplary Superintendents in Tennessee (BEST) at East Tennessee State University is to identify aspiring superintendents in the state of Tennessee and provide an intensive professional development program for their preparation for the superintendency.

Beginning in 1994, 50 people have been selected annually to participate in this program over a 3-year period. The BEST program was created by the project director, Dr. Donn Gresso, working with an advisory board of business executives, university faculty, state education officials, and superintendents. Practitioners, professors, business executives, and others conduct the learning sessions.

The BEST program emphasizes problem solving, consensus building, and cadre development. Participants meet as a cohort during a 3-year period. "Internship experiences, cultural events, and professional development sessions . . . involve a cohort in intensive opportunities to network and collaborate. . . . Change processes, collaborative decision making, and effective CEO strategies [are] part of the content covered during this period" (Gresso, 1995, p.1).

AASA National Superintendents Academy

The purpose of the National Superintendents Academy is to improve the skills of new superintendents or those who aspire to be superintendents. The American Association of School Administrators (AASA) sponsors the academy, which enrolls 30 to 50 educators each summer.

The agenda for the 1989 academy provides a sample of the curriculum and some of the nationally known instructors selected by AASA:

- Essentials of Leadership, Robert Tschirki
- Marketing Yourself, Jessie Kobayshi and Doyle Winter
- Curriculum Management and Development, Fenwick English
- Developing and Managing Staff, Marilyn Bates
- Superintendent's Contract and Legal Issues, Gerald Caplan
- School/Business Partnerships and Financial Management, Edna McDuffie Manning
- Men and Women Working Together, Charol Shakeshaft
- Educational Administrator Effectiveness Profile and Prescription for Change, AASA National Executive Development Center
- Politics and Education; School Board/Superintendent Relations, Richard L. Foster
- Media Skills for the Executive, Linda Crocker Moore
- Assessing and Changing Cultures, Terrence Deal
- Strategic Planning, Daniel Keck
- Assessing a District Before the Interview, Ruth Love

During the design of the BSS, Carolyn Hughes Chapman conducted a survey of participants in the AASA National Superintendents Academy in 1989, 1990, and 1991. She found that 28.8% of the 73 respondents were superintendents at the time of their academy; 42.5% were assistant superintendents; and 15.1% held other central office positions. Of the participants, 55% had applied for at least one superintendency and 5.5% had applied for an assistant superintendency by the time the survey was taken in 1992.

The academy participants were a mobile group, as shown by the fact that 21% changed jobs once and 5% changed jobs twice in the 3-year period. Of those who changed jobs, 20% became superintendent within 3 years of their participation in the National Superintendents Academy. Two of the BSS superintendents were among the respondents to the survey.

LOOKING TO THE FUTURE

In 1993, the American Association of School Administrators (AASA) identified eight main standards for the superintendency, which included 89 competencies and skills. The *Professional Standards for the Superintendency* include: (1) leadership and district culture; (2) policy and governance; (3) communications and community relations; (4) organizational management; (5) curriculum planning and development; (6) instructional management; (7) human resources management; and (8) values and ethics of leadership.

Baden (1995) examined how 24 first-year superintendents in Oklahoma perceived these standards. He found that they saw organizational management skills as most important, followed by time management, superintendent-board of education relationships, modeling appropriate judgment and actions, financial planning and management, and demonstrating ethical and personal integrity.

The message to universities is clear: Unless programs reflect current research and emerging professional standards, the programs will not be adequate. One alternative would be to consider traditional university administrator preparation programs as entry-level work on which university professors can build new processes and structures for the advanced preparation needed by superintendents.

Conceptually sound advanced programs might be developed incorporating continuing "seminars" scheduled to fit into the busy lives of administrators. These programs might be given, for instance, in a weekend format. New superintendents need opportunities to develop skills in areas such as strategic planning, budgeting, and group processes while gaining increased knowledge of current research in teaching and learning, organizational development, and instructional leadership. This is the essence of what the BSS superintendents identified as ways to strengthen university-based preparation programs. All of the innovative superintendent preparation programs presented here blend theory with emphasis on the practical elements of finance, policy and politics, and interpersonal skills.

If Glass (1995) is accurate in his estimate that the job-life expectancy of a superintendent is about six years, there is ample demand for superintendent preparation programs. The BSS superintendents identified the areas that they believed would have better prepared them for the first superintendency. These superintendents' recommendations are echoed in the current innovative programs.

Universities can no longer afford to ponder the question of what to do if they wish to remain vitally involved in superintendent preparation. Action is needed to provide leadership for the school districts of the nation. If universities do not develop programs that meet the needs of superintendents, non-university-based programs will develop and thrive.

QUESTIONS FOR REFLECTION AND DISCUSSION

1. Some traditional preparation programs have been criticized for being "too much theory and not enough practice." What do you see as an appropriate balance between developing clear understanding of research and theory to guide administrative decision making and hands-on skill building?

2. How does the time that elapses between graduate course work and entering an administrative position affect ability to function effectively? What can educators do to stay "on the cutting edge" after completing their graduate degrees?

3. What benefits might emerge from full-time graduate study in a concentrated period of time in contrast to being a part-time graduate student while holding a demanding, full-time job? How could you determine whether the benefits outweigh the time and fiscal resources required?

4. If a friend told you he or she was considering taking graduate courses to prepare to become a superintendent of schools, what recommendations would you make? How has what you have read in this book affected what you would recommend?

REFERENCES

American Association of School Administrators. (1989, July 9–21). *The 1989 superintendents academy, Colorado Springs, CO.* Arlington, VA: Author.

American Association of School Administrators. (1993). *Professional standards for the superintendency.* Arlington, VA: Author.

Baden, K. (1995, April). *The AASA standards and the first-year superintendent in Oklahoma.* Paper presented at the Fourth Annual National Conference on Creating the Quality School, Oklahoma City, OK.

Bridges, E. M., & Hallinger, P. (1991, Fall). Problem-based learning: A promising approach for preparing educational administrators. *UCEA Review, 32(3),* 3–5, 7–8.

Crowson, R. L., & McPherson, R. B. (1987). The legacy of the theory movement: Learning from the new tradition. In J. Murphy & P. Hallinger (Eds.), *Approaches to administrative training in education* (pp. 45–64). Albany: SUNY Press.

Foundations back efforts to train, place city supts. (1992, March 15). *Leadership News, 96,* 2.

Glass, T. E. (1992). *The study of the American school superintendency: America's education leaders in a time of reform.* Arlington, VA: American Association of School Superintendents.

Glass, T. E. (1993). Exemplary superintendents: Do they fit the model? In D. S. G. Carter, T. E. Glass, & S. M. Hord (Eds.), *Selecting, preparing and developing the school district superintendent.* Washington, DC: Falmer.

Glass, T. E. (1995). *Beginning superintendents: Who are they?* Paper presented at the annual conference of the American Association of School Administrators, San Francisco, April 19, 1995.

Goodlad, J. I. (1984). *A place called school: Prospects of the future.* New York: McGraw-Hill.

Gregg, R. T. (1969). Preparation of administrators. In R. L. Ebel (Ed.), *Encyclopedia of educational research* (4th ed., pp. 993–1004). London: Macmillan.

Gresso, D. (1995). East Tennessee State University-Bell South program for exemplary superintendents in Tennessee. Author.

Guthrie, J. (1990). The evolution of educational management: Eroding myths and emerging models. In B. Mitchell & L. Cunningham (Eds.), *Educational leadership and changing contexts of families, communities, and schools. Eighty-ninth Yearbook of NSSE. Part II.* Chicago: University of Chicago Press.

Hoyle, J. R. (1989, January). Preparing the 21st-century superintendent. *Phi Delta Kappan, 70,* 376–379.

Loredo, J. G., & Carter, D. S. G. (1993). Enter the neophyte: Preparing administrators for leadership roles. In D. S. G. Carter, T. E. Glass, & S. M. Hord (Eds.), *Selecting, preparing and developing the school district superintendent.* Washington, DC: Falmer.

Murphy, J. (1992). *The landscape of leadership preparation: Reframing the education of school administrators.* Newbury Park, CA: Corwin Press.

National Association of Secondary School Principals. (1985). Performance-based preparation of principals: A framework for improvement. Reston, VA: Author.

National Association of State Directors of Teacher Education and Certification. (1991). *The NASDTEC Manual, 1991.* Dubuque, IA: Kendall Hunt.

National Commission for the Principalship. (1990). *Principals for our changing schools: Preparation and certification.* Fairfax, VA: Author.

Peterkin, R.S. (1994). *The Harvard Graduate School of Education: Urban superintendents program.* Cambridge: MA: Harvard University Graduate School of Education.

Peterson, K. D., & Finn, C.E. (1985, Spring). Principals, superintendents and the administrator's art. *The Public Interest, 79,* 42–62.

Pitner, N. J. (1988). Training of the school administrator: State of the art. In D. Griffiths, R. Stout, & P. Forsyth (Eds.), *Leaders for America's schools: Final report and papers of the National Commission on Excellence in Educational Administration* (pp. 367–404). Berkeley, CA: McCutchan.

Schmuck, P.A. (1992, February). Educating the new generation of superintendents. *Educational Leadership*, 66–71.

Shibles, M. R., for the Subcommittee on the Preparation of School Administrators. (1988). *School leadership preparation: A preface for action.* Washington, DC: American Association of Colleges for Teacher Education.

A P P E N D I X

Beginning Superintendent Study Interview Guides

INITIAL INTERVIEW

Preliminary (Warm-up) Information

A. Tell me about your district. (Use whatever follow-ups are needed to gain information listed in B through F.)

B. What is your student enrollment? What grade levels are included?

C. How would you describe the demographics of your community?

D. Approximately what percentage of your students qualify for free or reduced-priced lunches?

E. What is the racial makeup of your student body?

F. How would you describe the district's financial situation?

Selection

1. How did you come to this position? Describe the process. When did you assume the position?

2. Why were you the one selected?

3. What were the keys to your deciding to take this job?

4. Where did your support come from during the selection process? (Check for specific individuals and their roles.)

NOTE: Many questions for the initial and periodic interviews were based on the Interview Guide in *Becoming a Principal: The Challenges of Beginning Leadership* by Forrest W. Parkay and Gene E. Hall, 1992, Boston: Allyn & Bacon. Adapted by permission. Additional questions were added, based on interviews with superintendents and former superintendents.

Personal Reflections

5. Was there anything about the decision to accept this superintendency that was difficult or problematic for you?

6. What are you thinking about as you move from one position to another?

Entry/Goals/Plans

7. What do you see as the opportunities and challenges of this superintendency?

8. What would you like to see happen in the school district this year? (Vision) How do you think this vision compares with what board members want to have happen?

9. At this point, who do you see helping you to implement the plans you have?

District Climate

10. What steps have you taken so far in order to learn about the school district?

11. What have you learned about your school board members?

12. How long do the board members who hired you have left in their terms of office? How are your board members chosen?

13. What have you learned about special connections between school board members and school employees? (If it does not come out in response to this question, ask, What do you know about who board members listen to?)

14. What organization negotiates for teachers in your district?

15. What have you learned about how that organization (or union) functions?

16. How would you describe the relationship between the board and the teachers' organization?

Key Steps

17. What have you done so far to make your entry successful?

18. What have been the critical incidents/turning points? What happened? What did you do next? What was the result?

19. Has anything happened so far that created a personal or professional (moral or ethical) dilemma for you? How did you resolve it?

Support Systems

20. What kinds of resources, ideas, and people have been helpful?

21. What has hindered or blocked?

22. What support would you like to have that you have not had?

Philosophy/Educational Platform

23. What do you plan to do in order to be a successful leader of this school district?

24. What do you see as priorities for your time this first year?

25. A basic controversy in education deals with how much autonomy/freedom teachers and principals have. What are your thoughts about this related to materials, teaching methods, school governance, etc.?

26. What are your thoughts about possible needs for staff development (district staff, principals, teachers, etc.)?

27. Do you anticipate the need for new rules or policies?

28. How much autonomy versus close connections to the district office do you think that principals should have?

29. How much autonomy versus close connections to the board of education do you think the superintendent should have?

30. What do you think are board members' perceptions of their role in relation to yours? How does that fit with your own views?

31. How do you see yourself as superintendent right now?

32. Is there anything you want to add, or are there any additional concerns you have?

GUIDE FOR PERIODIC TELEPHONE INTERVIEWS

1. Describe the critical events that are occurring.

2. How are you spending your time?

3. What community activities are engaging your time?

4. To whom did you turn for support, and who did you support?

5. What is happening with the school board?

6. What is happening with the teachers' organization?

7. What decisions have you made (major and minor)?

8. What joys, successes, and frustrations are you experiencing?

Name Index

Subject Index